THE DEEPER MEANING OF
ECONOMIC LIFE
Critical Essays on the U.S. Catholic
Bishops' Pastoral Letter on the Economy

The Deeper Meaning of ECONOMIC LIFE

Critical Essays on the U.S. Catholic Bishops' Pastoral Letter on the Economy

R. BRUCE DOUGLASS, Editor

GEORGETOWN UNIVERSITY PRESS
Washington, D.C.

ACKNOWLEDGMENTS

The editor would like to express his appreciation to William Gould and Dale Kuehne, graduate students in the Department of Government, Georgetown University, for their assistance in the preparation of this volume.

Library of Congress Cataloging-in-Publication Data

The Deeper meaning of economic life.

    Bibliography: p.
    1. Catholic Church.   National Conference of Catholic
Bishops.   Pastoral letter on Catholic social teaching
and the U.S. economy.   2. Economics--Religious
aspects--Catholic Church.   3. United States--Economic
conditions--1981-   . 4. Sociology, Christian
(Catholic)   5. Catholic Church--Doctrines.
I. Douglass, R. Bruce.
BX1795.E27D44   1986   261.8'5   86-27148
ISBN 0-87840-440-6
ISBN 0-87840-441-4 (pbk.)

Contents

FOREWORD

When Pope Paul VI in his Apostolic Letter, *Octogesima Adveniens,* asked the bishops of the world to take Catholic social teaching and apply it to their particular nations since the Popes could only speak in the most general of terms, he was asking much of us. Catholic social teaching has grown through the century because of new problems and new challenges to the church. Applying it would be easy if all the applications could be made in one place and time. These are, however, new times, and certain aspects of the body of doctrine will inevitably seem more relevant than others, and certain of the basic theories will require further penetration and elucidation. One cannot apply theories without rethinking them. Moreover, the body of doctrine called Catholic social teaching is less a unified and perfectly constructed whole than a series of repeated attempts to answer precise world problems in very definite historical contexts. It was with such a body of doctrine that the bishops of the United States had to work. Moral discourse is not done in the abstract.

It must also be stated that the bishops, in writing their pastoral letter, *Catholic Social Teaching and the U.S. Economy,* could not write a whole treatise on moral, economic and political philosophy. It had to be a limited document if it was to be serviceable. Many critics already feel it is far too long!

The proper category for the content of the letter from an academic point of view is certainly that of economic philosophy. But the term *pastoral* must be accentuated. Bishops do not and should not write philosophical treatises for or with their people. Since they write pastoral letters—and this is a genre of its own—they must at times just presuppose or hint at some of the philosophical issues that cannot be fully dealt with. Not all of the homework they do finds its way into a pastoral letter. Moreover, many times theorists have differed on salient points, and in these cases the bishops have had to use their better judgment about the pastoral implications of the various proposals and accept the one that seems most consonant with Catholic tradition. They could not give all of the academic arguments in favor of or against each point of view without again turning the document into something other than a pastoral letter. At most, they could refer the reader in the footnotes to the full set of arguments.

For these reasons a volume of commentary and critique like this is most helpful in outlining certain of the more pertinent philosophical questions involved and for discussing them at the level and in the depth they deserve.

The Economic Pastoral could be cited as the first attempt on the part of the teaching church in the United States to come to terms with what is left of Enlightenment philosophy, where the major theses of capitalism can be found. The church in Europe has had a long and bitter experience in battling the kind of Enlightenment liberalism that sought to choke off not just all the privileges of the church but all its rights as well. The U.S. experience of the Catholic Church has been quite different, but neither did it involve deep reflection on the ways liberalism agreed with or contradicted the main body of the Catholic philosophical and religious tradition.

In the Economic Pastoral there was no occasion to discuss at length these philosophical questions. Most readers would know, if only vaguely, that the church has always rejected communism as unacceptable because it deprives the church of its right to exist and function. It has also kept a certain distance from those aspects of capitalistic thought that were deterministic or mechanistic or that saw the human person as a mere variable component of the system rather than both its subject and object. The church has always tried to keep this strongly humanistic point of view before its eyes. Even without a long historical discussion of the philosophical questions underlying this approach, these points are clearly indicated in the Economic Pastoral. We should all, however, welcome such extended discussion of these philosophical questions, which I find generally takes place much more frequently in Europe than in the United States.

Some seem disappointed that the church does not propose a "third way" between capitalism and communism. But it is neither the duty nor the competency of the church to produce an economic third system; the most the church can fruitfully do is to allude to values that should be found in such a system and suggest certain general directions. That is the reason the church finds itself playing a more negative role, that of offering constructive criticism. No one should expect the church to embrace any one system as being perfectly in accord with Christ's teaching; the answer will always have to be "more or less" and carefully nuanced.

The pastoral letter comes at an opportune moment, when all over the world people are reflecting on the effects produced by a global or interdependent economic system. The philosophical roots of capitalism are not so deeply planted in many areas of the world (South America, Africa and Asia, for example) as they are in the United States. Thus, our system finds itself received in different ways in different parts of the world, with consequences that are both interesting to contemplate and important for our economic future. We tend to assume that capitalism is intrinsically wedded to our democratic tradition, because we feel that both were built on the same philosophical premises. But Third World nations have long since separated these two strands of the tradition. In addition, they have witnessed our alignment with militaristic and highly authoritarian, if not totalitarian, regimes in the Third World. Often taking a more speculative bent in their thinking than we do, they look for a deeper analysis of the values involved in the economic system. It should not surprise us, then, that even committed religious leaders look at times to modified socialist solutions to their problems rather than to capitalistic ones. Our letter has already had strong impact in those areas since it has stimulated new thought about the underlying philosophy of the U.S. capitalist system as it is experienced both in the United States and in other cultures abroad. Any future discussion of the U.S. economy must include that larger audience simply because our economic system is clearly international and intercultural.

A pastoral letter must be written with diverse audiences in mind. The first audience is the Catholic laity, now very diversified in terms of social strata and interests. If it comes out of the United States, it must also take into account the other nations of the world that are affected by our economic system and its underlying values. The third audience comprises those who share our concerns, are interested in the same issues, and are searching along with us for solutions. At the hearings held by the Bishops' Committee, most of them expected us to speak out of our own tradition and, indeed, often seemed eager to show how a convergence of values and ideas can take place even when one begins from different religious and philosophical premises. The dialogue with that third audience must be a continuing one.

They are correct who say that the Economic Pastoral is a beginning, not an end. The important point now is to continue the dialogue on the issues raised and to accept the challenge they present. We hope the church in the United States can make the heritage of Catholic social teaching its own and continue to contribute to its refinement and growth. I welcome books of this sort which try to do just that.

Most Reverend Rembert G. Weakland, O.S.B.
Archbishop of Milwaukee

Chairman, National Conference of Catholic
Bishops' *ad hoc* Committee on Catholic Social
Teaching and the U.S. Economy
September 1986

Introduction

MODERN ECONOMIC LIFE, like much of the rest of modern life, is based on a heresy. It is a heresy which, admittedly, has turned out to be very useful, but it is nonetheless a heresy. The heresy in question is autonomy. Orthodox Christian teaching, with its strong emphasis on the active presence of God in the world, has always insisted that the whole of life is to be lived in conformity to God's will, and that therefore all aspects of our existence should be ordered to serve the end of virtuous and pious living. But modern economic relations recognize no such higher purpose. They derive, in fact, from a deliberate declaration of independence from the influence of such "external" considerations. From the beginning of the modern period in the seventeenth and eighteenth centuries, when the foundations of economic activity as we know it today were laid, it has been part and parcel of the modern experience unto itself, governed by its own logic and pursuing its own discrete ends. "Economic man," the symbol of this way of thinking, single-mindedly pursues one end—efficiency—as though it were an end in itself. It is, in fact, a necessary condition of efficiency, his apologists have always insisted, to think and act in this way; and they have devoted much time and energy to the elaboration of complex theories designed to demonstrate why this is the case.

Not everyone thinks this way, of course. Economic man is an abstraction that fits only imperfectly the experience most of us actually have as economic actors, and there have always been significant pockets of resistance to what that abstraction represents. Still, it is not just an abstraction. It corresponds to something which is real and important in the world we inhabit—arguably, in fact, one of its most significant defining features. Among those whose views are important in the ordering and conduct of economic activity in societies like that of the United States, it is particularly influential. Those who make economic policy, whether in government or private institutions, as well as the commentators and analysts whose views they respect, would appear to be heavily influenced by the premise that economic activity is a world unto itself, following its own immanent logic. Virtually everything in their training encourages such thinking, and it is consistently reinforced by the norms of the institutions in which they go about their work.

It is bound to come as something of a shock, then, when this way of thinking confronts a serious challenge. By this I mean more than the simple affirmation that there is more to life than economic efficiency. The man or woman of affairs may well be in his or her private life a practicing believer, and accustomed to such general affirmations of the relevance of religion to worldly concerns. But it is one thing to encounter this claim in a form that preserves the de facto autonomy of the economic realm as now ordered, and quite another to confront it in a form that does not—a form that is almost certain to provoke resistance. Faced with a more specific challenge, especially one which attempts to subordinate economic practice to an alternative logic based on the priority of higher values, even the pious man or woman of affairs will be tempted to suggest that the clerics should mind their own business and to insist, on grounds of competence, that the church confine its pronouncements on these matters to generalities and leave the specifics to lay practitioners.

Up to a point, there is obvious merit in this suggestion. Modern economic life is filled with technical complexity, and it would be preposterous for the church to presume to give detailed guidance on the manifold technical problems confronting the makers of both public and private economic policy. The further the church ventures into the particulars of policy, the more it is bound to overreach its competence and to violate the spirit of its own teaching about the dignity of secular learning. At the same time, to accept uncritically the judgment of practitioners in this (or any other) field is to beg the very question which needs to be explored and to assume that the purposes which the church would have prevail in the economic order can, in fact, be well served without abridging the autonomy of economic man. The evidence that has accumulated on this matter since the emergence of modern economic relations is not self-evident, to say the least, which is why the church has not been content to confine its teaching simply to general admonitions to virtue and piety. All through the history of its response to the modern world there runs the sense that modern economic relations are likely to encourage ways of thinking and acting that are in tension, if not contradiction, with the ends it favors; for this reason, the church's teaching has taken the form of a fairly elaborate body of social and economic theory designed specifically to challenge the autonomy of economic man.

But a complete repudiation of modern economic life has not been at issue in this challenge — at least not since the pontificate of Leo XIII (1878–1903), when Catholic teaching first began to address these matters constructively. For all of the church's pointed criticism of modern economic practices, it has not taken the position that they are simply wrong. Even in the days when it sought to focus attention on the social costs of industrialization and to characterize the fate suffered by the working class as "a yoke little better than slavery,"[1] the tacit assumption of church pronouncements on the subject was that the revolution which had brought modern economic relations into being was an accomplished fact, and that for all of the attendant problems, it had resulted in advances in economic efficiency that, in principle, were of great value. Moreover, as industrialization has proceeded and as the social costs associated with its early phases have been overcome, there has been growing evidence of a tendency in Catholic teaching to treat existing economic institutions with respect. The standard of living attained in the industrialized world has come to be recognized for the extraordinary achievement that it is, and the role which such modern developments as the free market have played in producing this result is now taken for granted.

We do not live by bread alone, however, and the church has sought to recover an awareness that there is more to economic life than mere productivity. While acknowledging that efficient production is the primary task of those who invest time and energy in the manufacture of economic goods, it has insisted that there are other dimensions to this activity which must be taken into account if it is to be conducted in a way truly conducive to human well-being. Labor, for example, is more than just the means by which goods and services are made available. It is also a human activity that can profoundly affect the quality of life of the people involved. Given the central role of work in defining the worth which modern people attach to their lives and their access to economic benefits, it is vitally important, as papal teaching in particular has maintained, that those who are capable of working are given the opportunity to do so, and that their work is done under conditions that are appropriate for a human being.

Similarly, commerce is more than an economic transaction. The kinds of goods that are made available to consumers and the attitudes toward consumption that are cultivated have a significance which extends far beyond their effect on the strength and vitality of the economic institutions involved. Recent experience suggests that trade can become one of the key determinants of a people's way of life, affecting (sometimes profoundly) their most basic beliefs and values. Especially in recent decades, when mass consumption has begun to flourish in the industrialized nations, Catholic teaching has come to emphasize this, and in turn to challenge the assumption that more is necessarily better. The church reminds us that whatever the economic arguments for continuous cultivation of our acquisitive appetites may be, it is not at all self-evident that this cultivation is either morally or spiritually desirable.

In pursuing these concerns on the terrain of modern economies, the church has sought both to modify their functioning and to transform them. It has not presumed to offer a full-blown alternative to the existing order, but has insisted on the necessity of modifying the forms created by the advent of modern economic life in order to temper their essentially amoral and areligious character. Drawing extensively on its own theoretical heritage, it has developed a way of thinking about modern economic problems which, while not completely denying the need for autonomy, significantly qualifies it. It has continued to insist, for example, on the relevance of such moral standards as the just wage and just price, which, if taken at all seriously, would profoundly alter the play of market forces. It has made a point, too, of upholding the dignity of labor, and has actively defended the right of working men and women to form unions, engage in collective bargaining, and most recently, participate in governing the institutions in which they labor. Its teaching on the common good has led rather naturally to an embrace of the welfare state and economic planning.

Beyond such reforms, however, the church's real concern has been the transformation of attitudes. As Keith Breclaw observes in his contribution to this volume, the purpose of Catholic teaching is not well understood if it is viewed simply as an apology for a series of structural reforms in market economies. Important as such reforms are, the church's fundamental purpose in confronting the challenge of modern economies has been to transform their character by changing the way in which people conceive of the meaning of their activity as economic agents. Consistently, the thrust of the church's teaching, ever since it began to address these issues in a serious way, has been that the root of the moral and spiritual disorders which have accompanied the rise of modern economic relations is attitudinal; and it has attempted, in turn, to provide a corrective by elaborating a view of economic life that makes clear the necessity of its subordination to higher purposes.

UNTIL VERY RECENTLY, however, the contribution made by the church in this country to this enterprise was minimal. The American hierarchy followed the lead of the larger church, to be sure, and sought faithfully in its own way to apply Catholic teaching to the conditions prevailing on these shores. But it did so, typically, in a way that involved little fundamental challenge to the more important institutions in American public life. There have been exceptions—the public schools, for example—but for the most part the church here has refrained from adopting any position that might suggest principled opposition to the "American way." It has been anxious, for reasons which are transparent to anyone familiar with the history of Catholicism in this country, to affirm its loyalty to the characteristic ideas and institutions of this society. The hierarchy has tended to be reluctant, moreover, to engage in actions that might give the appearance of any significant degree of political partisanship. As Elizabeth McKeown demonstrates in her contribution to this volume, when the bishops have found it necessary to venture overtly into public affairs, they have almost always done so in a way that could be construed as apolitical. Rarely has there been much emphasis on those aspects of Catholic teaching that entail significant criticism of the principles on which our political and economic life is found. Nor, in turn, has there been much evidence of an inclination to contribute constructively to the development of the body of ideas with which the church addresses the social and economic problems of industrial societies. Reading the statements issued by the U.S. conference of bishops since its inception in 1919, one notices an almost systematic avoidance of any attempt to engage in serious theoretical analysis.[2]

Now, however, things are obviously beginning to change. Catholics are coming of age as political actors in this country, and as they do so, the hierarchy is increasingly inclined to play an active—and even activist—role in public affairs. The old misgivings about partisanship are fading rapidly as the church aggressively seeks to influence policy on a number of important and highly controverted issues. Unmistakably, the tone of what it has to say reflects a growing sensitivity to the distance which separates existing institutions and policy from what the bishops believe to be morally and theologically defensible. The more active they become in the public arena, the more they are inclined to stand in judgment on the beliefs and practices which are common among their fellow citizens, and to press the case for change. Whether the issue be abortion or national defense or, more recently, the fate of the poor, the trend is toward an increasingly "prophetic" posture, and as this takes place, there is evidence of much greater interest in theory as well. For the first time, the American hierarchy appears not only to make a point of the theological and philosophical grounds on which its views on public issues rest, but also—and perhaps even more important—to attempt to make its own contribution to the development of Catholic teaching on these matters.

The most prominent manifestations of this new mood are the two major pastoral letters which have been issued under the auspices of the conference of bishops in the last two years. First came *The Challenge of Peace*, published in final form in 1983, which challenged the basis of national policy on an issue no less consequential than nuclear strategy.[3] It did so, moreover, in a manner that involved a significant adaptation of the church's traditional just war teaching. While by no means abandoning that teaching, the letter emphasized the novelty of the situation created by the existence of nuclear weapons, and refused, in turn, to countenance the possibility of their just use. To this has now been added another statement — of comparable length, partisanship and ingenuity — on the economy. *Catholic Social Teaching and the U.S. Economy*, first issued in November 1984, just after the election that returned Ronald Reagan to the White House for a second term, is still, at this writing, in process of revision;[4] but it is easy to see that it follows the same pattern. Once again, it is a matter of a sharp challenge to existing practice, this time on grounds primarily of distributive justice; and once again, the structure of the argument is such as to give the appearance, at least, of significant innovation. Instead of simply repeating the familiar themes of what is by now a well-established body of traditional doctrine, the letter invokes new concepts and seems to reflect an inclination to break fresh ground.

The response has been predictable. Both letters have elicited wide comment in both religious and secular fora, and their principal claims have provoked extended debate. Surely, no statement on a public issue by an ecclesiastical body in this country has ever received as much public attention as has *The Challenge of Peace*, and now the letter on the economy is beginning to acquire a comparable status. It has generated the first serious discussion of the relationship between religious belief and economic practice in American public life since at least the 1930s; and in the process, Catholics themselves are being led to think more deeply than ever before about the meaning and significance of the church's teaching in this realm. Both letters have also provided a stimulus for an outpouring of scholarly writing in the relevant disciplines; as with the popular debate, this scholarly discussion is by no means confined to Catholics.

What will come of all of this remains to be seen. Cynics will say that it is just talk, and that precisely because what is at issue in both cases is of great practical consequence, nothing will change. But cynics have a tendency to exaggerate the durability of the status quo. Sometimes things *do* change, because of precisely the sort of change in attitude the bishops seek to promote. This much, in any case, can be taken for granted: having begun to establish, at long last, an accepted place for itself in American public life, the Catholic hierarchy is not about to turn back. If anything, its activism can be expected to grow and become increasingly ambitious; and the more the legitimacy of their public role is taken for granted, the more the bishops are likely to be emboldened to challenge even well-established features of this society which they find objectionable. And the importance of the issues they are now seeking to address, on both practical and theological grounds, is such that it is highly unlikely that these concerns will fade away.

It is one thing, however, to identify a challenge and quite another to address it successfully. In speaking as it has in these recent letters, the hierarchy has begun to establish for itself a role and an agenda in public life that are potentially of great importance. But in order for this potential to be realized, more—much more—is needed than just a point of view and the will to enunciate it. For the church to achieve the role to which it now aspires in this society, it needs, above all, well-reasoned arguments capable of commanding the attention and respect even of those who are not predisposed to respond favorably to what it has to say. It needs a coherent and informed moral vision, to insure that its criticism of existing practice and the alternatives it proposes not only are plausible but carry enough weight to be taken seriously. It must make good, in short, on the aspiration to develop a body of teaching that will "stand up to public scrutiny."[5] I think it is reasonable to conclude that this has not yet been achieved. Partly because of the novelty of the enterprise in which they are engaged and partly because of their unwillingness simply to repeat traditional formulae, the bishops in these two recent letters have done little more than establish a basis for discussion. They have taken an important step toward recovering a sense of the utility of thinking theologically about defense and economic issues—which, in the context of American public life, is no mean accomplishment—and they have established a presumption in favor of pursuing that reflection in a certain direction. But they have not made a compelling argument for the specific conclusions which they wish to draw.

The more one reflects on the two letters in the light of the debate they have elicited, the more appropriate it becomes to think of them as exploratory statements. Both have a vigorous affirmative character, to be sure, but the way in which the drafting process has been conducted suggests that the bishops have been as much concerned with developing a discussion as with speaking authoritatively on the issues in question. The degree to which they have encouraged criticism and sought to give at least the appearance of openness to revision of their arguments suggests that they recognize the impossibility of even pretending to speak with finality on such issues at this particular time in the life of both the church and the nation. In any case, if they did not begin with this intent, one would assume that by now they have come to appreciate the point. As even staunch defenders of the two letters must acknowledge, they raise as many questions as they answer, and even the answers given need much greater refinement.

ABOVE ALL, the foundational issues need further discussion. As noted, one of the most striking features of these recent statements by the American Catholic hierarchy is the attention they devote to theological and philosophical considerations. Unlike many past statements by the conference of bishops on public affairs, these letters do not confine themselves simply to offering judgments about the details of policy. Both of them contain a great deal that bears directly on particular problems of policy, and ultimately they are designed to influence the formation of public policy in certain directions. But neither is read properly if it is seen simply as a brief for particular positions in the policy debates of the present moment. If they are taken as written, that is, and not with the obsession for the "bottom line" that so often dominates our public discourse, it should be readily apparent that they are concerned primarily with something else — something of far more fundamental and lasting significance. The real issue in both letters is not so much what we should do about certain policy proposals of current interest, but rather the frame of mind with which we approach *all* of the problems that confront us in these areas. The purpose of the letters is, in turn, to alter the way in which we think at this most basic level. As with the church's social teaching in the past, they are meant to reconstruct, or at least reform, our public philosophy.

The American mind being what it is, however, it has been difficult for this part of the argument to be taken seriously. There has been a recurring tendency in the discussions generated by both letters to focus on the policy recommendations they provide, to the neglect of the larger argument. Commentators in the secular media have been inclined to act as though the theological and philosophical claims made by the bishops did not exist, and insofar as they acknowledge them at all, to treat them as mere window-dressing. The inevitable result is a caricature, which not only badly distorts what the Catholic hierarchy is about but also sacrifices what is of greatest value and importance in the enterprise they have undertaken.

The lack of attention to these themes is particularly troublesome in view of the impression of innovation which the letters convey. There would be less need for critical scrutiny of the bishops' more fundamental claims if these letters were simply a straightforward recitation of familiar teaching. At least there would be less urgency about it. But since the bishops have chosen to convey their message in a form which suggests a new departure, it is especially important that the argument be subjected to critical review.

To provide such a review, or at least to begin to do so, is the purpose of this volume. To a large extent, that work has already been done on the pastoral on defense issues. The authors of that document could (and did) draw on a well-developed scholarly discussion of the moral problems created by nuclear weapons; and once the letter was released, the theologians, ethicists, and others who had been active in that discussion provided a ready audience for the bishops' theoretical claims. Thus it has been difficult for religious people, at least, to ignore the larger argument.

The pastoral on economics, however, has suffered a rather different fate. Unlike the letter on defense, it is not the product of a great deal of prior theological and philosophical discussion, and so it has not met with the same kind of response. Numerous replies have been made to the letter's claims about the U.S. economy, and some of these have addressed the deeper issues raised by the bishops. But such comments have been the exception rather than the rule. More often than not, the responses have been far less sophisticated than those elicited by *The Challenge of Peace*.

We seek here to redress this imbalance. A single volume is unlikely, of course, to be a substitute for a whole discussion. But it can serve as an example. By focusing on the more fundamental theological and philosophical issues raised by the pastoral on the economy, we hope to show the utility of thinking about our activity as economic actors in these terms, and in the process to encourage others to undertake such reflection as well. Economic philosophy (as one of our contributors aptly characterizes our theme) is a subject badly in need of revival. Perhaps these essays can be a step in that direction.

For the most part, the papers speak for themselves and need little introduction. They are the product of an interdisciplinary (and interconfessional) faculty colloquium at Georgetown University which we have found to be of great value in exploring the issues at stake here. Though each essay aims to interpret the pastoral letter and make sense of its claims, none is intended to be simply a commentary. Each author seeks to provide a critical perspective, to enable the reader to understand more fully what is at stake in the various claims made by the bishops. On the whole, the mood is respectful and even supportive of what the letter represents. But at the same time there is a clear sense, which has become more pronounced the longer our discussion has gone on, that the letter is best understood as a point of departure, and in no sense as the last word.

The book does not deliberately seek to be disputatious. There is much on which the contributors agree, and our agreements are every bit as important as our disagreements. Nonetheless, we are by no means of one mind. The papers reflect serious differences of opinion concerning some of the most important issues the letter raises. The reader will easily identify most of these issues, but the following are of particular note.

1. For all the attention devoted by the authors of the letter to exposition of the theological and philosophical affirmations on which their position is based and for all the appearance of novelty which this exposition creates, the real character of that position is anything but clear. Those who focus on the emphasis placed on the fate of the poor and the obvious parallel to liberation theology which this entails are inclined to take the impression of innovation at face value, and to conclude that the letter does, in fact, represent a new departure. That point of view is reflected in several of the papers, but so, too, is another view which suggests that in this instance appearances are deceptive. There is no doubt, say the proponents of this alternative opinion, that there are some elements of innovation in the letter, and that it employs an idiom which has not been customary in Catholic social teaching. But at the same time the essential logic of the argument is that of the tradition, and few, if any, of its important features are sacrificed. Far from being a new departure, therefore, the letter is simply old wine in a new vessel, and the innovations are best understood as adaptations dictated by the need to take into account new circumstances.

2. More is at issue in this debate than just the identity of the existing text. For it quickly becomes evident, as the possibility of such adaptation is discussed, that there is a significant difference of opinion about both the value of the church's traditional teaching and its adaptability. Some of what the reader will encounter in this volume obviously reflects an appreciation for the body of thought developed since *Rerum Novarum* based on the assumption that it is still worthy of respect and capable of being adapted successfully to the new circumstances of our time. Especially when the traditional teaching is compared with the alternatives, so this argument runs, it still appears to be the best resource available for making theological and moral sense of the phenomena the church must address in its social teaching. But there are skeptics. Several of our number have been led, in the course of analyzing particular issues raised by the

pastoral letter, to doubt whether the ideas on which the church has relied in the past really suffice any longer. Since Vatican II, there has been a striking renaissance of theological creativity in the church, and this, combined with emergence of new social and economic conditions which severely test certain of the assumptions on which the traditional teaching is based, give rise to the conclusion that it may be time for major innovation. More than once in this collection the reader will be left with the impression that the author believes the traditional teaching is so wedded to outdated assumptions that it must be superseded, and that the real challenge confronting the American hierarchy is to provide leadership in this regard.

3. Much of the same sort of disagreement arises out of the methodological innovations which the letter introduces. Once again, the meaning and significance of these innovations is anything but obvious. But the fact that the letter employs a different mode of theological and philosophical discourse is indisputable. Gone is the traditional natural law idiom, and in its place is substituted a combination of themes derived from Scripture and modern rights theory. The obvious question is whether this new mode of reasoning (and expression) is well advised. This question needs to be addressed on both substantive and tactical grounds, since the stated objective is not only to address the faithful but also to speak in a manner that will be comprehensible and persuasive to nonbelievers as well. In reading this book, one will encounter very different responses to the letter in this respect. Some of the papers clearly reflect approval for this new turn in the church's method of speaking on such matters, and they convey the impression that it needs to be pursued even more vigorously. The accent on Scripture in particular is appealing to some of our number, and they imply that the church would be better served, on both substantive and tactical grounds, if it embraced distinctively biblical themes more fully and consistently. Others have just the opposite reaction. Some question whether this emphasis on Scripture makes any sense at all in the light of the bishops' desire to speak in a way that effectively influences the general public, and still others worry about the appropriateness of Scripture as a basis for trying to make theological sense of economic practice. Both the historical conditions reflected in the Bible and the comparative indifference of its authors to economic considerations make it highly improbable, they suggest, that a credible economic ethic can be built on such a foundation.

4. Hardly less important in our deliberations has been the relationship of the letter to liberalism as a political and economic ideology. For at least two reasons we have found ourselves returning to this theme again and again. First, liberalism is clearly the dominant

ideology in American public life, and as such, defines the terrain on which any attempt to influence public opinion and policy must proceed. Second, obviously in response to this, the bishops seek to construct their argument in a manner that is congenial to at least some of what liberalism historically has represented. This is particularly evident, for example, in the stress placed on rights. But it immediately gives rise to critical questions. In seeking such rapprochement with themes familiar to the American public, have the bishops conceded too much? Are they in danger, as some critics charge, of simply baptizing liberalism, albeit in a highly revisonist form, and in the process, of simply sweeping under the rug some of the important objections to liberalism which Catholic teaching has enunciated in the past? Most of what is said in this volume about this issue aims to refute this criticism. Indeed, much of it can be read as commendation for the bishops' position on the precise ground that it *challenges* the characteristic claims of liberals. But there remain the dissenting voices of those who suggest that for all of the distinctions which can be made between the bishops' argument and a comparable liberal view, the letter has too much affinity with liberalism at key points for the distinctions to make much difference.

FINALLY, A WORD about thought and action. Implicit in all of this is the assumption that further reflection and discussion provide an appropriate response to the concerns which the letter raises. The bishops obviously mean to convey a strong sense of urgency about these matters—as well they should—and from this it might be concluded that the only appropriate response is one of action. Some will be impatient with the invitation to further reflection which this book represents, on the ground that we already know what needs to be done and it is time to get on with doing it. Why persist in talking—much less writing scholarly papers—while people starve? The question is a serious one and may not be dismissed casually. Intellectuals all too easily fall into taking for granted the importance of what they do. We are convinced however, that there is still a place for extended discussion, in a variety of forms, of the issues explored here; indeed, we would even go so far as to propose that this is essential if the bishops' letter is to achieve its purpose.

We say this because we do not believe it is clear what precisely is the right course of action to follow in dealing with many of the practical issues the letter raises. If the letter conveys a different impression, then it simply misleads. Beyond certain rather obvious and elementary moral imperatives, informed observers clearly disagree, often profoundly, about how best to approach the policy choices involved in meeting the economic challenges of our time. This disagreement must be respected if the church's attempt to deal with these themes is to be taken seriously. But it is not only the policy recommendations of the letter that need discussion. As this volume demonstrates, there is not always a clear idea of precisely what the church should say when it attempts to shed theological light on current economic problems. The bishops' letter speaks rather matter-of-factly about "the Christian perspective" on the meaning of economic life, as though this perspective were self-evident; but in point of fact, it is not. Now more than ever, it is an open question what the church's teaching in this realm should be; and for this reason, too, it is important that the letter be treated more as a point of departure than as the last word.

But above all, the letter needs discussion in order for it to achieve the change in attitudes to which the bishops aspire. For change in basic assumptions about something as consequential as our daily work and bread cannot take place overnight. Surely, it is not likely to take place on the scale which the bishops have in mind on the basis of a single statement—no matter how eloquent—on the importance of justice. Only gradually will the faithful relinquish deeply rooted assumptions such as those the bishops have chosen to challenge; and they will do so only if they can be persuaded, through an extended process of education, of the wisdom of the alternative. The more one reflects on what is actually at stake in the letter, the more formidable becomes the task the bishops have set for themselves. It is the work of a generation, if not longer; and it will succeed only if the bishops can combine persistence and vision with a capacity for taking seriously the doubts and reservations of those who do not completely agree with what they have to say.

There is an enormous pastoral challenge here, one which is as important as any the church has ever faced in the United States. For the country badly needs a careful critical appraisal of the way in which it conducts its economic affairs. The church can provide leadership in this regard only if it speaks with informed respect for the complexity of the topic. It is our hope that this volume will serve that end.

R. BRUCE DOUGLASS
Washington, D.C.
April 1986

xxiv INTRODUCTION

NOTES

1. *Rerum Novarum (The Condition of Labor)* (1891), no. 2.

2. Cf. Hugh J. Nolan, ed., *Pastoral Letters of the United States Catholic Bishops* (Washington, D.C.: United States Catholic Conference, 1984), vols. I–IV.

3. National Conference of Catholic Bishops, *The Challenge of Peace: God's Promise and Our Response* (Washington, D.C.: United States Catholic Conference, 1983).

4. National Conference of Catholic Bishops, *Catholic Social Teaching and the U.S. Economy* (Washington, D.C.: United States Catholic Conference, 1984–85).

5. Ibid., second draft, no. 32.

JOHN LANGAN, S.J.

The American Context of the U.S. Bishops' Pastoral Letter on the Economy

JOHN LANGAN, S.J., is a Senior Fellow at
the Woodstock Theological Center. He
received his Ph.D. in philosophy from the
University of Michigan. He also holds
degrees from Woodstock College in
theology and Loyola University of Chicago
in classics and philosophy as well.

GRAND CENTRAL STATION in New York is one of the great monuments of the age when railroads were the dominant form of transportation in the Western world. Built in 1913, it stands in the center of Park Avenue, a defining point for one of the places that symbolize American opulence. The firm that built it, the New York Central Railroad, was the source of the wealth and power of the Vanderbilts, one of the greatest of the plutocratic dynasties of America in the late nineteenth century. The New York Central, however, is no more: after it merged in 1968 with its longtime rival, the Pennsylvania Railroad, the new combination, the Penn Central, went into a spectacular bankruptcy in 1970. The building, however, continues as a central hub for ground transportation in New York City; intercity

1

trains, commuter trains, subways, airport buses all converge here and bring thousands of people into the station en route to their offices and shops in midtown Manhattan. The building has one of the greatest interior spaces in the city and a grandiose facade in the Beaux-Arts style. Directly above the terminal and its underground rail yards towers the Pan-Am Building, one of the largest and tallest office buildings in New York and an apt symbol of the combination of greed and ingenuity that makes New York go. Inside the waiting rooms of the terminal and on the streets around it are dozens of homeless men, unshaven, ill-clothed, smelly, with vacant or angry and occasionally menacing looks in their eyes. The terminal is the center both of frenetic activity and of passive despair, a magnet for the destitute and a meeting place for the industrious, a refuge overflowed by the madding crowd.

Let us take this remarkable building as an image for the America that the Catholic bishops are addressing in their pastoral on Catholic social teaching and the U.S. economy. American society, behind the classic facade of its constitutional and legal structure, contains both an aging and financially vulnerable industrial base of manufacturing industries and an innovative information-driven technology. At the same time, it includes large numbers of people who have no active part in the production of wealth and very little security for the future. Like the terminal, it is monumental in scale ($4 trillion a year) and indispensable in its functions. It is a prime feature of the contemporary world and yet is still relatively new. It is the locus of past accomplishments and of future anxieties, of present pain and pride.

In New York City both the rich and the poor are more clearly visible than in most other parts of the United States; and it has become customary for the homeless to seek shelter in areas that are surprisingly close to the centers of financial power and commercial glamor in the city. But the United States remains overwhelmingly a country of the middle class. Ronald Reagan may exemplify the style and beliefs of the southern California rich; but it is his ability to communicate with millions of his fellow Americans, including many unionists and blue-collar workers, that has made him president. Surveys routinely show that 80 to 85 percent of Americans regard themselves as middle class, a category which includes well-paid business executives and retail clerks, doctors and computer programmers, lawyers and bus drivers. It is to this vast middle class, which defies simple categorization but which must be persuaded if any significant changes in public policy with regard to the poor and the jobless are to be made, that the Catholic bishops have chosen to address the draft of their new pastoral letter.

The Catholic constituency which the bishops have in mind as one of the two primary audiences for their letter is itself predominantly middle class. The days when the Catholic community in the United States consisted mainly of blue-collar ethnic groups (Irish, Poles, Italians, Hungarians, Czechs, Croatians) in the large industrial cities of the East and North are over. There has been geographical dispersion and upward social mobility. As a result of internal migration, the Catholic sees of Houston, Atlanta, and Phoenix have grown quite rapidly; and many of their members are "upscale," in the current jargon. Such prominent corporations as Allied, Chase Manhattan, Johnson and Johnson, and Metropolitan Life Insurance are now led by Roman Catholics. The most prominent businessman in America today, Lee Iacocca of Chrysler, is both a proponent of government activism in economic matters and a devout Roman Catholic. Blacks, who are the ethnic group that is most afflicted by poverty, are for historic reasons much less Catholic (3 percent) than is the population at large (22 percent).

The two great exceptions to the picture of increasing levels of education and of financial success in the American Catholic community are the large and rapidly growing Hispanic community and the increasing number of older ethnic blue-collar workers who have been affected by the decline of the old manufacturing regions in the Northeast. The Hispanic migration takes different forms, depending on different countries of origin, and affects different parts of the United States in different ways. Thus the Puerto Ricans and Dominicans have concentrated in New York City; the Cubans, who are mainly middle-class opponents of Castro, have achieved a dominant position in the life of Miami; Salvadorans now constitute the largest immigrant group in the archdiocese of Washington, while Los Angeles is the great center for the Mexican migration. Unlike earlier ethnic groups, the Hispanics have not brought priests with them; and many of them are likely to affiliate with various Protestant churches. But Hispanics are and will continue to be the largest body of poor Catholics, a population that confronts the many stresses of living in an alien, competitive, and often violent urban environment and that at the same time makes a continuing and immediate appeal to the Catholic bishops. If one thinks only of Hispanic immigrants and of unemployed workers in manufacturing industries, one can readily see that most of the major dioceses of the United States will have significant numbers of poor people whose problems will have a direct impact on pastoral activity and whose situation is clearly the result of social factors and not merely of personal faults or errors of judgment. So it is not surprising that the bishops, at the beginning of the first draft of their pastoral letter, state the priority that the poor have in their reflections:

> The poor have a special claim on our concern because they are vulnerable and needy. We believe that all—Christians, Jews, those of other faiths and no faith at all—must measure their actions and choices by what they do *for* and *to* the poor. As pastors and as citizens we are convinced of one fundamental criterion for economic decisions, policies, and institutions: they must all be at the service of human beings. The economy was made for people, *all* people, and not the other way around.[1]

This paragraph is of particular interest for six reasons. First, it reminds us of the notion of human dignity, which has been fundamental in contemporary Catholic social teaching. This notion also underlies John Paul II's teaching in *Laborem Exercens* on "the principle of the priority of labor over capital," a teaching which the bishops reaffirm in par. 75 of their first draft. The central and decisive importance given to this principle is closely connected with the continuing criticism of the subordination of human persons and their needs to systemic exigencies in both capitalism and communism. Second, in this paragraph the bishops present themselves as concerned in a special way with the poor, and they urge their audience to share this concern. But neither the bishops nor the audience are strictly identified with the poor. Some critics on the religious left regard this as disappointing. But, as we have seen, such an expectation is not in accordance with a realistic picture of how most Catholics have fared in the U.S. economy or with what the bishops are trying to accomplish as leaders of a large, hierarchical organization.

Third, both bishops and audience are implicitly distinguished from "the economy" which exists to serve persons. Some critics have argued that the bishops, when they took as their fundamental questions, "What does the economy do *for* people? What does it do *to* people?" (par. 1), were showing a tendency to reify the economy, forgetting that the economy is nothing more than an aspect of the ongoing relationships and activities of persons. Without going into the metaphysical aspects of this line of criticism, I would observe that "the economy" must always confront any particular audience or any particular group of decision-makers as a reality with which they are intimately involved but which is at the same time independent and external. It has a history, a normative structure, and patterns of complex decentralized interactions which make it largely independent of direct commands and acts of will, even virtuous acts of will by very powerful persons. At the same time, serious dangers arise when "the system" is reified and then either attacked or absolved. Precisely because the economy is an extraordinarily complex historical and social construction, it is not to be equated with an order of nature that requires our unchanging fidelity and that is never to be tampered with or deviated from. Precisely because the economy is a collaborative construction intended to meet the needs and desires of persons, who are either similar to or identical with ourselves, it is not to be regarded as a purely external source of evil in the manner of those late sixties radicals who denounced "the system" and who saw those who managed the system only in negative and depersonalized terms, while presenting themselves as both powerless and uncorrupted. The general reformist tone of the bishops' letter, their insistence on reminding all of their responsibilities, and their avoidance of sweeping condemnation all make it clear that they do not think of the economy as a fixed and impersonal reality. More positively, their understanding of the economy sees it as an opportunity for human beings to express and to fulfill themselves and also to contribute to the common good.[2]

Fourth, this paragraph, along with a great deal of what the bishops say about the problem of unemployment, presents the moral problems of the economy in terms of omission and exclusion. In many American suburbs, the poor are simply invisible; in many political discussions, they have no power; and in the advertising and entertainment worlds, they do not count except as an insignificant part of the vast American audience whose dreams they are presumed to share. The issue is no longer exploitation and expropriation, the using of labor and the taking of its fruits away from the workers. Nor is it merely survival and the distribution of those goods necessary for survival. The images that we have of earlier stages of the industrial economy — the coal mines of Wales and Pennsylvania, the sweatshops and textile mills of Lancashire and Massachusetts, the steel mills of Essen and Youngstown, with all the human experience of heroic toil and patient saving which they evoke — can be profoundly misleading in our efforts to read the shape of current economic conflicts and to discern the shape of solutions to come. This is not to say that unsafe and unhealthy working conditions, inadequate wages, intimidating efforts to prevent the formation of unions, and serious economic anxiety cannot be found in the United States of America in 1985. Unfortunately, they are all there. But they do not shape the experience of American industrial workers as a group. The auto workers of Detroit, the garment workers of New York, and the aerospace workers of California and Georgia have other worries on their minds: credit payments to be made and not merely on houses and cars (in some cases, second houses and second cars and boats), the funding of pension programs, possible cutbacks in medical and dental benefits, and the steadily rising cost of appliances, vacations, and college educations for their children.

In mentioning all this, I do not want to disparage the affluence of blue-collar workers or to minimize the real problems and frustrations they encounter. Rather, I want to underline the fact that the great difference in the current U.S. economy is not between the propertied class and the working class or between the bourgeoisie and the proletariat, but between those who have an opportunity to participate effectively in the U.S. economy at some level and those who do not. The bishops' concern in their letter is very much for those who do not, that is, precisely for those who lack real leverage or influence within the economic system. Most of the American poor cannot alter the course of events by striking, since the economy shows that it does not need or want their labor. Their best hope for altering this situation is by political organization, and their best chance for doing this is when they are sufficiently concentrated in a given geographical area or can cluster around an ethnic or racial community. But they still face the fact that the poor in the United States are a minority and will remain so, barring catastrophic developments in the future.

It is also a mistake, a mistake which is partly encouraged by the image of Grand Central Terminal with which I began, to equate the predicament of the poor in America with the plight of the homeless. For homelessness is only one facet of poverty in the United States, though it is the most dramatic and the most visible one precisely because the homeless are likely to be found around Grand Central or sleeping on grates near the State Department in Washington or in similar places. But homelessness frequently originates in psychological factors which cannot be overcome in any simple or direct way by bureaucratized social programs. It is a condition which responds more to care and patience (which involve commitments of both personal and economic resources) than to macroeconomic management. The condition of the homeless, with its pathos and its challenges to both pragmatism and complacency, is an important factor in public awareness of the problems of the poor. But to focus on it is profoundly misleading if it leads us to think of the poor as the psychologically or socially inadequate or as unable or unwilling to work. It can also create false expectations about what government programs can do to resolve the problem; for it is very unlikely that so long as the courts and liberal opinion oppose involuntary hospitalization of the mentally ill, and so long as American cities continue a policy of permissive neglect, the homeless will disappear from our midst.

What is different about the problem of the homeless in contemporary American society is their increased visibility and the comparative absence of sustaining or containing institutions and networks of aid. It is, however, not to be expected that the kinds of programs recommended by the bishops in the second half of their letter dealing with policy questions will alter the problems of the homeless in any fundamental way. These recommendations call for national standards for welfare benefits, for greater respect for family values and personal dignity in the administration of welfare programs, for government job-creation programs aimed at the structurally unemployed, for improved job-creation strategies and job-placement services. These are recommendations that can reasonably be expected to bring some benefits to people at higher levels of the social ladder than the homeless and the destitute, and they may bring some marginal or indirect improvements even to them. But the effective resolution of their problems will require a combination of humble charity, social imagination, and scientific progress in treating personality disorders, a combination which goes beyond anything the bishops propose or can command.

Fifth, the paragraph under consideration sets the task of the letter in pragmatic terms. The test of the economy is not its conformity to a priori rules or conceptions of human nature and society or even to divine commands, but its effects in the lives of all human beings and especially the poor. This is one example of a fundamental tendency in the development of the letter, that is, its turning from more abstract categories to more specific ones. Originally, as the letter was conceived in November 1980, it was to be a letter on capitalism. It was proposed by Bishop Peter Rosazza, an auxiliary bishop of Hartford, Connecticut, as a counterpart to the letter on Marxism which had just been adopted by the bishops in their annual meeting that year. The decision was taken at that same meeting to authorize preparation of the letter on war and peace; and two ad hoc committees were set up, the one on war and peace being under the chairmanship of Archbishop Joseph Bernardin of Cincinnati (who has since become cardinal archbishop of Chicago), and the one on capitalism being led by Archbishop Rembert Weakland of Milwaukee, a musicologist and former abbot primate of the Benedictines. The Weakland committee included bishops from Atlanta, Salt Lake City, and St. Cloud (Minnesota), as well as Bishop Rosazza of Hartford. It did not have clear or sharp internal divisions on the issues it was considering (unlike the Bernardin committee); and it has generally presented a united front to the outer world while doing its work in an atmosphere free of tension and confrontation.

The committee did, however, change its original mandate from the preparation of a letter on capitalism as such to a letter on the U.S. economy and Catholic social teaching. There are three aspects of this change that deserve comment. In the first place, it enabled the bishops to avoid the difficulties that would have inevitably arisen if they had taken an inherently universal topic such as capitalism. For capitalism is a different social and economic reality in Latin America, East Asia, and Europe than it is in the United States. The bishops would have had a more complex subject to deal with and also a subject about which they had less knowledge. They would also have seemed to be pronouncing on institutions and problems that are more properly the concern of other bishops' conferences or of those responsible for governing the universal church. In the second place, the shift in the topic made for a more direct connection between the teaching of the bishops and public policy, for public policy discussion has to focus on the U.S. economy and not on a general system which is at most imperfectly exemplified in the actual structures of the U.S. economy. Third, the bishops were able to avoid some of the fundamental philosophical and theological problems about capitalism, problems which have been puzzling thoughtful people ever since the outlines of the capitalist system of political economy became evident in Western Europe in the eighteenth century. How the pursuit of self-interest is to be reconciled with the common good and Christian love, how free enterprise is to be harmonized with public order, how the virtues and attitudes appropriate to Christians are to be reconciled with the needs and practices of corporate life, what the connection should be between historical experience and our visions of ideal community in the shaping of a morally satisfactory society in the circumstances of justice — these are all interesting topics of fundamental importance which the letter does not address in an extended or explicit way. Rather, it takes as given the existing institutional structure of American society and the distribution of roles within it. Thus at the end of the first half of the draft, in a section dealing with the responsibilities and rights of diverse economic agents and institutions, the bishops offer a series of reformist admonitions in which we can easily see the influence of both Catholic institutional conservatism and American pragmatism on the formulation of demands for a more just and more participatory society.

A sixth point that should be made about this important early paragraph in the bishops' letter is that it is addressed not merely to the Catholic faithful but also to the public at large. Thus the treatment of the poor is proposed as a criterion for the actions of all, not merely for Christians. Here, in fact, the bishops could have quoted the words of Dr. Samuel Johnson: "A decent provision for the poor is the true test of civilization."[3] As in the letter on war and peace, which was approved at the bishops' meeting in Chicago in May 1983, the bishops wished both to remind Catholics of their moral responsibilities and to make an effective contribution to the public policy debate on matters of current concern. They state their objectives in the following terms:

> We write with two purposes. The first is to provide guidance for members of our own church as they seek to form their consciences and reach moral decisions about economic matters. The second is to add our voice to the public debate about U.S. economic policies. In pursuing the first of these purposes we argue from a distinctively Christian perspective that has been shaped by the Bible and by the content of Christian tradition, and from a standpoint that reflects our faith in God: Father, Son, and Holy Spirit. The second purpose demands that our arguments be developed in a reasoned manner that will be persuasive to those who do not share our faith or our tradition.[4]

This is a statement which closely parallels the description of audiences, objectives, and premises of argument given in the letter on war and peace. It manifests a desire to combine two theological approaches: The conciliar and postconciliar reliance on biblical faith and the methods of biblical theology in understanding moral and social questions, along with the traditional Catholic reliance on philosophical modes of argument in the natural law tradition which do not presuppose Christian faith and which parallel the more abstract levels of public policy discussion.

This double conception of audience, objective, and method of argument in the two letters has been both a major strength and a continuing source of difficulties. It is a major strength because it recognizes the breadth of the task of Christian social ethics, which cannot be either purely religious or fundamentally secular with a few religious overtones; and because it enables the bishops and their writers and advisors to draw on the whole range of relevant social and religious considerations. It also places the work of the bishops within the continuing Catholic theological tradition, which has customarily been willing to draw on nonreligious sources. The double conception also gives rise to certain difficulties, some of which are simply the reverse of its virtues. Thus, its complexity provokes questions about consistency of argument, about the criteria for modifying either religious or secular elements in the argument in case of conflict, about the secular competence of the bishops, and about the purity of the bishops' motives in attempting to influence public policy.

Some difficulties that were raised about the letters have faded as the discussion developed. For instance, one of the first reactions to the war and peace pastoral was that it violated the separation of church and state, a hallowed principle of American constitutional law. Further reflection convinced nearly everyone that such an interpretation of the separation of church and state would restrict the freedom of speech which the bishops have along with all other citizens and would be a barrier to the free exercise of religion which the Constitution explicitly guarantees. The difficulty about the competence of the bishops on such secular topics as nuclear deterrence and economic policy has been at least partially resolved by the procedure that they have followed in the preparation of the letters. For they have consulted widely with academic experts in various disciplines and have met with representatives of various groups whose interests would be affected by their policy recommendations. They have encouraged open discussion and criticism of the successive drafts of the letters. They have also made it clear that they do not wish to impose their policy conclusions with the full weight of their religious authority, a point which was particularly important both to proponents of the autonomy of the laity and to those non-Catholics who feared a divisive religious intrusion into political life. The procedure and the encouragement of open discussion fit well with the values of American culture but are less acceptable to those theological conservatives who prefer for the mysteries of the ecclesial kitchen to remain concealed and for its products to be seen as beyond public criticism.

Two interesting difficulties, however, remain in this area. The first has to do with the selection of the relevant secular sources and principles which, as the bishops admit, need to be brought into the argument. They describe their use of these materials in the following terms:

> Our second purpose in issuing this letter is to influence the public policies of our nation, and so we must also persuade those who do not share our faith or our tradition. Therefore we appeal to many sources of analysis and judgment which are not strictly religious or theological. In doing so we necessarily have

to make judgments about which philosophical frameworks, economic theories and explanations of particular problems are more rationally defensible. We are convinced that these judgments will stand up to public scrutiny, though we acknowledge that persons of good will may in some cases reach differing conclusions.[5]

Some selection among contending economic theories and philosophical interpretations of economic life is plainly necessary once one acknowledges, as the bishops do, that "the Bible, taken alone, does not provide direct solutions to complex policy questions."[6] There are two main suggestions in the pastoral itself about the basis for making these judgments and selections. The suggestion found in the text quoted from par. 20 is rational defensibility under public scrutiny. The other suggestion is that the selection is to be made on the basis of religious convictions about the dignity of the person and the communitarian character of human life. (pars. 23, 24) The bishops tell us that "our discussion of U.S. economic life today is rooted in this vision of human dignity and social solidarity." (par. 25) More specifically, they tell us that their argument is "shaped by an overriding concern for the impact of decisions and policies on the lives of people, especially the poor."[7]

If one does not expect to arrive at a value-free form of social science that will be used for the shaping of public policy, then a suggestion that economic analyses and theories might be chosen for their compatibility with moral and religious values should not be dismissed out of hand. But the process of making such choices needs much more careful scrutiny than the bishops have been able to give it. The bishops seem to maintain that neither suggestion gives a unique satisfactory result. Some element of subjective selection enters into the rational scrutiny; and at the same time "good will" and commitment to sound moral principles do not ensure agreement on the analytic level. This is a pattern of inconclusive argument and more or less informed choice that can be duplicated in many other policy debates and in the decision processes that public officials carry on.

The bishops are dealing with a problem that has two different levels. On the one level, there are fundamental issues in the theory of knowledge and the theory of action in their social aspects. The connection of rationality and commitment, the problem of ideological influences on objective policy assessment, the relationship of faith and reason are all involved on this level. It would be unreasonable to expect the bishops to give a comprehensive and satisfactory account of these matters in a pastoral letter. But there is also another less ultimate level on which the problem of choice among approaches to the economy arises and on which criticisms are made about what the bishops are doing. Briefly, the claim is made by conservatives (though a similar claim could also be made by radicals on the left) that the choice of analytic perspectives by the U.S. bishops in both their major letters shows the influence of the liberal academic establishment. In fact, conservatives have taken delight in pointing out that the analyses and recommendations of the two letters have been applauded by Harvard professors and by public figures from the center to the left of the Democratic Party. In the spring of 1985, for instance, there was a debate on the pastoral at the Berkeley campus of the University of California in which John Kenneth Galbraith argued in favor of the letter's policy recommendations and Milton Friedman argued against. Some critics pointed out that many of those who strongly endorse what the bishops are saying on economic and security questions are less responsive when the bishops speak on abortion or in defense of traditional family values. This is true, and it underlines both the complexity of the bishops' agenda for American society and the shifting ideological coalitions found in a pluralistic society. It is also the obverse of a point that is made by defenders of the pastorals, namely, that many who invoke the authority of the pope and the bishops on moral issues of human sexuality and the family often disregard their teaching and the values it proposes when they deal with larger social issues.

The fact remains that the bishops in these two pastorals are in an informal ideological alliance with the liberal (in the American sense of moderately left) academic establishment. This is not in itself discreditable. A fundamental factor to bear in mind here is that it would be difficult to find a major Western political movement or intellectual school that had no affinities in either form or content with Christian teaching or that had no areas of convergence with important Christian values. If this can be true for explicitly antireligious movements such as Marxism, then it should be even more likely when we consider more neutral or permissive movements or schools of thought. The bishops themselves are in effect saying that they are looking for the best ideas that they can find. When they are dealing with social policy questions, this means ideas that will be rationally defensible in public debate, that will be applicable in a very imperfect world, and that will contribute to the embodiment of Christian values. So it is not surprising that Catholic social teaching should make use of analyses and policy recommendations from secular sources.

The problem the bishops have is that their choices have put them on one side of a vigorous ideological battle that is currently being waged by neoconservatives, libertarians, and laissez-faire economic theorists against a well-entrenched interventionist and internationalist liberal consensus which looks back to the accomplishments and aspirations of the New Deal of Franklin Roosevelt and the Great Society of Lyndon Johnson. The Reagan presidency has given media visibility and political influence to a whole series of critical proposals which deny the effectiveness of government intervention in the economy and challenge many liberal assumptions about the goals of government policy. Liberals, whether in the think-tanks and research institutes of Washington or in the elite universities or in the upper ranks of the government bureaucracy, have found that they have had to reexamine ideas that had guided them for a long period of time as well as ideas that they had been encouraged to reject as undergraduates. The assumption of the superior effectiveness and superior righteousness of the liberal way of thinking has been badly shaken, along with the conviction that the Democratic Party, which has been the majority party since 1932, was, despite temporary reverses and dissensions, the natural party of government. Thus there is a distinct likelihood that the bishops have adopted ideas that were once powerful and attractive but that have now lost their political vigor and usefulness. This can be regarded as evidence of the prophetic character of what the bishops are doing and its essential independence of intellectual fashions or as evidence of the church's knack for "discovering" ideas that are past their prime.

The bishops would, I think, reject both interpretations and would affirm that they are making a conscientious choice of what seem to them to be the best available theories and proposals. This choice puts them at odds with the present administration and its ideological supporters. The bishops might gain by more explicit reflection on the factors shaping their choices and by a stronger sense of the irony and complexity of such choices, but it is difficult to believe that they would choose differently. For they and their staff people approach the whole problem of meeting human needs through economic activity from the perspective of Catholic social teaching, which has always been interventionist and anti-laissez faire and which has been more than ready to remedy the deficiencies of the market through government programs. If the bishops were going to enter into the American public policy debate on these issues at all, and if they were going to do so in conformity with the development of Catholic social teaching in the papal encyclicals and in Vatican II, they were bound to be in opposition to significant aspects of the Reagan program. If they wanted to take stands on specific policy issues, the bishops would have to make some such choices as they did. And I would add my own opinion that their choices in this area and on national security issues in the earlier pastoral, while not beyond all criticism, meet the test of being "rationally defensible." But did they have to enter the public policy debate? And were they wise to get so deeply involved in making specific recommendations?

This brings us to the fifth and final difficulty confronting the bishops' project in the pastoral letters, namely, the specific policy recommendations which they make in the second half of the first draft of the pastoral and in the third chapter of the second draft. These recommendations have to do with employment policy, reform of the welfare system, preservation of the family farm, and international development assistance. The original fourth policy section, which concerns the necessity of collaboration in shaping the economy, and which is now a separate chapter, has virtually nothing to offer by way of specific recommendations. The principles which it proposes could lead to a radical restructuring of the American economy and society or to a series of collaborative reforms.

The policy sections of the letter do not attempt to provide a comprehensive treatment of morally compelling topics in the U.S. economy. The bishops themselves observe that "numerous important issues which one could legitimately expect to be here will not be treated in the document" and that the issues actually treated are "illustrative topics intended to exemplify the interaction of moral values and economic issues in our day."[8] Thus the bishops have not attempted to deal explicitly and in detail with such vexing problems as the continuing high level of interest rates, the U.S. budget deficit, the U.S. trade deficit, the economic effects of U.S. defense policies, and the reform of the U.S. tax system. Since no one today seems to be in a position to write a *Summa Theologica Economica*, the bishops should not be faulted for their failure to address all the major issues in current economic debates. The topics that they actually chose do meet criteria that the bishops propose, namely, they "deal with U.S. economic policies that are basic to the establishment of economic justice" and they "serve to illustrate key moral principles and norms for action from Catholic teaching."[9] The necessary incompleteness and selectivity in this half of the pastoral does mean that, since the bishops are dealing with a very complex system whose parts interact with each other and in which gains legitimately sought by one group or element may have intended and unacceptable consequences for others, there has to be a certain tentativeness in the policy recommendations.

In fact, the bishops approach this part of their task with a strong sense of the limited character of what they can say. Thus they affirm that "the movement from principle to practice is a complex and sometimes difficult task" and that "ethical principles in themselves do not dictate specific kinds of programs or provide blueprints for action."[10] The bishops acknowledge that other participants in the debate who hold the same moral principles may reach different policy conclusions because they interpret the principles differently or because they adopt different assumptions about the relevant "historical, social, and political realities," or because they rely on different prudential judgments. For these reasons, the bishops refrain from imposing the specific conclusions they reach as a matter of religious authority. At this point they quote the assertion of their previous pastoral letter on peace that "not every moral statement in this letter has the same moral authority."[11] The response that the bishops expect to their specific proposals is not unquestioning obedience but "serious attention and consideration." This does not sit well with those who prefer church teaching to be presented in a more authoritative mode and therefore to be confined to those topics on which the church can speak authoritatively. It does avoid the risk of producing anger and bitterness in those who disagree or in those who regard the specific economic and political agenda of the bishops as an alien addition to their own religious concerns.

But even if we grant that the bishops are diving into the tank of political and economic sharks from a low diving board and with lifejackets and other precautions and qualifications, the question still remains: why do they dive in at all? There is, I think, one fundamental answer to this question. It is that, as they themselves say, they desire "to influence the public policies of our nation."[12] In dealing with so pragmatic a people as the citizens of the United States, it seems necessary to show that general principles can make a difference on the level of policies and actions. Furthermore, the bishops are moved by concerns about the actual needs of real people, not by a desire to achieve a fuller formulation of church teaching as such (interesting and important though that might be). The ultimate objective has to be to meet the needs of human beings in a way that respects their dignity and nurtures their ability to function in a free and creative way. Cries for real bread and real jobs cannot be stilled simply by better or safer documents. The economic problems and the unmet human needs of American citizens are less stark and less dramatic than those of people in most Third World countries; and they are less massive and less urgent than they were at the time of the Great Depression.

But the point remains that there is a qualitative difference between effective social and the moral discourse which urges us to such action. There is, as Thomas Aquinas observed long ago, a movement in our practical life from the mind to things. In the public life of a pluralistic democratic society, this involves a complex, open-textured debate in which arguments have to be advanced and reasons have to be given with a shifting background of premises, on many of which there is no stable public agreement. Public debate has to be polymorphic and is not confined to the unfolding of straightforward deductive arguments. Persuasion itself is less than a fully rational process. The building of a consensus and the enactment of a policy usually require some combination of compromise and skillful leadership. Successful implementation of policy requires agreement by the majority and serious commitment at least by the group that sees the need for change and by the officials who will carry out that change. All this means that between the tip of the peninsula which is the limit of reasoned argument from common moral principles to the opposite shore which is the achievement of the desired social good there is a complex and difficult passage across the shifting currents of an ocean which is not fully charted and which is in many ways unpredictable. The American bishops have chosen to initiate this voyage on behalf of the church, which is an important decision on their part and not without risks; but the concern that they have for the goal to be obtained makes this decision appropriate, even if it is not logically required or uniquely justifiable. The bishops have been concerned to minimize the risks of their decision; and they would probably be content if, in the long run, they were seen as contributing to a public debate which resolved some of the problems they were concerned about, even if their specific policy recommendations were not implemented.

This is a general line of reflection that supports the decision to deal with specific policies. It can be supplemented by more pragmatic considerations such as the greater pedagogical effectiveness, in the American context, of statements which have a clear bearing on current policy debates or the usefulness of statements which can maintain alliances between church groups and labor unions and minority groups. But these are, I believe, quite secondary considerations.

But beyond the general question of dealing with specific policy issues, there are more specific questions about how these issues are dealt with in the letter. Here I will confine myself to one example; it is, however, an example which has been widely discussed. The first recommendation that the bishops offer in their discussion of unemployment is the following:

We recommend that the nation make a major new policy commitment to achieve full employment. We believe that an unemployment rate in the range of 3 percent or 4 percent is a reasonable definition of full employment in the United States today. ... In the light of the possibilities for reducing unemployment and the criteria for doing so successfully, we believe 6 percent to 7 percent unemployment is unacceptable and is not the best the United States can do. While a zero unemployment rate is clearly impossible in an economy where many people are constantly entering the job market and others are changing jobs, appropriate policies and concerted private and public action can improve the situation considerably, given the will to do so. No economy can be considered truly healthy when so many millions of people are denied jobs by forces outside their control.[13]

A Catholic businessman remarked to me about this passage: "When the bishops say things like this, I am ashamed for the church." Certainly, as he went on to argue, there is no text in Scripture or in the defined doctrines of the church which dictates that we should accept 2 to 3 percent instead of 6 to 7 percent. One plausible reaction is to say that providing more people with jobs is indeed a praiseworthy goal, but the church should not attempt to make lower unemployment rates obligatory. Another reaction is to say that the bishops are inconsistent. For if unemployment is such a great evil that we should change policies and spend large sums of money to reduce it, then we should eliminate it altogether. After all, no one thinks that the bishops would be content to accept a comparable reduction in the number of abortions. Both of these reactions have hold of important points, but they strike me as incomplete responses. For joblessness is a serious social evil which blights the lives of those it affects. Each percentage point in U.S. unemployment levels represents a million persons. The goal of reducing unemployment is morally more urgent than simply bringing about a desirable state of affairs such as making video-cassette recorders generally available. Talk of accepting a higher "natural" rate of unemployment blunts that sense of urgency. One the other hand, there are limits to what can be done in any economy which allows significant freedom to either capital or labor. Unemployment, precisely because it involves underlying trends in the economy and lies beyond the reach of individual decisions by employers and employees, cannot be equated with those evils which it is in principle possible to avoid by individual decisions. So the

2–3 percent goal represents an adjustment of the good to the possible; an impossible good cannot be made obligatory.

But the bishops also offer a supporting comment for their position. They say: "Toleration of present unemployment rates would have been unthinkable 20 years ago. It should be regarded as unacceptable today."[14] The bishops are certainly right in their historical claim, but their inference to the proper present attitude is suspect. For it suggests that it is both possible and wise to restore the conditions of twenty years ago, that the major economic changes of the last twenty years are of relatively little moment, that the good old days of American industrial supremacy can be restored even while worthy but costly programs for creating jobs and providing social and economic benefits are extended to millions. In fact, in the course of preparing the second draft of the letter, the bishops eliminated the specific unemployment target, even while keeping most of their argumentation.

Among the most difficult questions about the bishops' letter and the future of the U.S. economy are whether the bishops have really come to terms with the creative destruction that Joseph Schumpeter saw as characteristic of capitalism and whether they really grasp the altered situation and prospects of the U.S. economy within the global economy. What may well stand out when we look back at the letter ten or twenty years from now is not the extent to which it criticized the U.S. economy, but the extent to which it accepted it. Certainly, the desire of the bishops to shape that economy in a more humane way is deeply felt and is highly laudable. This has not silenced all critics, or ensured the acceptance of the bishops' proposals; but it does mean that the bishops have not generally encountered violent or bitter criticism. With regard both to this letter and to the previous letter on war and peace, there is a widespread sense in many parts of the American public that the bishops are addressing troubling and difficult aspects of contemporary American society and that even if their solutions are inadequate, they deserve serious consideration for the statement of the problems and for the way in which they connect these unresolved problems (which Americans normally discuss in provincial and ahistorical terms) with the tradition of Christian theology. Roman Catholicism in the United States represents a unique combination of institutional power, religious yearning, intellectual definiteness, and historical memory. To these the current generation of bishops has now added a very American willingness to explore difficult practical issues and to enter into public debate in a pluralistic society. In all likelihood, it is the public theology of American Catholicism that will be its major contribution to the universal church and to ecumenical life in the United States. The pastoral letter on the U.S. economy, in its first draft and its subsequent revisions, will be an important part of that contribution.

NOTES

1. National Conference of Catholic Bishops, *Catholic Social Teaching and the U.S. Economy*, first draft (Washington, D.C.: United States Catholic Conference, 1984), 3.
2. Ibid., 231–40.
3. James Boswell, *The Life of Samuel Johnson*, ed. George Birkbeck Hill (New York: Bigelow, 1894), II, 150.
4. *Catholic Social Teaching and the U.S. Economy*, 17.
5. Ibid., 20.
6. Ibid., 65.
7. Ibid., 21.
8. Ibid., 152.
9. Ibid., 153.
10. Ibid., 151.
11. Ibid., 155.
12. Ibid., 20.
13. Ibid., 179.
14. Ibid.

R. BRUCE DOUGLASS

First Things First: The Letter and the Common Good Tradition

R. BRUCE DOUGLASS is an Associate
Professor and Chairman in the
Department of Government of
Georgetown University. He received his
Ph.D. from Duke University in political
science and a theological degree from Yale
University as well.

I. Introduction

LET ME BEGIN at what I think is the beginning, focusing your attention on a question that should have been asked — and seriously discussed — long before now. The debate which the U.S. Catholic bishops' pastoral letter on the economy has elicited to date has not been particularly edifying, in my judgment, and the reason is in large measure the neglect of the question that I have in mind. This question concerns the standards that are appropriate in evaluating a document of this kind. How should it be judged? What constitutes a fair and intellectually responsible way of assessing the argument and point of view which it seeks to articulate? To be critically self-conscious in this regard is vitally important, I would submit, because of the peculiar character of a document of this sort in the context of our public life. It is not, after all, like most of the other contributions to public discourse with which we are familiar. Even though it addresses issues which are the staples of public debate in a modern society like the United States, it does so in a quite distinctive way. It seeks, specifically, to articulate a theological perspective on economics, and it therefore entails a deliberate effort to bring together two modes of thought that, in recent memory at least, have had very little to do with one another. Indeed, the separation of economics from the influence of Christian theology and its concerns is so integral to modern consciousness as to be part of the very definition of the word *modern*. Any attempt like that entailed by the bishops' letter to bridge this chasm requires, in turn, an evaluation which takes both sides of the argument seriously. Insofar as it embraces particular economic analyses and policies, it must be judged on those terms, to be sure, but not on those terms alone. It must be judged theologically—and philosophically—as well, and given the nature and function of a pastoral letter, I would even argue that primacy should be given to the theological component of the evaluation. Good theology is certainly no compensation for bad economics, but the document is first and foremost a theological statement and needs to be judged accordingly.

The primary consideration should be, therefore, the adequacy of the theological (and philosophical) interpretation of the nature and purpose of economic activity which the letter offers. Does it really do justice to what reason and revelation today tell us about the place of economics in our lives and about the standards appropriate for ordering that part of our existence? But nothing could be further from the way the public discussion of the document has in fact proceeded. Theology has been largely ignored, and the focus has been almost entirely on the economic adequacy of the position(s) the bishops have embraced. One would think, reading much of what has been written in the press, that the letter were just another pronouncement by the Democratic National Committee or the AFL-CIO. Given the unfamiliarity of most of our pundits with theological arguments, this is predictable, of course, but it has skewed the discussion in a highly unfortunate direction. The critics have had a particular tendency to focus on a few of the letter's more controversial policy proposals, to the almost complete neglect of the theological and philosophical foundation on which those proposals rest. Much of what has been said about this part of the document has simply been an effort to pin the bishops with the appropriate ideological label, that is, whether they should be called "liberals" or "Social Democrats."

Such trivialization of a serious argument is, of course, one of the best ways of deflecting its thrust, and I suspect that explains much of the treatment the document has received. Some of what it says is not at all welcome news to the audience it seeks to address. For a long time Catholic social thought has been out of step, in varying degrees, with the attitudes and behavior that come naturally to modern people, and the present letter, precisely because it is in its own way a rather traditional statement, conforms to this pattern. What better way, in turn, to avoid the challenge it poses than to dismiss its claims as the belief that "God subscribes to the liberal agenda"?[1] Whatever the motives of such innuendo, it needs to be stoutly resisted, particularly by Catholic intellectuals, whose very vocation is implicitly at issue. Regardless of our final conclusions about the letter's merits, it deserves better treatment solely on the grounds of the importance of the general issue it raises. In addition, there are, as I shall seek to show, good reasons for appreciating certain of its arguments on their merits as well.

I.

WHAT, THEN, ARE the merits of the statement? Does it articulate a theology of economic life that is relevant to the present phase of American history? More broadly, does it articulate what men and women who seek today to live out the demands of godly living — whether they be Catholic, Orthodox, or Protestant — ought to believe and do with respect to the production and distribution of economic goods? The answer I propose is in principle affirmative, but with certain significant qualifications.

In making this judgment, I presuppose a particular way of interpreting the character of the letter's argument. There is more than a little uncertainty about the letter in this regard, principally because of the strong emphasis it places on the fate of the poor. As a result of this emphasis, some critics have charged that the position of the bishops represents a new departure which owes more to certain ideas currently fashionable in secular philosophy (most notably, the Rawlsian "difference principle") than to the church's historic teaching. I do not find this allegation persuasive, however. There is, to be sure, an unmistakable element of novelty in the theological part of the argument, and it is of no small consequence. Indeed, I shall argue that is of great importance in defining the position the letter embraces. But this innovation neither violates nor supplants traditional Catholic social teaching. And treating it as a foreign element will not help us understand it.

The fundamental theme of traditional Catholic teaching in this field has long been the idea of the common good, and that theme is very evident in the letter. Indeed, this theme provides the real foundation of what the bishops have to say about the "deeper meaning" of economic life. The stress they place on the fate of the poor can well be understood as an extension of this traditional teaching. In similar fashion, the emphasis on the fate of the industrial working class in the encyclicals *Rerum Novarum* and *Quadragesimo Anno* derived from an application of Catholic principles to the conditions of the times. Far from breaking with tradition, the bishops may be read as simply applying to the poor in this society things which the church has said about the disadvantaged for a long time. Insofar as there is an innovative element in the argument, it owes much more, I believe, to developments that are internal to the evolution of Catholic theology in recent decades than to any alien philosophical or political influence. I refer in particular to the increasing importance attached to Scripture and the new "critical" way of reading it.[2] This is clearly reflected in the design of the letter, especially in Part I, and it is of more than stylistic significance. The heavy reliance on Scripture affects the substance of the argument as well, and this above all, I believe, explains its character. The theology which the bishops are proposing as the proper basis for understanding economic life is the fruit of an effort to update the common good tradition, an updating whose principal motif is a more complete integration than in the past of the social theory which common good teaching entails with resources drawn from Scripture.

I shall return to the consequences of this attempt to give Scripture a larger role. As will become evident, I do not think these consequences are altogether salutary. First, however, I want to elaborate on the place of the common good tradition in the bishops' letter. Given the controversy about the nature and purpose of the theological claims which the bishops make, I want to be as precise as possible about the way in which I see this tradition reflected in the document. This is hardly the place, of course, to enter into a detailed discussion of the social theory which the common good tradition entails.[3] But three of the claims made by the letter are so significant and relate so directly to the common good tradition that they are worth emphasizing, however briefly.

One claim is that economic activity is to be understood as a means to serve higher purposes and not as an end in itself. Economic institutions are not to be evaluated solely in terms of economists' considerations—i.e., productive efficiency—but also by the contribution which they do (or do not) make to the well-rounded development of the human person.[4] The clear implication is that economic activity must be put in its place. It is important to human welfare, to be sure, as the letter clearly acknowledges, but it is not *ultimately* important. A well-ordered society, therefore, is one in which economic considerations are not the be-all and end-all of human existence; and where economic efficiency conflicts with the pursuit of other "higher" goods, it can and will be compromised.

Second, the proper way for human beings to relate to one another is in *community*—i.e., as self-conscious collaborators in enterprises of mutual interest and concern. This pertains to economics as well as to everything else. We are to think of the economic means at our disposal as common resources with which we have been entrusted in order to seek the good of the whole community. The document stops short of carrying this idea to the point of advocating collective ownership of the means of production. On the contrary, it affirms, in a very traditional manner, the utility and even virtue of private property. But at the same time, it insists on the necessity of viewing the property with which individuals (and other private economic actors) find themselves entrusted as just that, a trust, given to them to serve the common good and not just private interest. Those who dispose of the means of production on behalf of the community, says the letter (striking a very biblical theme), are to view themselves as stewards of the earth, responsible to God and the community alike for its proper use.

Third, the letter insists, again in highly traditional fashion, that the common good should be consciously willed and pursued in the design of social institutions and public policy. There is not a hint here of confidence in an Invisible Hand bringing the common good out of individual self-interest exercised independently of the wider good of the community. The common good, unmistakably, is a good which must be deliberately sought, and the implication is that in the absence of such conscious pursuit, it will not, in fact, be achieved—or at least not achieved very well. This implies, in turn, a substantial role for government. As the text correctly observes, Catholic social thought has long held that one of government's prime tasks is "the coordination and regulation of diverse groups in society in a way that leads to the common good and the protection of basic rights."[5] But the principle is not confined to government alone. It implies the conscious design—or at least cultivation—of the whole institutional fabric of a society to achieve the common good. Not only government, but industry, the schools, the arts, the family, etc. should all be structured and maintained to enable people to live together in a way that promotes the full well-being of one another.

Much more could be said on this subject. But these summary remarks are enough to establish an impression and to convey a sense of what is involved in thinking in these terms. The key question is whether those responsible for drafting the letter have chosen wisely in continuing to uphold, albeit in an adapted form, this essentially traditional way of thinking. I am inclined to answer affirmatively. I am, in fact, very favorably impressed with the letter's general theological orientation. I know of no comparable statement on the same topic in recent memory that comes close to matching the cogency of the theological and philosophical parts of its argument.

To explain this judgment, however, I must comment briefly on what I understand to be the general challenge which confronts anyone seeking to undertake what the letter entails. The basic, underlying issue in any such attempt to make theological sense of economics, consonant with the distinctive theological claims of Christianity, is how to reconcile the competing claims of godly living and economic efficiency. Unlike some of the other great world religions, Christianity — in its Western mutations, at least — is not in principle world-denying, nor does it deprecate material well-being. On the contrary, as an extension of Judaism, it affirms the goodness of human efforts to take control of the earth and exploit it for human benefit, and it treats as part of God's providence the goods and services which human beings acquire through their labor to improve their lot. There are different emphases among the Christian communions in this regard, to be sure, but in principle Christian teaching has supported consistently efforts to improve the material conditions of life. On the other hand, Christian thought has long recognized that true human fulfillment lies beyond material well-being, and that there is always a danger with economic activity and material prosperity that mundane pursuits and pleasures may distract us from our true vocation. Especially in the New Testament, with its tendency to interpret godly living as the single-minded pursuit of one thing, is the danger of flirtation with Mammon apparent; but this has almost always been a part of orthodox Christian thinking. Even Calvin, who is perhaps best remembered for opening Pandora's box with respect to work and usury, spoke eloquently (and critically) of the spiritual dangers involved in the pursuit of riches.

The question for most of the history of Christian thought has been how to do justice simultaneously to both of these concerns. Economic efficiency has a certain theological dignity in Christian thought, but so, too, does living one's life in accord with the demands of piety and virtue (however defined). How do we bring the two together in a way that does not entail sacrificing one for the other? The common good tradition developed, in its economic aspect at least, precisely to meet this demand, and it prevailed as long as it did because it was reasonably successful in this regard. It provided a way of acknowledging the intrinsic worth of economic pursuits without allowing them to become the be-all and end-all of human existence. The tradition was not, however, geared to economic *growth* in the sense to which we have subsequently become accustomed; and this ultimately proved to be its undoing. For the rise of "economic man" in the later Middle Ages and the possibility of the steady multiplication of capital provided by the instrument of the free market, the thinking embodied in the common good tradition was increasingly perceived as restrictive and even reactionary.[6] If only, said the early apologists for capitalism, we could be free of the restraints imposed on economic activity by the church and the state in the name of the common good, a new dynamism could be introduced into our economic life that would enhance in unparalleled ways the material benefits available to us.

Subsequent history has shown this claim to be well founded. A dynamism *has* been introduced into the conduct of economic activity in the West that has resulted in an enormous and relatively steady advance in the standard in living. We live better in a material sense today—far better—than our predecessors in the age of Aquinas because of the late medieval and early modern revolt against the common good tradition. And much of this material well-being must be considered progress by any reasonable standard. The fact that people in the industrialized world have access to good medical care, that food is plentiful and available, that we can afford to educate (for years at a time!) almost every citizen—all of this enhances human well-being in ways that are both profoundly important and beyond dispute. The question, then, which naturally has arisen as the church has sought to adapt itself to these conditions, is whether it should abandon the common good tradition in favor of some more modern and "progressive" alternative.

This question is especially apt with respect to economic liberalism, which is the primary (though by no means the sole) source of the new dynamism that entered the Western world in the seventeenth century. If indeed the set of economic relations which developed from the liberal triumph over Catholic social teaching in the early modern period has been so successful in promoting economic growth and improvement of the material conditions of life, so the argument runs, perhaps the church should reconsider its position. Perhaps it should embrace liberalism, in one form or another, as its own. This argument has never made much headway, however. Instead, the tendency has been to adapt the common good tradition to the new conditions presented by the modern world. The social encyclicals of the modern period have reiterated the characteristic themes of the old tradition, albeit in a modified form to take into account the innovations in economic policy which have fueled modern prosperity; and they have generally been followed in this practice by the architects of modern Catholic social thought.

Why has there been this resistance to adopting a new position? The question is particularly pertinent at a time when, in this country at least, a vigorous effort is being made to reformulate the basic tenets of Catholic teaching on grounds more congenial to liberals.[7] In part, the answer must lie in the role which tradition has played in the development of Catholic thought. But more is involved. The fundamental reason, I would submit, lies in the conviction that all of the modern alternatives to the common good tradition somehow involve claims that are theologically and philosophically unacceptable. Liberalism does indeed provide an extraordinary dynamism in the economic sphere, especially if certain social conditions can be assumed, and it is, moreover, conducive to liberty in a manner that has few parallels. But at what price? It unleashes a competitive spirit which can easily militate against both social justice and community. Furthermore—and this may be the most important consideration of all—it has a well-established tendency to make the pursuit of economic goods the primary aim of existence.

Liberalism, therefore, fails the crucial test: it does not in any way strike a real balance between the twin concerns of spiritual and moral well-being on the one hand, and material well-being on the other. It is what its early apologists said it was: a defiant assertion of the primacy of worldly materialistic concerns over the more complex—and balanced—view of the human good represented by the common good tradition. No amount of celebration of the value of freedom will gainsay this fact. Much the same applies, too, though in a very different way, to socialism, the major competitor to liberalism in today's world. To be sure, socialism meets directly some of the concerns raised in the Catholic critique of liberalism, and seems therefore in some respects to be a viable substitute. This affinity to certain aspects of the common good tradition explains why Catholics tend to be more easily attracted than, say, Protestants to socialism. But unless one is willing to forget spiritual concerns, this alternative, too, is ultimately unsatisfactory. For socialists tend to share with liberals the characteristic "economism" of the modern world, though in a different way. They, too, are inclined to treat economic productivity and related concerns as the heart of the human good, and to treat with contempt or indifference the moral and spiritual concerns which must be preeminent, I would think, in any authentic Catholic social theory.

II.

THE LETTER, THEREFORE, rests on a defensible foundation. Moreover, the common good tradition provides, in my judgment, the best perspective on the nature and purpose of economic activity which is available to Catholics—and, to go further, to Christians generally. It makes far better theological sense of economic life than any of the alternatives currently proposed. Even though it antedates the modern period by several centuries, it can be successfully adapted, I am convinced, to the conditions we now face, and can thus illumine the problems and opportunities of the present era without at the same time adopting wholesale the characteristic biases (and illusions) of modernity. It is valuable precisely because it is not altogether consonant with the ideas and practices currently in vogue. The way of life to which we are accustomed may be comfortable in many respects, but there is much in it that is not at all theologically defensible. Any Christian theology of economics worthy of the name should make us sensitive to this in just the manner the bishops attempt to do in their pastoral letter.

The letter has much to offer which should commend it to anyone, Catholic or not, who is seriously concerned about the general issues it raises. Merely to have articulated anew certain of the themes of the common good tradition as forcefully and effectively as it does, and to have drawn attention, implicitly, to the contrast between that tradition and prevailing assumptions in the economic life of this nation, is a major achievement. For this reason alone, the letter deserves careful study, and anyone who disputes its fundamental claims must be prepared to show that there is a preferable alternative. I for one am skeptical that this can be done.

Granting the soundness of the foundation on which the bishops have chosen to make their case, it is not, however, satisfactory in every respect. To agree with the foundation is not to agree with every particular inference drawn from it. I find the more specific details of the argument unpersuasive in several respects, and I want to indicate briefly some of the more important of these.

(1) One of the more important characteristics of this letter, considered against the background of earlier Catholic social teaching, is, as I have indicated, its reliance on Scripture. This is not just a matter of form; it affects the substance of the argument as well. Those familiar with recent trends in Catholic theology will recognize immediately that this is not accidental. It derives from developments in the post-Vatican II era that are having a profound effect across virtually the whole range of the theological agenda. As a Protestant, I can only applaud in principle what this represents. It meets what has long been an important theological criticism of Catholic social teaching by Protestants, and in the process it adds a vitally important dimension to Catholic theology. The result is that for the first time in a long while Catholic thought is beginning to take on the character of the synthesis of reason and revelation that it has always claimed to be.

Progress in method, however, does not automatically mean progress in the substance of the analysis and argument being advanced. In the case at issue here, I would contend that it clearly does not—certainly not with respect to the coherence and plausibility of one of the letter's essential claims, at least. I refer to the emphasis on distributive justice and the particular interpretation given to that concept. It is in this regard more than any other, I would submit, that the new attention to the claims of Scripture is reflected in the claims the bishops make. For what they propose is that justice is virtually identical with the biblical concern in the ordering of economic relations, and that this is intended in a very specific sense—i.e., care for the well-being of the least advantaged. Critics have alleged, as I have noted, that this reflects the influence of modern philosophy and/or political ideology, such as the Rawlsian "difference principle," but I do not think this charge will bear close scrutiny. Its real source is exactly what the citations in the text suggest—that is, recent scriptural studies, which have established a solid foundation for this part of the letter's theological claims.

But what is scriptural may not necessarily be satisfactory for the purposes of moral and political philosophy. The great strength of Catholic social teaching in the past—a strength which has always compensated for its tendency to give short shrift to Scripture—has been the stress placed on philosophical coherence. For this reason Catholic social thought has tended to have greater philosophical plausibility than Protestant thought, with the difference varying in direct proportion to the extent to which Protestant bibliolatry prevailed. But now, as Catholic teaching begins to incorporate themes deriving from Scripture in a more direct and complete manner, the danger is that it will be afflicted with the same tendency to sacrifice philosophical coherence for scriptural dogmatism from which Protestant thought has so long suffered.

The problem is not the insistence of the priority of justice as the standard by which social—and especially economic—institutions are to be judged. That is hardly a uniquely biblical claim, and it could well be articulated in a philosophically coherent form, a form consonant with the common good tradition which is the foundation of the letter. The problem lies, instead, with the other claim—the notion that justice means, simply, a concern for the well-being of the least advantaged. I have no doubt that there is very good biblical warrant for making this claim (especially in the prophetic literature and the Gospels), but I do question whether it readily can suffice as the sum and substance of the definition of justice in a document meant to encompass the totality of economic life. If the theme of the text were simply the problem of poverty, one might judge this differently. But it is not. The aspiration is to provide a general statement about the nature and purpose of economic activity, and a definition of this sort, which is so narrowly focused on only one aspect of the problem, is inappropriate for this purpose.

Why do I say narrowly focused? The general question of who deserves to get what in the allocation of economic goods—and burdens—has many dimensions. Certainly, the fate of the "disadvantaged" is part of this, and a very important part. But it is still only a part. Equally important are considerations like the following: Who should pay—and in what proportion—for the benefits which go to the least advantaged (the key philosophical issue in the relevant tax policies)? How much—and what kind of—equality in the distribution of benefits among those who are *not* the least advantaged is desirable? To what degree is social mobility a part of social justice?

Merely to raise such questions is to demonstrate the inadequacy of a single-minded attention to the role of the least advantaged. But let me press the point. One can well imagine a society devoting itself very seriously to the task of providing for the welfare of its least advantaged and still falling short of justice in a more complete sense because of its way of dealing with these other issues. Indeed, such a society could actually be judged *unjust* because of the way in which the resulting costs were imposed on the rest of the population. For example, the sacrifices imposed by affirmative action policies fall, typically, not on upper middle-class white males but on their lower middle-class and lower class brothers. Any philosophically coherent concept of distributive justice recognizes this many-sided character of the problem and the need to take all sides into account in an integrated way; to the extent that some biblical passages suggest otherwise, they are simply misleading. On this point in particular, Scripture needs what Catholic teaching has usually required—philosophical refinement, if not correction; and the absence of this makes the current text deficient on a crucial point.

(2) A second issue which needs to be treated with greater sophistication than the present text reveals has to do with the polarity discussed earlier between the competing demands of piety and virtue on the one hand, and economic efficiency on the other. The strength of the common good tradition is that it represents a serious effort to do justice to both demands. But its modern critics would say, justifiably, that ultimately this tradition tended to sacrifice economic efficiency for religious concerns. The question which has been at issue in recent efforts to revise Christian economic (and political) philosophy so as to come to terms with the modern concern with economic growth, is how to make the required changes without creating a new imbalance of the opposite sort. The present document is clearly meant to do this, but it pursues this objective in a way that, in my judgment at least, does not really recognize the seriousness and complexity of the problem. The principal reason for this, I suspect, is that the authors are reluctant to acknowledge what may, in fact, be an unavoidable dilemma—that the sort of prosperity to which we are now accustomed in the industrialized world (and the growth that is part of our expectations) may simply be incompatible with the notions of human fulfillment and virtuous living that are commonly assumed in Catholic moral philosophy and theology.

This, I readily admit, is a controversial claim; and it is one that I obviously cannot develop here in the detail it deserves. But what I have in mind is something that does not require a great deal of exposition, in its initial formulation at least. The point is simple and straightforward: it is very difficult to reconcile the obsession with economic activity and material well-being which has been characteristic of the industrialized societies ever since their "take-off" with the sort of devotion to the higher goods that is central to almost any of the definitions of godly living that are taken seriously in contemporary Catholic theology. This is not to say that economic activity, well-being or growth are per se undesirable. The point is rather that the particular *way* in which they are defined and pursued in modern societies—capitalist and socialist alike—tends to be directly subversive of those qualities of mind and heart that are inherent in a theological understanding of what human existence is suppose to be.

The document occasionally recognizes this tension, but it never really wrestles with the more fundamental issue it raises. It seems to suggest that we can somehow have our cake and eat it too; that we can continue to maintain a huge, growth-oriented economy, in which each generation expects to have a greater standard of living than its predecessor, while at the same time modelling our lives on images which encourage simplicity, frugality, putting the things of this world in proper perspective, etc. But can this really be done? I am not at all sure that we can have it both ways, and it is misleading not to acknowledge the tension, if not contradiction, between the two lines of thought. Such an acknowledgment would be especially useful and welcome in a document with a pastoral function.

This is such a sensitive point that I cannot resist adding a further comment. If, indeed, the simplicity of life which the document rightly recognizes as growing out of theological and ethical claims that are increasingly central to Catholic teaching is to be encouraged as a general norm for virtuous living, then whose purchases will underwrite the millions of jobs that are necessary for realizing the letter's objectives regarding employment and wages? The goal of reduced consumption is altogether appropriate in a document of this kind, even more perhaps for theological than ethical reasons, and it should probably be given even more emphasis. But it can hardly be reconciled with a highly ambitious set of employment goals, unless one is thinking of an economy that is fundamentally different from the present one. It may well be that at least some of the thinking that went into this letter reflects a sense of an economy of the future very different from what we know today in the industrially advanced societies. But this thought is not developed, and thus one of the most important challenges of the document remains unexplored.

(3) The final critical observation I want to raise here concerns, in still another way, the adaptation of the common good tradition to modern conditions and the role assigned to the state in the ordering of economic life. An essential part of the social theory which this tradition entails is, as noted, an insistence that the common good be consciously defined and pursued, and that government play a major role in this process. The bishops' letter, fully in keeping with this tradition, assigns a considerable — though by no means all-encompassing — role to civil authorities in achieving the end it prescribes. Many of the specific policy recommendations it offers simply reiterate the now-familiar steps that have been taken in the social encyclicals and other Catholic pronouncements to adapt this tradition to the logic of the modern welfare state. This occurs, however, in a context in which there is now considerable controversy about the role of the state, and in which long accepted assumptions about the role which the letter proposes for government are increasingly disputed.

There are many complex reasons for this new debate about the role of the state. In part, they have to do with objective political and economic problems which the welfare state has encountered, in one country after another, in recent years. But they also have to do, in no small measure, with the desire of ideologues of a certain sort to impose a particular interpretation on these problems, one which will have the effect of discrediting the whole enterprise that the welfare state represents.[8] The bishops have generally chosen to ignore this view with good reason, in my judgment. Most of the claims that conservative and neoconservative critics are making today about the significance of the welfare state's current troubles are enormously exaggerated, and are not supported by anything like the necessary argumentation and evidence. They deserve to be dismissed without extended comment. The problems themselves, however, which are at issue in this controversy over the role of the state are quite a different matter. There is, in fact, a fiscal crisis of the modern state, and because of this, issues of political economy are attracting much attention these days from political scientists and economists alike. There is also a crisis of delivery, as a result of which both practitioners and analysts of social policy are much less confident now than they were a few decades ago (remember the Great Society?) that the intentions reflected in governmental efforts to produce certain social results can, in fact, be fulfilled. Regardless of what one believes about the conservative interpretation of these problems, they are not merely figments of the conservative imagination. They are real, and are likely to endure. Moreover, it is not at all unreasonable to conclude that we are now entering a new era in the discussion of the role of the state under modern conditions. The hallmark of this era, in turn, will be the requirement that every proposal which entails a significant role for the state be accompanied by careful, self-critical analysis of its feasibility in relation to fiscal policy, on the one hand, and the actual delivery capabilities of public agencies, on the other.

The letter, however, reflects little awareness of these new realities. Even though it speaks eloquently in the introductory paragraphs of the need for theological reflection to be sensitive to "the signs of the times" and in so doing acknowledges the novelty of this particular moment in American economic history, most of its discussion of particular economic issues reads like similar pronouncements of twenty, thirty and even fifty years ago. I refer here primarily to the domestic side of the argument; the international is another matter. Social problems are identified and familiar public policies are proposed as remedies with hardly any acknowledgment of the complications that have been introduced into the appraisal of such recommendations by a half-century of experience. The policy proposals scarcely hint at the ambiguity which increasingly afflicts all of the old cliches about government serving as the agent of the popular will. This is one of the main reasons why the document has been so easily dismissed as nothing more than another ideological statement.

The letter badly needs an infusion of sophistication about the complexities of social policy today. It needs a theory of the state which reflects the realities of the 1970s and 1980s rather than those of the 1930s and 1940s. The difference which this makes may be more a matter of mood than essential substance — although it is by no means simply that — but in this case the nuance is of considerable importance. We are living in a new time. The electorate senses it, as do many politicians; and scholarly analysis is beginning to capture what the difference actually is. In this setting the bishops can ill afford to appear as well-meaning dogmatists who cannot bring themselves to give up outworn clichés. There is no good reason, in any case, why they need appear so. The tradition of thought which they have chosen as the basis for their argument is probably better equipped to respond constructively to these new realities than are most of the alternatives.

The letter, then, is hardly the last word. Much work remains to be done, and some difficult issues must be confronted if the bishops are to meet the challenge which they have posed for themselves. But they have already accomplished a great deal — far more, certainly, than most of their critics have been willing to acknowledge. Simply to have clearly and forcefully raised the issue of the uneasy fit between Christian faith and the current American economy is itself a signal accomplishment. Beyond this, they have gone a long way toward establishing the possibility of a coherent contemporary Christian understanding of the meaning and purpose of economic life. They are on to something which is potentially of great significance for the nation as well as the church, and one can only hope that they pursue this project in the years ahead with the dedication it deserves.

NOTES

This paper is an expanded version of an article which first appeared in *Commonweal*, June 21, 1985, 359–63.

1. George Will, "The Vanity of Bishops," *The Washington Post*, November 15, 1984.

2. Cf. Thomas Sheehan, "Revolution in the Church," *The New York Review of Books* XXXI (10), June 14, 1984, 35–39.

3. I have treated this topic elsewhere in "The Common Good and the Public Interest," *Political Theory* XIII (1), February 1980, 103–117.

4. The key claim which the letter makes about the evaluation of economic systems is *not* in fact what it says about the fate of the poor, but rather the proposition that "The dignity of the human person, realized in community with others, is the criterion against which all aspects of economic life must be measured . . . " A bit later in the text, this is amplified with the affirmation that "Human personhood must be respected with a reverence that is religious . . . Economic life must serve and support this dignity which needs to be realized in relationship and solidarity with others." Cf. "First Draft—Bishops' Pastoral: Catholic Social Teaching and the U.S. Economy," *Origins* 14 (November 15, 1984), secs. 23 and 24, 343.

5. Ibid., sec. 124, 355.

6. The revolt against medieval economic philosophy on these grounds in very well summarized in R. H. Tawney, *Religion and the Rise of Capitalism* (London, 1926).

7. I have in mind here in particular Michael Novak and those associated with him at the American Enterprise Institute. For a convenient summary of the argument they advance, cf. *Toward the Future—Catholic Social Thought and the U.S. Economy: A Lay Letter*, which was issued by a self-appointed lay commission at about the same time as the bishops' letter.

8. A good example of this sort of argument is the highly popular tract by George Gilder, *Wealth and Poverty* (New York, 1981), which derives most of its plausibility from combining worst case assumptions about the consequences of pursuing current trends in the development of the welfare state with best case assumptions about the "supply side" alternative.

ANTHONY J. TAMBASCO

Option for the Poor

ANTHONY TAMBASCO is an Associate
Professor in the Department of Theology
of Georgetown University. He received
his Ph.D. from the Union Theological
Seminary of New York and holds
degrees from the Catholic Institute of
Paris and the Pontifical Biblical Institute
of Rome as well.

I. Introduction

ONE OF THE KEY THEMES recurring throughout the bishops' pastoral letter on the economy is that of the preferential option for the poor. It is
a theme that is in some ways a traditional principle of Catholic social
ethics and in some ways a new emphasis in the teaching.[1] Much of
the background and the sources that influenced this theme developed
especially in Latin American liberation theology and papal teaching
as influenced by liberation theology. However, the letter seems to
draw explicitly on only some of the meaning and implications of the
theme as it is developed in these other sources of Catholic social

teaching. This essay will discuss the meaning of the phrase and draw out implications of the principle as it has evolved in liberation theology and papal teaching, while also making comparisons with the use of the phrase in the bishops' letter on the economy.

II. Hermeneutic Privilege of the Poor

THE TERM "preferential option for the poor" is one that came to prominence when the Latin American bishops' conference at Medellín, Colombia, in 1968, encouraged the development of a new theology that we have come to know as liberation theology.[2] By the time of the next bishops' conference in Puebla, Mexico, in 1979, the phrase was used as the title of an entire document.[3] Gustavo Gutierrez, considered the "father" of liberation theology because of his pioneering and popularizing work, gives a description of the phrase which helps us begin to understand it as it is accepted generally by Latin American liberation theologians. He says, "To opt for the poor is to enter the world of the oppressed race, culture and social class, to enter the universe of their values and cultural categories."[4]

This understanding of the term emphasizes a point not stressed in the bishops' pastoral on the economy and raises the question of how comprehensive a meaning the bishops want to give to the phrase. As understood by liberation theologians, "option for the poor" includes as a primary ingredient what they describe as the "hermeneutic privilege of the poor," i.e., that the poor have a privileged position for interpreting the meaning of their poverty and for judging the work of justice that addresses itself to that situation. As Gutierrez says:

> History (in which God reveals himself and we proclaim him) must be re-read from the viewpoint of the poor.... Remaking history means subverting it, that is to say, "turning it upside down," and seeing it from below instead of from above.... This subversive history involves a new experience of faith, a new spirituality and a new proclamation of the Gospel.[5]

The bishops' pastoral letter does allude quickly to seeing things from the side of the poor. However, the heaviest emphasis seems to be on doing the works of justice *to* the poor and *for* the poor, rather than justice being done *with* the poor and *by* the poor. The bishops undoubtedly stress the former over the latter because they are writing for a wealthy country and for a Christian audience that is by and large middle class. Moreover, the bishops, writing in such a North American context, need to speak out of that specific interpretative context and perspective. Nevertheless, we will better appreciate even the bishops' injunctions if we understand that much of what they write about justice for the poor has been influenced by what the church of the poor has been saying through Latin America. Making this link more explicit will show us that we will more readily know what to do *for* the poor, if we can identify in some way *with* them in their view of reality.

We need to explore, then, the option for the poor as implying a hermeneutic privilege of the poor. This hermeneutic privilege of the poor is not uniquely the claim of liberation theologians. It is the development and application of insights that are widely espoused in Western culture. Liberation theologians find their own implications out of what scholars have described as the sociology of knowledge and out of current trends in the science of textual interpretation.

Sociology of knowledge developed as a reaction to the Enlightenment, and its overconfidence in the possibility of obtaining objective truth and unbiased knowledge of reality through reliance on reason, especially scientific reason. Nietzsche, Freud and Marx all showed in different ways that even in our attempts at objectivity we bring presuppositions to our efforts to understand reality which influence our view of the facts. It is a falsity to establish a sharp polarity between the knowing subject and "the facts" known. Our answers about what is going on depend in large part on how we ask the questions; we most often find just what we are looking for. Our insights are partial and limited, capable of ongoing clarification and enrichment, but we never fully comprehend the objective reality we seek to know. Liberation theologians enter into this discussion by highlighting the particular Marxian insights, namely, that economic presuppositions influence the way in which we see reality. Where one stands in a society and its structures will have an important effect on how one perceives the political and economic order and the issues of justice related to them.[6]

One profound effect of the sociology of knowledge has been in the science of textual interpretation. Scholars like Hans Georg Gadamer and Paul Ricoeur have shown how texts have a life of their own, once released by their authors to the community. Such texts bear meaning far richer than that intended by the authors. Texts begin, as it were, a dialogue between the author and the reader. In such conversation both parties contribute to the communication ultimately given. What the reader brings to the text is as important as what the author does. It is even more the case when dealing with classical or foundational texts. There we find material which, rather than becoming more obscure as it leaves the thought world of the author, becomes more and more luminous as it enters new thought worlds in history.

The Bible is such a document, and current textual interpretation has focused on this "surplus-of-meaning" in a text. Until recently, modern biblical scholarship devoted its skills to deciphering the intention of the author, and equated the meaning of the text with this intention. Now we have entered a period described as postmodern biblical criticism which distinguishes the intention of the author from the meaning of the text, at least insofar as the two are not identical.

Liberation theologians enter into this theory of textual interpretation with their own reading of biblical literature.[7] The poor are a specific group of readers who themselves enter into dialogue with the biblical text. When they ask their particular set of questions, they open the Bible to their world and to a new horizon of meaning. They can draw out of the Bible insights perhaps not recognized before or at least not emphasized before. The hermeneutic privilege of the poor indicates that the poor are especially situated to hear the Word of God as a word addressed to those in oppression and as a word of justice and liberation from that oppression. To undertake the option for the poor is, then, to listen to the Word of God as the poor listen to it. It means acknowledging a hermeneutic privilege that derives new *meaning* from the text, at least as new emphases, and not just new *applications*.

These methodological considerations provide some of the background, but remain, as we said, largely implicit in the bishops' letter. Indeed, the bishops seem cautious in accepting this claim of liberation theologians about a hermeneutic privilege of the poor, a caution arising from the questions that yet remain over this issue. Who says the poor have a better view of reality than anyone else? By what criteria and controls do we ascertain that they view reality accurately? How does one resolve the inevitable conflicts between their viewpoint and those of others? There are no easy answers to these questions, if indeed we can find answers at all at this moment in history. Several observations may be helpful, however, in trying to make sense of this debate. First of all, the solution to these problems cannot be a simple return to a naive realism that assumes we perceive objective reality free of all presuppositions. Whatever we do now, we have no practical alternative but to face up to the influence of our subjective experience and seek to raise to consciousness our own presuppositions. From that we then enter into dialogue with other positions and out of such dialogue we should expect to nuance, qualify and sometimes change our own views, moving toward a fuller grasp of the truth of our situation. The quest for truth is ongoing, presumably, and never complete.

In any case, liberation theologians do not intend the hermeneutic privilege of the poor to mean that the poor have an exclusive insight into the meaning of biblical texts. All that they propose is that theirs is a vantage point which is unique and which makes a special contribution to the theological enterprise. Even liberation theologians observe that the poor need to be challenged and drawn into deeper awareness of their situation, but they also observe that, while one challenges, one must also listen to what the poor have to say.[8] At the very minimum, such dialogue, while it does not immediately resolve all our questions about objective truth, alerts us to the dangers of absolutizing our own perspectives.

Sociology of knowledge warns us not only that presuppositions influence the ways in which we view reality, but also that our presuppositions can often prevent our coming to an accurate view of reality at all. Liberation theologians have spoken frequently of this problem as a problem of ideology, stressing its importance especially on the political or economic level. There is a strong tendency for those in power to hold tenaciously to a view of things which enables them to justify (above all to themselves) keeping the poor in oppression. Ideology can be defined as a predisposition to see things in a certain way, operating prior even to conscious reasoning, which makes it difficult if not impossible to see things clearly.[9] Theology itself can serve as an ideology when presuppositions are brought to it in such a way that theology no longer reflects what justice really demands, but becomes one more tool by which the rich and powerful oppress the poor and powerless, maintaining the status quo of the society.

There seems to be such an ideology when, for instance, Christians in the United States explain wealth as simply a reward for hard work and the sign of God's blessing for such virtue. Or when Christians identify the kingdom of God with American culture and its political and economic system. While the bishops seem hesitant to acknowledge a hermeneutic privilege of the poor, they do show at least implicitly an attentive listening to the poor, making them the center of our attention both within this country and abroad. There seems at least an implicit awareness of the dangers of ideology even within Christian theology and ethics.

Becoming conscious of the pull of ideology makes one alert, moreover, to what are ultimately weak objections to elements of the bishops' letter. For instance, objections to the hermeneutic privilege of the poor, with denial that the poor can speak authoritatively about their own situation, may be nothing more than the fear of some in dominance that the status quo and their own position are likely to be threatened. The same applies to the contention that the Bible speaks, not of an option for the poor, but of "spiritual" matters. Surely, the poor are not the only ones who have a view of the economic and political problems of justice, and surely the Bible speaks of more than the option for the poor; but the poor do have perceptive insight and the Bible does, as we shall see, emphasize the option. Liberation theology is often dismissed as simply not "realistic." Robert McAfee Brown has pointed out that ideology lurks behind many criticisms of liberation theology, and his point may be applied to much of the criticism that will be leveled against what the bishops have heard liberation theology saying.[10]

III. The Biblical Data

IF WE ARE on somewhat uncertain ground in analyzing the bishops' evaluation of a hermeneutic privilege of the poor, we can feel more certain about their acceptance of what the hermeneutic privilege discovers, namely, new emphases in the biblical data itself. Near the beginning of their document the bishops show that they are listening to what the poor hear in the biblical text, namely, that God himself expresses preference for the poor in history and gives priority to their well-being. This theme has attained wide acceptance in biblical scholarship, as well as having been emphasized by liberation theology, and has thus been adopted by the bishops. This above all is the reason for contending that liberation theology is not merely a political campaign making a tool of theology, and in turn that the bishops' letter is not simply left-wing politics under the guise of theology. Both are founded on themes which are central to Scripture, which dictate that care for the poor is a special and indeed primary concern of the faithful. The option for the poor is more, therefore, than just one option among others, all of which are equally valid, but a priority that *should* be recognized as such for anyone who seeks truly to be a disciple of Christ.

This matter is so important that it warrants elaboration. In the Old Testament the themes of creation and covenant both illustrate the point. Whereas we have often enough understood the dominion over creation of which Genesis speaks as the right to manipulate creation for our purposes, the poor (and the bishops) read the stories as implying something more: stewardship respectful of the purposes of creation. This perspective is hardly unique to the poor, moreover.

In a culture praising individual initiative, where creativity can be seen as nothing more than private enterprise for personal profit, there is much merit in reminding ourselves that the early church fathers saw the earth's goods as belonging in principle to all, and they condemned the appropriation of these goods by a minority of the population as though they were theirs alone to enjoy.

The divine concern for the poor and oppressed is especially apparent in the story of the Exodus and the founding of the covenant between God and Israel. Whereas we are often inclined to interpret the movement from slavery to freedom in very spiritual terms, the biblical story is quite explicit in showing that it has political and economic dimensions as well. The initial revelation of God to Israel is that of one who recognizes the cry of people suffering under unjust oppression and enters into history to liberate them, and the liberation is obviously in very worldly terms. While it surely is spiritual as well, the text of Exodus highlights a God who reaches out especially to the poor and marginalized to make them the special recipients of his grace. Moreover, the mode of activity established in the Exodus becomes the pattern for God's initiative throughout the rest of the history of Israel. The people of the covenant are told to put themselves in harmony with what God is doing by themselves reaching out to care for the orphan, the widow, and the victims of injustice, as God himself is doing. Hardly a text of the prophets can be read without hearing a call to give special attention to the fate of the poor in the land.

The New Testament has these same emphases, but puts them into a new context of eschatology, i.e., theology about the final time of redemption. New Testament eschatology has often been seen as hope in an other-worldly reality, so that the final conquest of poverty would be only a hope offered after this life. Marx based his criticism of Christianity on this perspective, when he accused it of offering a "pie in the sky." Liberation theology has been especially sensitive to this accusation, and working out of a hermeneutic of the poor, has shown how the New Testament also stresses that the final time of redemption has already begun in some ways with the coming of Jesus.[11] The pastoral letter clearly reflects such an eschatology.

What this means is that the kingdom of God is not just coming in the future, but has already begun to change things here and now, as a consequence of the life, death, and resurrection of Jesus. This promise of change in the present in anticipation of the kingdom comes especially as good news to the poor. For it provides new possibilities of justice and for the conquering of poverty now in this world. Eschatology thus offers a vision of the future which can serve as a source of hope in the midst of pessimism. It draws those of us who live in the present to begin the works of justice as God's work in this world. More than in any other biblical teaching, the present and future dimensions of eschatology converge in the mystery of the resurrection of Jesus. In his resurrection Christ offers hope of a final reality yet to be achieved, but he offers equally a presence which already begins that transformation. Christians are thus called to the demands of discipleship of Jesus, to living those demands of justice and concern for the poor which are the hallmark of what God has done from the very beginning of biblical revelation and is bringing to final fruition in the risen Christ.

Our consideration of the meaning of the preferential option for the poor, in the light of the background and sources of the term, has shown a complex concept with various elements mutually influencing each other. We may state the interrelationship by saying that it begins with thinking with the poor and being *with* them, so that we may ultimately see the priority of doing something *for* them. Or, conversely, we may recognize that truly to do something *for* the poor, we need first to enter their world and understand *with* them the poverty that we seek to eradicate. The bishops' letter leaves implicit part of their methodology, but what they say about the biblical mandate of the option for the poor gives strong indication that they have been listening to other sectors of the church, such as Latin America, and have learned from what the poor themselves see in the Bible.

Of course, much of the debate over the preferential option for the poor has to do with considerations which go beyond the basic meaning as we have just considered it. It would be difficult to deny absolutely that the poor have any insight into their situation, as it would also be difficult to deny the simple biblical command to give special consideration to the poor in works of justice. The debate really begins when one considers *how* the poor exercise their privilege, and *how* the biblical data gets translated into contemporary theology and ethics. It is worthwhile considering these points in more detail to understand better the implications of the option for the poor and to see how many of them are taken over by the bishops' letter.

IV. Dependency Theory and Institutional Change

WHEN ONE BEGINS to elaborate the hermeneutic privilege of the poor, it becomes obvious that the poor cannot interpret their situation and the implications for justice purely out of the raw experience of material poverty. This experience must be mediated by some tools of analysis of that experience which illumine its meaning and significance. Latin American liberation theologians speak in this context of social analysis and usually have in mind the specific method of analysis called dependency theory. They find this theory the most helpful tool currently available to counter the prevalent development theory which informs First World assumptions about poverty.

An outgrowth in particular of the "development decade" in the 1960s, in which the First World countries poured resources into Latin America to help it move out of poverty, development theory is based on the assumption that the way to prosperity for these poor "underdeveloped" countries is to imitate the technology, efficiency, political institutions, and, above all, the economic arrangements of the developed countries. After years of failure, the poor nations increasingly are concluding that this assumption is false. Underdeveloped countries are not on the way to development. Rather, their unemployment is caused by the development policies of the First World in such a way that one may speak more properly of a chronic and worsening dependency of the poorer nations on the wealthier.[12]

Liberation theology is almost uniform in accepting this way of viewing the causes of poverty, and it becomes, in turn, a central theme of its interpretation of the option for the poor. The Latin American bishops' conference at Medellín adopted this theory, in effect, as the most fruitful way to understand the root causes of Third World poverty. The bishops embraced a position which dictates that dependence is the natural result of the relationship which now exists between the First and Third Worlds, and that it cannot be expected to be overcome as long as these relations remain as they are now. They point to one-crop dependencies of some countries, the disparity between cheap export of raw materials and expensive import of manufactured goods, the draining of capital from the poor countries by foreign business in collusion with the elites of Latin America, and the increasing national debts.[13]

In fact, this development in the Medellín documents has had a significant influence on the general social teaching of the church as it is presented in Vatican documents. Two years after Medellín, for example, Pope Paul VI sent a message to the United Nations addressing the beginning of the Second Development Decade. The message criticized the development strategies of the first decade, which tended to widen the gap between the rich and poor nations, and left intact domestic and international injustices which interlock and reinforce each other.[14] The Latin American bishops' conference at Puebla reaffirmed the situation of dependency with reference to multinational corporations and whole economic systems that do not regard the person as the center of society.[15] Pope John Paul II draws on these insights when he refers, for instance, to the "links between individual States" which "create mutual dependence," and calls into question the effects of the behavior of such institutions as the multinational corporations.[16]

Social scientists in various disciplines in the First World take issue with this theory of dependency. It is fair to say that among economists in this country there are only a minority who accept and work on the basis of dependency theory. General papal social teaching has recognized this reluctance and has seen some merit in it. From the time of Pope Paul VI, papal teaching has been increasingly forceful in pointing out the interdependence that exists between rich and poor nations, but it has by no means repudiated categorically the capitalist system. The problem remains, however, of determining just how much of the capitalist system can be retained and what can be substituted for it as a more just system. Church social teaching has refused to prescribe a specific economic system, since it is beyond its competence to do so, but has insisted that dependency theory helps define the realities that need to be addressed in any such effort.

The bishops follow this approach in their letter. They extol the great benefits that have derived from the capitalist economy in this country, but they also stress its negative by-products. They warn in particular about dependencies created by multinational corporations which tend to compound the disadvantages of the poor in the Third World. In making their judgment, they leave open many questions that need further study. For instance, they do not explicitly adopt nor formally discuss dependency theory. This is likely because the jump from acknowledging a hermeneutic perspective of the poor to acknowledging dependency theory as a part of that perspective is subject to debate. They are surely aware of the risk of capitalist ideology preventing North Americans from seeing this perspective, but nevertheless, they are obviously willing to run that risk in the absence of a stronger support for the theory.

By avoiding the debate over dependency, the bishops also avoid two other dangers. First of all, they avoid the risk of alienating their North American audience, which would surely be offended by their adoption of what is still a debated theory that has the effect of dismissing their economic system. Second, they avoid the trap of having North American obligations toward the poor depend solely on the status of a contested theory. The bishops recognize that both national and international dependence of the poor on the rich is a fact no matter what the economic system, and even if one were to disprove dependency theory, that would not remove the obligations of the wealthy toward the poor. In sum, the bishops appear to be influenced by liberation theology's hermeneutic of the poor as it has filtered through papal teaching, so that they are willing to criticize capitalist practices, but they also identify with the hesitancy of papal teaching unconditionally to adopt liberation theology's use of dependency theory as the framework on the basis of which analysis is done.

At this point in the debate, it may be best to say that dependency theory is most useful in qualifying the claims of those theories of development which are built on complete confidence in the capitalist economic system of the First World. It is also helpful in connecting the fate of the poor to structures, so that the option for the poor becomes a recognition of the need to change structures or systems of oppression. As Gutierrez says:

> The option for the poor and the oppressed through a liberating commitment leads to the realization that this commitment cannot be isolated from the social set-up to which they belong; otherwise we would not go beyond "being sorry for the situation."
>
> The poor man is therefore someone who questions the ruling social order.
>
> Solidarity with the poor implies the transformation of the existing social order.[17]

In many ways this concern for the change of structures is traditional in modern Catholic social teaching from Leo XIII onward. It represents the insight that personal conversion is not sufficient to achieve the works of justice; institutions need to be changed as well. However, the option for the poor as it has now developed puts more and more emphasis on the need to change structures. Leo XIII assumed that a change of heart would be sufficient to induce people to change what was unjust in the structures. He also presumed that the structures were unjust principally because of the sinful attitudes of individuals and that the existing capitalist structures could be adapted to create a just society. Now, however, this is less and less taken for granted.

Optimism about capitalism perdured through the reign of Pope John XXIII and the Second Vatican Council. Then the reality described by liberation theology came to the fore and with Pope Paul VI came the realization that sinful economic structures are not always eliminated by conversion of individuals. Changes in institutions need to accompany personal conversion. So the Pontiff admitted, "That is why the need is felt to pass from economics to politics," and in the same document cautiously offered a possibility of dialogue with socialism as a healthy critique of capitalist economic assumptions.[18] Pope John Paul II has moved papal teaching to a situation where he is now forthrightly critical of some capitalist assumptions. He writes, for instance, "We all know of areas in which there is a consumer civilization, involving a surplus of the goods needed by individuals and entire societies (in this case, affluent and highly developed societies), while the other societies, or, at least, large sectors of them, are plagued by hunger and not a few people die each day of starvation and malnutrition."[19]

We must note, however, that the present pope is equally skeptical of socialism as an alternative. Nor does he overtly embrace dependency theory. From this one might infer that while dependency theory is not altogether satisfactory as a means of explaining world poverty, it is at least helpful in identifying certain assumptions within capitalist countries about development that are problematic. The option for the poor includes seeing poverty as the poor do, namely, as a structural problem as well as an individual one, with the demand for changing structures. The bishops' pastoral letter stands in this tradition with its challenges to some of the structures of capitalism as well as with its call to personal conversion.

One final point needs to be developed in our consideration of how the hermeneutic privilege of the poor is worked out in the specific details. It is the growing recognition that the poor need to take possession of their own destiny. This follows directly from what we have already discussed: if the poor have a privileged position in analyzing their situation and in finding new meaning when they read the Bible, they also have, in turn, a privileged position in determining what to do about their situation and how to apply the biblical text. Self-determination for the poor is thus another central theme of liberation theology. Gutierrez writes:

> Traditional Christian circles often have a concern for the poor, provided always that it not raise any questions. What was novel in Medellín and Puebla was the concrete nature of their interest. ... Puebla bishops express their satisfaction with the attempts the poor have made to organize themselves, in recent years, so as "to live their faith in an integral way, and hence to reclaim their rights."[20]

In Latin America, this initiative of the poor has taken concrete shape in the development of base communities, small groupings of the poor and marginalized within local areas and with local leaders, which provide the context for discussion of the Bible and which provide support for efforts to change oppressive structures. The influence of such base communities has had a discernible effect, through Medellín and Puebla, on the general social teaching of the church. We can detect a marked shift from Leo XIII to John Paul II in the encouragement given to the oppressed in the face of their difficulties. Whereas Leo was quite reluctant to promote unrest by the poor, and preferred to reform society "from the top down," John Paul has preached to the poor that they must see themselves as the prime authors of their own advancement and take an active part in shaping their own destiny. Others are to see themselves as cooperating with the poor, rather than simply doing something to or for them.[21]

This aspect of the option for the poor has some echo in the bishops' pastoral letter, though with a different emphasis. The bishops are writing for a wealthy country and not one with an immense number of oppressed people. They are not addressing those who most feel the effects of poverty, but rather those who can do most to eliminate the causes of poverty. Rather than concentrating, then, on the need for self-defense or self-determination, they emphasize the need for self-criticism and self-denial. The option for the poor in this setting turns out to be consistent, but not identical with the option as it is interpreted in Latin America and in certain aspects of papal teaching.

Having said this, however, we do find in the bishops' letter some concern for the poor to assume control of their own destiny. It is combined with the call to self-denial on the part of the rich and the middle class. The bishops give, in fact, strong emphasis to allowing the poor to participate in the making of those decisions that determine their fate. Perhaps the bishops could have expanded their brief statements about the role of grass-roots organization and could have been more emphatic about the necessary role to be played by the marginalized of society in shaping their own destiny within this country. Nevertheless, the call to self-denial does concentrate on the most important obligation of the First World in making the option for the poor.[22]

V. Definition of Justice

THE DRIFT OF WHAT I have had to say is that much of what liberation theology says about the option for the poor as a hermeneutic privilege of the poor has been implicit in or omitted from the bishops' letter. I have also indicated that more than anything else, the bishops have taken over the results of the perspectives of the poor in the biblical statements about the option for the poor. The final part of this study explores how the bishops apply the biblical data to the contemporary scene. Standing with the poor, recognizing structures that can be oppressive, feeling the need for the participation of all in shaping the future, they then apply the biblical injunctions to do something for the poor by seeking to elaborate a specific standard of justice.

Justice is commonly defined as giving every person what is his or her due. The problem over the course of human history has been to define who is due what. This notion of desert refers, of course, most often to what is necessary for the preservation and protection of human beings, and tends today to be framed in terms of rights. What this means has taken, in turn, various specifications, depending on how one defines the human person and basic human dignity. The liberal philosophical theory which is so prevalent in our country in economics and politics has focused on individual rights and freedoms. Too often insistence on these rights is translated into a myth of equal opportunity which masks a reality of highly unequal competition for scarce goods and services. Too often the theory of individual rights has turned into an ideology of self-interest used by those with power to justify their retaining control at the expense of the less fortunate.

Catholic social teaching has always challenged the inadequacy of such a one-sided emphasis on individual rights because of its inadequate definition of the human person.[23] From the very beginning of modern papal teaching, there has been insistence that the human person is defined by communal relationships, and that therefore rights are also relational and justice has communal requirements. Respect for the dignity and freedom of individuals does not mean simply avoiding any interference with their activity, but also taking steps to help those who are in need and to establish the structures that promote genuine community of persons. Traditional Catholic teaching has expressed this by insisting that justice has multiple dimensions, consisting of commutative justice (obligations of persons to respect the rights of other persons), distributive justice (obligations of society to respect the rights of persons to share in community), and legal justice (obligations of persons to respect the societal structures which facilitate distributive justice). The latter two, which express communal concerns, are customarily grouped together in modern times under the heading of social justice.[24]

While these communal dimensions of justice have been traditional to Catholic social teaching, we can also detect an evolution of thought within that tradition. The preferential option for the poor has become a way of encapsulating this further evolution of thought, which has also been adopted by the bishops in their pastoral letter. The option for the poor expresses a relative egalitarian theory of justice.[25] This view tends to stress the need for structures that actively attempt more equal allocation of resources, rather than allow more room for competing claims of rights and simple equality of opportunity, and seeks redistribution from the rich to the poor to establish more of a mean. The mean is described as relative because the concern is not to achieve perfect redistribution, but rather to hold the allocation within limits so that there are not enormous gaps between rich and poor and communitarian bonds are strengthened.

A shift to this emphasis came because of the realization that while people were debating the relative merits of different theories of justice, the rich were getting richer and the poor poorer. While even Catholic teaching was struggling to reconcile the claims of the three fold elements of justice, the gap was widening between rich and poor. The hermeneutic perspectives of liberation theology were certainly no small influence in recognizing increasing inequality as the overriding problem of our times. Hence, the development of an option for the poor which says, in effect, that any redistribution of resources to the advantage of the poor will lessen the disparity between rich and poor and promote genuine community.

We can see this movement toward a relatively egalitarian theory of justice in the shift in Catholic social teaching about private property. Under Leo XIII, the emphasis was on the individual right of private property. He was reluctant to challenge that right even in the struggle to meet the demands of social justice. By the time we reach John XXIII, the right of private property is made relative to the social function of property. Paul VI is quite clear about subordinating the right of private property to the principle that the goods of the earth are for the benefit of all. He insists that none have the right to keep for their exclusive use what they do not need, when others lack necessities.[26]

It would appear that the option for the poor is moving the church's social teaching in the direction of a more conflictual model of justice.[27] Whereas previous teaching assumed that maintaining the principles of justice for an individual would achieve also the communal goals of justice, more recent teaching has recognized that, in our given world, imperfect structures can only approximate full justice, and individual and communal claims can conflict. In such a setting, priorities need to be established. The option for the poor as a relative egalitarian principle would maintain that in conflict situations priority must be given to social justice over commutative justice. Rights that promote the communal dimensions of the person have priority over rights as individual.

In what we have been discussing about a relative egalitarian concept of justice, we have put the emphasis on the distribution of goods in a more equitable fashion. This is, perhaps, the first step that is necessary in the demands of justice. However, a full concept of justice must also recognize the right of persons to share in the production of goods and services within an economy. The bishops have this view of justice as well, since they frequently emphasize a principle of participation, pointing out that justice is measured by the degree to which the marginalized and the poor are allowed to share in the economic process of a society. I have already discussed this aspect of justice in the section above where I spoke of the rights of the poor to participate in their own destiny, so I will not repeat that point here.

Finally, the option for the poor as a relative egalitarian principle would demand more government intervention to achieve a reasonable balance of resources between rich and poor. This would be an understandable insight from a hermeneutical perspective that saw oppressive structures as part of the context of poverty. Traditional Catholic teaching has always seen the state as more than a coercive force against injustice or an arbiter of conflicting claims in society; it is also a positive force for the promotion of justice and the establishment of institutions to that end. Nevertheless, prior teaching put the emphasis on the autonomy of the economic realm from the political, and was reluctant to have government intervention in the economic system.

Gradually, under pressure from the Third World, papal teaching began to recognize that the economic system was not simply neutral, but was in some ways structurally part of the reason for the widening gap between rich and poor. Pope John XXIII spoke of the reality of socialization, i.e., the growing interdependence of people in society with the accompanying need to establish social institutions to deal with these new complexities. He gave cautious approval to the state intervening in the economic order. Paul VI made the move more categorically, saying that the need is felt to move from the economic to the political.[28] The bishops follow in this tradition.

There are, of course, many ways in which the state can intervene in the economic order, not all of which are desirable. This general principle needs, therefore, to be cautiously applied. The bishops themselves proceed cautiously, qualifying the role of the state by other principles which are squarely in the Catholic tradition. Throughout the development of recent papal teaching about the role of the state, for instance, there is the concern to avoid the opposite risk of government intervention, which would be statism or government control of every sector of society. The principle of subsidiarity is maintained, which says the state is not to arrogate to itself what can be achieved by a voluntary institution within the society. Nevertheless, there is seen the growing need both nationally and internationally for intervention to make structures more just and to reform the imbalanced world economy according to a relative egalitarian basis of justice. That is the context for what the bishops also have to say about the role of government in their discussions of the meaning of justice.

VI. Conclusion

IT IS THE HOPE of this essay that the reader has come to see that the option for the poor is a complex reality which means much more than a pious sentiment of charity toward the unfortunate of society. Much of its meaning has been expounded by liberation theologians who have brought it to the fore. It presumes a hermeneutic perspective that comes from standing with the poor, listening to what they say, seeing the full context of their poverty, and joining with them in their struggle. This leads to a challenging reading of the Bible that urges one to adopt the poor as the central object of human and Christian concern. It leads further to renewing the concept of justice in today's world to mean primarily the effort through various institutions to reallocate human resources so as to bring a relative equality to the enormous inequality that now exists between rich and poor. The United States bishops have been informed and influenced by this multifaceted concept of the option for the poor. While they do not speak of a privilege of the poor, they implicitly acknowledge the vantage point from which the poor speak, for the bishops have embraced much of the teaching that comes out of that vantage point. They have heard the poor in their reading of the Bible as a call to justice especially for the oppressed.

Likewise, the bishops appear reluctant to embrace dependency theory explicitly, but they show the influence of liberation theology, at least as it has filtered through papal teaching, when they point out the problems within capitalism, the effects of First World economics on the Third World, and the need for institutional changes, as well as the participation of the poor in these institutions. Finally, there seems at least an implicit influence of liberation theology when the bishops move toward an egalitarian concept of justice that measures this virtue above all by what is done for the poor and oppressed of a society. In summary, liberation theology has expounded a rich concept and, whether implicitly or explicitly, much of this concept lies behind what the bishops teach in their ever recurring phrase "the preferential option for the poor."

NOTES

1. See Donal Dorr, *Option for the Poor: A Hundred Years of Vatican Social Teaching* (Maryknoll, N.Y.: Orbis Books, 1983).

2. See the Second General Conference of Latin American Bishops (Medellin), *The Church in the Present-Day Transformation of Latin America in the Light of the Council: Conclusions* (Washington, D.C.: United States Catholic Conference, 1973).

3. See John Eagleson and Philip Scharper, eds., *Puebla and Beyond: Documents and Commentary* (Maryknoll, N.Y.: Orbis Books, 1980).

4. "Liberation, Theology and Proclamation," *Concilium* (1974): 60.

5. Appendix in Julio de Santa Ana, *Towards a Church of the Poor* (Maryknoll, N.Y: Orbis Books, 1979), 124–25.

6. See Juan Luis Segundo, *The Liberation of Theology* (Maryknoll, N.Y.: Orbis Books, 1976).

7. See J. Severino Croatto, *Exodus: A Hermeneutics of Freedom* (Maryknoll, N.Y: Orbis Books, 1981), especially 1–11.

8. Paolo Freire, *Pedagogy of the Oppressed* (New York: Herder, 1970).

9. Anthony J. Tambasco, *The Bible for Ethics: Juan Luis Segundo and First-World Ethics* (Lanham, Md.: University Press of America, 1981), 91–133.

10. Robert McAfee Brown, *Theology in a New Key* (Philadelphia: Westminster Press, 1978), 101–131.

11. José Miguez Bonino, *Doing Theology in a Revolutionary Situation* (Philadelphia: Fortress Press, 1975), 132–53.

12. Theotonio Dos Santos, "The Structure of Dependence," *American Economic Review* 60 (1970): 231–36; Fernando Cardoso, *Dependency and Development in Latin America* (Berkeley: University of California Press, 1979).

13. A good summary of Medellin's view is found in the conclusions of its document *Peace*, in *Church in the Present-Day*, nos. 1–13.

14. "Message of His Eminence Maurice Cardinal Roy, President of the Pontifical Commission 'Justice and Peace,' on the Occasion of the Launching of the Second Development Decade," in *The Gospel of Peace and Justice*, ed. Joseph Gremillion (Maryknoll, N.Y.: Orbis Books, 1976), especially 477–82.

15. See especially the final document in Eagleson, *Puebla and Beyond*, nos. 64 and 66.

16. *Laborem Exercens (On Human Work)*, no. 17. The text of this encyclical may be found in *On Human Work: A Resource Book for the Study of*

Pope John Paul II's Third Encyclical (Washington, D.C.: United States Catholic Conference, 1982).

17. "Liberation," 60.

18. *Octogesima Adveniens*, in *The Gospel of Peace and Justice*, ed. Joseph Gremillion (Maryknoll, N.Y.: Orbis Books, 1976), 499–501; 507.

19. *Redemptor Hominis, The Pope Speaks* 24 (1979): 123.

20. Gustavo Gutierrez, *The Power of the Poor in History* (Maryknoll, N.Y.: Orbis Books, 1983), 154.

21. See, for example, the sermon preached by the pope to the poor in Favela dos Alagados, during his visit to Brazil, published in the English edition of *L'Osservatore Romano* (August 4, 1981): 7.

22. See a fully elaborated treatment of this topic in Marie Augusta Neal, *A Socio-Theology of Letting Go* (New York: Paulist Press, 1977).

23. See David Hollenbach, "Modern Catholic Teachings Concerning Justice," *The Faith That Does Justice*, ed. John C. Haughey (New York: Paulist Press, 1977), 207–31.

24. Eberhard Welty, *Man in Society*, vol. 1 of *A Handbook of Christian Social Ethics* (New York: Herder and Herder, 1960), 281–324.

25. See Drew Christiansen, "On Relative Equality: Catholic Egalitarianism after Vatican II," *Theological Studies* 45 (1984) 651–75.

26. See a summary of this development in Gremillion, *The Gospel of Peace*, 23–37.

27. See David Hollenbach, *Claims in Conflict* (New York: Paulist Press, 1979).

28. For a summary of this development, see Gremillion, *The Gospel of Peace*, 39–46.

HENRY W. BRIEFS[1]

The Limits of Scripture: Theological Imperatives and Economic Realities

HENRY W. BRIEFS is a Professor and Chairman of the Department of Economics at Georgetown University. He received his Ph.D. in economics from Georgetown University.

I. Overview and Orientation

IN A REFLECTION on *Gaudium et Spes*, the Constitution on the Church in the Modern World, Karl Rahner, S. J., asked the question, "Is there a properly Christian ideology of the future?"[2]

For Rahner, this searching question remained open. For the American bishops, the answer seems to be a confident "yes." Furthermore, judging by certain passages in their letter on the U.S. economy,[3] they seem to believe they know how their vision can be realized.

I address two main topics in the following pages. In Part II, I delineate the letter's "Christian ideology" and its approach to implementing it. The essentials are found mainly in chapter 2, addressed to the faithful. As I read these passages, they urge a subtle but significant shift in Catholic social thought, compared with traditional teaching. However, because the presentation is complex and intended meanings are often difficult to disentangle, the letter may contain as well a much more traditional message, which others strongly argue *is* the message. Notwithstanding, I confine myself to those parts of the letter which seem to outline a new way of understanding Catholic social teaching. At issue is a U.S. post-Vatican II conception of what it would mean and require to build a new Christian socioeconomic order.

Part III concerns the contribution social economics can make to thinking about the "Christian Vision of Economic Life" and about the advocated approach to its implementation.[4] Is the vision in the form urged—namely, that of a "true commonwealth" structure of participatory arrangements—feasible in today's world? Insufficient consideration seems to have been given to real-world limits on what is proposed, that is, to reality dimensions in economic activity that any change of institutional arrangements must take into account. The problem, I think, stems from grounding the essentials of what the letter urges in a rather literal reading of biblical sources with emphasis on the eschatological promise of the Second Coming, and from deemphasizing at the level of basics the kinds of reflection that could mediate between the "then" and the "now" of efforts to restructure the social order. Certainly in our time, economic reality considerations and emergent technical-organizational possibilities ought to have a part in the bishops' pastoral reflection about a future more worthy of human persons.

To identify my point of departure in what follows, let me add a note on the relationship between economic considerations and Catholic pastoral theology. That relationship hinges on how the common good is understood. The alleged shift away from traditional teaching has a key bearing on this understanding and is thus a central point of interest. The better to track what seems to me to be new in this shift, it may help to outline the traditional common good understanding of Catholic social teaching before turning to the pastoral letter itself.

The modern understanding of the church's social justice teaching is best put in *Quadragesimo Anno*, Pope Pius XI's great encyclical of 1931. Reflecting on the economic disorganization wrought by the great depression and, more broadly, on the strains of industrial modernization, Pius sought to bring the economic, societal, and political interdependencies of modern societies into just coherence.[5] Regarding the economic process, the guiding principle of action and governing virtue for each participant at his/her respective level and place of responsibility should be service to the common good. Applied also to activities in the other domains of social life, to politics and the various areas of private societal involvement, the common good covers the choices and actions of individual persons and groups in their various social relationships. It indicates to them in a structured way what their respective obligations are in and to the society whose members they are. Society, in turn, is conceived as a network of functionally differentiated, hierarchically ordered societal units, each contributing to the other and to the whole what is its due. State and society are sharply distinguished from one another, with the former playing a strategic but limited function in accordance with the principle of "subsidiarity." Subsidiarity requires that primary responsibility for addressing those social tasks which can be successfully performed by lower-level units should be left in their care. The state, meanwhile, takes up those major social tasks which it alone is equipped to perform, and, to the extent needed, extends the help required by subsidiary units if appropriate. Thus, depending on the particular issue, the state may be the first or last resort, or responsibility may remain at the level of the family, local group, or perhaps some other unit, depending on the needed expertise. The preservation, indeed the revitalization of these structures and their worth is an essential dimension of subsidiarity, lest the network of such relations and their bases come to be absorbed by the political regime. Animated by the virtue of social love, these principles of social organization formed the lodestone and rudder of "social justice" in Pius' sense.

No summary of this view is complete without an indication of how commutative and distributive justice relate to the common good. Commutative justice is clear enough. Because economic activity is largely organized through markets and market prices, justice in exchange is bound to be a feature of the common good norm. A great many social transactions, however, are not facilitated by markets or market-oriented arrangements. These interactions take place in a framework of family and governmental structures as well as of various intermediate bodies referred to above. Distributive justice speaks to the obligations of all such social units vis-a-vis their members regarding the social goods they serve to provide. Thus, justice in distribution, too, is a constitutive aspect of social justice. Its role, however, is not that of an architectonic principle; it does not guide toward nor return to, a just coherence of all dimensions of justice in society. That role is reserved for social justice.

It is important to add that nothing in the above understanding stands in the way of according particular urgency to distributional issues. The bishops' emphasis on the "option for the poor" fits easily into such a conception of social ethics. Whether such a judgment warrants direct moves to redistribute, more roundabout approaches, or some mix of these depends on concrete circumstances and available knowledge about likely consequences of proceeding one way or another.

II. The Vision and Where It Is to Lead

"THE CHRISTIAN VISION OF ECONOMIC LIFE"

CONCERNED AS WE ARE with the letter's core position, we can limit our discussion to chapter 2, "The Christian Vision of Economic Life," and to selected passages in chapter 4.

Two propositions ground the vision: first, that all are called to communion with God and with one another; and second, that Sacred Scripture offers guidance so that men and women may enter into full communion with God and each other, and so give witness of God's will for all mankind. The corresponding biblical categories are: God's creation of man in his image; man's redemption by Christ's death on the cross, and the new covenant so brought into being. Moreover, the meaning of this triad is to be understood as integral to the whole of God's saving history, so that Israel's beliefs about creation, God's will communicated to his people Israel in the first covenant at Sinai, and the promise of a saving history to be experienced in community, are all fully integral in the Christian understanding of God's salvific action in history. The whole of Scripture, the old and the new, must be taken as guidance so that men and women may enter into communion with God and each other.

What is taken from the covenant at Sinai? That he is their God and they are his people; that God wants his people to worship him alone; and that they live according to his justice. Yahweh is the God of justice. It is a justice measured by the treatment of the vulnerable and the powerless in society.[6] The letter explains that this justice must be understood in a deep, biblical sense, concerned with the rightness before God of the human condition and within society. "Justice so understood is a manifestation of love and a condition for love to grow."[7] Social relations are to be judged by this divine imperative.

What, then, is injustice? Two transgressions are emphasized: The "misuse of the world's resources" and "the appropriation of them by a minority of the world's population." To act in these ways is a "betrayal of God's gifts ... What belongs to God belongs to all."[8]

The significance of the New Testament—the new covenant—is Christ's entry into God's saving history. The new covenant brings into the world God's will, manifested in the life and teaching of Jesus. Its deepest meaning is that "a Christian ... now walks in the newness of life and is a member of a new creation."[9] Life has thereby been fundamentally changed in a way that provides the very ground of "our action in behalf of justice." The goal and the way are there in Christ proclaimed.

The goal to be realized is the eschatological kingdom to be established step by step, which Christ will bring to perfection at his Second Coming. Christ's call to all the faithful is to follow the way of the cross as a community of disciples. In this, they are to take as their model the life of the apostles and the early Christian communities. The pastoral points to the Jerusalem community for emulation, saying that its members distributed their possessions, holding "all things in common," so that "there was not a needy person among them."[10] The modern-day application is the preferential option for the poor. Interpreted religiously, " ... it calls for an emptying of self, individually and corporately, so as to allow the church to experience the power of God in the midst of poverty and powerlessness."[11] The call is to a deep identification with the poor and the powerless, the better to see, trust, and respond to God's way of salvation and liberation.[12] For the poor and powerless " ... are not blinded by wealth or tempted to make it into an idol. They are open to God's presence and their powerlessness makes them a model of those who trust in God alone ... Conversely ... the rich are wise in their own eyes ... are prone to apostasy and idolatry ... as well as violence and oppression."[13]

Together, the way and the goal describe the Christian vision of economic life. They also imply a method of discernment and an empowerment. "His power and presence ... will enable Christian communities to commit themselves to a solidarity with those suffering and to confrontation with those attitudes and ways of acting which institutionalize injustice ... Doing so involves a diagnosis of those situations which alienate the world from God's creative love as well as presenting hopeful alternatives which arise from living in a renewed creation."[14]

To "do justice," the letter seems to be saying, comes down to active participation in a struggle of the church in the midst of the world's powerless and poor against the world's powerful and rich. The main strategy, it appears, is to target the institutions which enable these minorities to appropriate and waste the God-given riches of the world, his gift to all. The implicit action model seems to be a conflictual one; as such, it would be very different from the common good understanding central in the church's traditional teaching about social justice. I shall return to this important issue at the close of Part II.

THE CHRISTIAN VOCATION AS SACRAMENT

THE FOREGOING RAISES questions about the relationship between the various activities of Christian communities and the church: one, holy, and apostolic. These questions apply especially to actions taken along the general lines urged in the letter, and to what various Christian communities assert as they proclaim the kingdom. These are issues of ecclesiology—the church's theological self-understanding—and as such need not detain us. One aspect of the view taken does, however, have a bearing on the letter's social ethics message. Consider paragraph 64 of "The Christian Vocation in the World," the second section of chapter 2:

> Christians are to respond to the Gospel by worship and prayer, by participating in the sacramental life, so that " . . . in the eucharist they hear the words of God proclaiming hope for the poor and oppressed and accountability of the powerful and more fortunate . . . thus the one bread, one body, one spirit makes the Christian community a sacrament or visible sign of the unity of justice and peace that God wills for the whole of humanity . . . For this faith community to be an effective sign to the world it must ceaselessly pursue an end to divisions in its own life and society."[15]

Taken into the contexts in which the social teaching is to apply, the message is easily read to say that the faithful alone are fit to be the carriers of the Christian transformation envisioned. In such an interpretation, other persons and groups are invited to participate in this labor, but their role in any strict sense must remain an instrumental one.

JUSTICE BY PARTICIPATION[16]

THE THIRD PART of chapter 2 bears the heading: "Ethical Norms for Economic Life." Its introductory paragraph describes what follows as a "complementary" mode of understanding, intelligible to non-Christians. It goes on to say that the ethical norms put forward are "faithful to the Gospel" and are "shaped by human experience and reason."[17] Anyone familiar with the tradition of Catholic social teaching would expect just such language in an introduction to Catholic social ethics.

The remainder of this text, in conjunction with the material on poverty and unemployment which follows in chapter 3, can be read as fulfilling this expectation. The same is true of a good deal of chapter 4 which explains what working for justice would mean for the organization of economic life. Father John Langan, S. J., made a point of praising this aspect of the letter. "The second draft in the discussion of poverty and unemployment makes more clear both the logical subordination of the option for the poor to the common good of all (as well as its special urgency in practice) and the necessity of assessing economic decisions not merely in terms of what they do to and for the poor but also in terms of what they enable to the poor to do for themselves."[18]

I shall argue that the norms in chapters 2 and 4 conform to another characterization. I do so, not because of any claim that my reading of the letter's core argument is the correct one, but because I believe that the text supports two distinct interpretations.[19] Though each takes account of the other, and not merely as a matter of rhetoric, the two arguments are at odds with each other in important respects. These differences are likely to feature in the exegetical dialogue about what the bishops meant or did not mean.

In the reading I have chosen to emphasize, the very passages citing the traditional teaching lead the way to a significant departure from it. The governing conception of "basic justice," put forward under the heading "Justice and Participation," defines it as requiring " ... the minimum levels of mutual care and respect that all persons and communities owe each other."[20] True, this is said to be less encompassing than the biblical justice requirement identified earlier; but the core notion to which it leads is the same: a deep, interdependent equality among persons in all their social and economic interrelationships. And when this understanding is connected with the concept of human sinfulness — the monopolization of God's gift to all and the resulting waste — it is clear that basic justice is the governing principle of distributive justice, not the common-good oriented social justice of traditional teaching.

The implications are profound and far-reaching. Commutative justice remains and is briefly explained. The common good principle, however, traditionally the very rudder and lodestone of the pursuit of social justice, is asked to play an instrumental, supporting role. Its raison d'etre is to call for organizational changes to achieve the âllocation of income, wealth and power that basic justice demands. Distributive justice is now the measure of justice in social relations.

Consider the content of this new conceptualization of distributive justice. The baseline is "the establishment of minimal standards, ... a floor of material well-being for all" as a duty of the whole society. True enough, but furthermore, distributive norms " ... call into question extreme inequalities of income and consumption when some lack basic necessities ..." because these inequalities are "... a threat to the solidarity of the human community ..." And although "flat, arithmetic equality of income and wealth" is not required,[21] distributive norms "... challenge economic arrangements that leave large numbers of people impoverished...." Finally, the norms of distributive justice call "... for a more systematic approach by business, labor unions and the many other groups that shape economic life—as well as government. The concentration of privilege ... today results far more from *institutional relationships* that distribute power inequitably than from differences in talent or lack of desire to work. These institutional patterns must be examined and revised."[22]

What is the governing principle under distributive justice so understood, its rudder and lodestone? That of overcoming marginalization and powerlessness. "The ultimate injustice ... is to be actively treated or passively abandoned" as if one did not belong to the human community, whether by political and/or economic exclusion."[23] The letter refers here to paragraph 18 of *Justice in the World*,[24] the document issued by the 1971 Synod of Bishops. Its text is worth citing because of the light it throws on the concept of basic justice as participation:

> It is impossible to conceive true progress without recognizing the necessity—within the political system chosen—of a development composed both of economic growth and participation; and the necessity too of an increase in wealth implying as well social progress by the entire community as it overcomes regional imbalance and islands of prosperity. Participation constitutes a right which is to be applied both in the economic and in the social and political field.

We see here the notion of justice as participation in seminal form: on the one hand, it calls for a redistributive thrust toward greater wealth equalization, " ... as the community ... overcomes regional imbalances and islands of prosperity." On the other, the thrust is toward greater power equalization in the economic, the social and the political field, i.e. presumably wherever the distribution of power makes any difference. Admittedly, other interpretations are possible. "Participation" can mean many different things in different contexts. However, this oft-quoted passage from *Justice in the World* has become a legitimating text for the proposition that justice in society requires the sharing by all in the community's life-sustaining and enriching goods, *and* the sharing by all in the community's different decision processes. The former fits the biblical vision. The latter does not. It is an alien idea, one that fits more easily into a socialist ideology in search of a way to avoid state bureaucratic centralism.

REALIZING THE BIBLICAL VISION

HOW ARE THE FAITHFUL to respond to these norms? How should the vision be implemented? Pope John XXIII's list of human rights, and especially the economic ones he set forth, provides a point of departure. But rather than treat these as criteria for judging situations calling for reform while leaving open how best to approach them — as would be traditional — the letter calls for the embodiment of "economic rights essential to human dignity . . . in the cultural and legal traditions of this nation . . ." The letter asserts that these are ". . . as essential . . . as are the political and civil freedoms granted pride of place in the Bill of Rights of the Constitution."[25]

The several discussions of this proposition suggest that formal institutionalization of basic justice as affirmative economic rights is intended. They are to be secured by ". . . the creation of an order that guarantees the minimum conditions of human dignity in the economic sphere for every person."[26] More telling for the interpretation being developed, implementation is to be governed by a threefold national priority: fulfilling the basic needs of the poor is first; providing increasingly active participation rights for the presently excluded or vulnerable is second, and the third, for the long pull, is directing the nation's wealth, talent, and energy to benefit the poor and economically insecure.[27] The goal is deep equality;[28] the key to basic justice is undoing the unjust patterns of institutional power.

The remainder of chapter 2 and chapter 4 concern the approach to realizing the second and third of these norms. Though it is not at all obvious from the exposition, the model guiding this discussion, so it seems to me, is a solidaristic form of democratic syndicalism.

What *content* should one look for in a package bearing this label? For reasons already introduced, we must adjust our sights by returning to the biblical vision of Christian economic life. Taken seriously, that understanding has three implications. First, because social sin is exclusively made to turn on the monopolization (and resulting abuse) of God-given resources by an acquisitive minority, the institution of private property is problematic. This conclusion follows as well from the conception of justice as participation in community based on love, i.e., it follows from biblical descriptions of the kingdom Christ will establish at his Second Coming. In this perspective, the eschatological striving of Christians should be directed toward communal property sharing. It should not acquiesce in relationships turning on arms-length agreements and exchanges among owners of private property rights.

The second implication is that government as chosen instrument in the process of realizing participatory justice must be able to respond accordingly. This requires that "private/public" or similar distinctions embodied in institutional constraints on the scope and reach of government be readily adjustable. In the long term, guaranteeing affirmative economic rights in dynamically changing circumstances *and* restructuring the relational interdependencies of myriad contributing persons and groups can brook very little in the way of such restrictions.[29]

The third implication is that the agents and institutions of "government" itself are problematic. Social sin as conceptualized could not be the kind of problem described, were it not for the complicity of attitudes, patterns, and structures at the level of government. Thus, the true principals in the struggle to guarantee basic justice are the faithful in their various communities, motivated and enlightened by social love in their quest to establish the Christian economic order. They—really they alone—are qualified to be the carriers of the struggle for basic justice. On my reading, that would be the logic of declaring that the social mission of the faith community is a sacrament to the world.

What statements in the letter conform to this three-part logic? Regarding the first implication, we begin with the parts of the letter that would seem to be least promising in this respect, namely, those in chapter 3. Its general introduction eschews proposing a "third way" of setting things aright in the U.S. economy in favor of one that " ... is pragmatic and evolutionary in nature."[30] In the next paragraph, however, the bishops " ... emphasize that our moral vision has direct bearing on larger questions concerning the economic system itself." The issues are telling. They are, in order, whether "the economic system" stresses profit-maximizing rather than meeting human needs and fostering human dignity, whether it tends to "concentrate power and resources in the hands of a few" rather than distribute benefits equitably, whether it promotes excessive materialism and individualism, and whether it directs too many resources to military purposes while failing to give adequate protection to the environment.[31] The systemic issue is: does the economy promote monopolization of power and of economic resources, thereby leading to the waste of God's gifts to all?

Succeeding sections deal with U.S. unemployment, poverty, farming problems, and U.S. responsibilities in the world economy. I limit the discussion to the first two. True, the agreeable spirit of searching for workable solutions and of learning from experience is present in these discussions; but there is also another structure and thrust in that argument. It is determined by the concept of social sinfulness on the one hand and by the vision's affirmative mandates clustered around justice as participation on the other.

We begin with poverty because it is pivotal, and the pastoral's main thrust. The introduction makes a brief reference to different forms of privation, but moves quickly to narrow the notion of poverty to " . . . the lack of sufficient material resources required for a decent life." Poverty, however, " . . . is not merely the lack of . . . financial resources . . . it is a more profound kind of deprivation, a denial of full participation in the economic, social, and political life of society and an inability to influence decisions that affect one's life . . . Poverty means being powerless in a way that assaults not only one's pocketbook but also one's fundamental human dignity."[32]

Who are the poor so defined, and what accounts for this condition? One large group consists of children in poor families, in very many cases families headed by women who raise their children alone. A major explanatory factor is said to be wage discrimination against women. The second large group of the poor are minorities. In relation to their number they suffer the highest rates of poverty. The reason is prejudice, and " . . . discriminatory practices in labor markets, educational systems and electoral politics."[33]

These themes are elaborated in the section dealing with employment and unemployment. Technological change and international competition are combined with corporate plant closings to account for a dramatic job loss for American workers. Job creation has shifted to " . . . traditionally low-paying, high-turnover jobs" and "discrimination in employment is one of the causes of high rates of joblessness and low pay among racial minorities and women."[34] Finally, high levels of defense spending effect serious economic distortions, among others a net loss of jobs and other forms of " ... a massive drain on the U.S. economy as well as a serious 'brain drain'."[35]

To deal with these problems, " ... we must first establish the right to a job for every American who wants to work." This is not an impossible task, according to the letter, although it " ... may require major adjustments and creative strategies that go beyond the limits of existing policies and institutions. ..."[36]

The policy suggestions that follow are familiar ones, many in the spirit of pragmatic problem solving. The items under "new strategies," however, suggest a return to systemic issues. They include trying to spread jobs so as to provide a job to everyone who wants to work (by job sharing, workweek reduction, limitations on overtime); and wage income equalization (by discouraging part-time employment, reducing wage differences between men and women, training the hard-to-employ, supplying the special needs of the handicapped, and generally by "upgrading traditionally low-paying jobs"). The bishops add here that greater efforts should be made to retool industries, retrain workers, and aid community adjustment, all matters that fit well under the heading of pragmatic problem solving; but here these admonitions are tied to the conversion of "some of the nation's military production to more peaceful and socially useful purposes."[37]

Clearly, the core concept of poverty and the characterization of employment and unemployment issues are intimately related. What remains to be shown is how the bishops relate this to economic inequality. Their opening sentence on this subject is telling. "Important to our discussion of poverty in America is an understanding of the degree of economic inequality." In describing their understanding, the bishops repeat the moral strictures we cited earlier. The offense is not merely that many are in need while relatively few enjoy a surfeit; it is also against " ... the development of solidarity and community, for large inequalities in the economic sphere mean that the degree of power and the level of participation in the political and social spheres are also very uneven."[38] The poverty problem, it seems, is systemwide and importantly rooted in economic structures. Existing inequalities of wealth and income are mainly symptomatic of institutionalized injustice.

What would be better, structurally? As we know, the last section in chapter 2 and all of chapter 4 deal with the new experiment in bringing democratic ideals to economic life. The call is for " ... serious exploration of ways to develop new patterns of partnership. ... "[39] This governing theme is repeated at the level of the business firm, local and regional agencies of all kinds, at the national level, and finally the international level as well. Where, in all of this, are the statements about private property and the scope of government? What special role are Christians to play in the struggle for basic justice?

Regarding the first, consider the following: "Every business, from the smallest to the largest ... depends on many different persons and groups for its success: workers, managers, owners or shareholders, suppliers, customers, creditors, the local community and the wider society ... Each contributes ... and each has a stake in its growth or decline. Present structures of accountability do not acknowledge these contributions or protect these stakes."[40] Most of what follows in chapter 4, even though timely and constructive in its own right, is tilted toward this passage. It sets the goal.

What is the nature of this goal? It is a syndical form of economic organization, one in which property rights and their respective assignments to different persons and groups are, in effect, jointly owned. That is, the exercise of these rights by any one "owner" would require the consent of all the others, which in turn implies that virtually all economic decision making—what is to be produced, by what technology and where, who gets to contribute what and how much, the timing and coordination of all the activities involved now and over future periods, the distribution of claimant shares, saving and investment decisions, etc.—ought to be explicitly consensual and thus participatory. If ongoing mutual accountability all round is meant to be real, this is the guiding ideal. It is the image of what is to take the place of private property, the market system with its price mechanism, and the various forms of business organization made possible by existing legal institutions. The private property language remains, but its content and meaning are to be replaced by something very different.

Is there textual support for the second and third conclusions above? To *guarantee* everyone's affirmative socioeconomic rights would require a government of far- and deep-reaching powers. At the same time, the biblical theology understanding of justice and injustice, together with its call to discipleship and vocation in the world, would have to imply a sharp differentiation between the powers assigned to the governmental regime and the identity, attitudes, and practices of those who are to activate them in behalf of basic justice. Strictly, only the faithful can be the carriers of the new justice. We must therefore look at the paragraphs that focus on the obligations of citizens. The second and third considerations above must be read in conjunction with one another if one is to understand what the letter says regarding the scope and reach of "government."

Approached with this understanding, the argument unfolds in line with the logic of this basic position. First, all citizens have obligations over and above the obligations of their particular roles in the social economy, simply as members of the social community. "By fulfilling these duties, we create a true commonwealth." One way of responding to these duties—as an expression of Christian love and social solidarity—is by voluntary efforts to overcome injustice in the various communities in which people live.[41] More importantly, every citizen has as well the responsibility to work " . . . to secure justice and human rights through organized social response. The guarantee of basic justice for all is not an optional expression of largesse but an inescapable duty for the whole community."[42] Then, given the "social pluralism of the United States . . . the Church insists that *government has a moral function: protecting human rights and securing basic justice for all members of the commonwealth.*"[43] "More specifically, its moral function is to assist and empower the poor, the disadvantaged, the handicapped, and the unemployed."[44]

Matching passages in chapter 4 can be read so as to flesh out this design. These stress (1) the " . . . inescapable social and political nature of the economy";[45] (2) the principle of subsidiarity, but as a two-edged principle which also " . . . calls for government intervention when small or intermediate groups . . . are unable or unwilling to take the steps needed to promote basic justice";[46] and finally, (3) that "society" provide for overall economic planning to produce a reasonable coordination as a condition of basic justice.[47] Nonetheless, the scope and reach of government must remain an open issue. "The precise form of government involvement . . . will depend on an assessment of specific needs and the most effective ways to address them."[48]

What of the injustice potential of governmental agents with powers of such scope and reach? This will be disarmed by citizens' mutual involvements. Action by Christian communities, and the practice of participatory deciding, cooperating, responsibility sharing, etc. with people of good will, are expected to double in brass as justice-guaranteeing and consensus-building processes.[49] From this perspective, the new order appears to be imagined as integrally solidaristic and "political" in its modus operandi, but in a sense that obscures distinctions between the communitarian and societal on the one hand, and the properly political on the other. Earlier, I termed these attributes "solidaristic democratic syndicalism." The bishops prefer calling it "true commonwealth," a form of social organization they seem to want extended to the whole family.[50]

A final issue remains. The interpretation put forward follows from the goals of basic justice, namely, the sweeping redistribution of goods and services, the dismantling of barriers to participatory rights, and the step-by-step process of reorganizing economic (and sociopolitical) life so as to institutionalize a more egalitarian society all round. Taken in conjunction with the emphasis on but two forms of human sinfulness, namely, the monopolization of God's gift to all and the resulting waste, one would expect—as we did above—that the road to basic justice would be marked by continuous conflict. Indeed, a sign-of-the-times reading casting the church as the David of the impoverished in their struggle for rights with the Goliath of wealth and power would suggest nothing so much as covert Marxism.

That is not the direction chosen by the bishops. On the contrary, they express a belief that the steps toward basic justice can be implemented as social transformations called for by common good considerations. But as pointed out, on our reading of their common good notion the latter has only an *instrumental* significance, not that of the architectonic principle. Why this role reversal with distributive justice, and what are its consequences? The role reversal seems to be grounded in the logic of the biblical approach set forth in chapter 2. Biblical references to justice and injustice frequently concern distributive issues or issues that can be said to have distributive aspects. The biblical emphasis on distributive justice should not be surprising, given the theocratic/monarchical regimes by which the Israelites were governed and their traditional organization into twelve extended family groups. With this as point of departure, and a form of pastoral theologizing that seeks its understanding of justice more or less directly in biblical reflection, common good considerations cannot but be cast in a subsidiary role at the level of application.

In contrast, *the common good principle of social justice with its subsidiarity dimension is the result of an effort to mediate between the scriptural call to justice in the treatment of one's neighbor and the understanding of this justice requirement in large-scale societies undergoing industrial modernization.*[51] From the latter standpoint, common good demands express gospel commands in systemic twentieth century terms. The point here is no quibble of interest to experts only. The issue is far reaching. In the traditional, architectonic conception, common good considerations belong in theological reflection about what justice in society demands because mediation is integral in such reflections. Natural law reasoning "complements" reflecting on Scripture in this sense.[52] A merely biblical understanding of pastoral theologizing excludes systematic mediation at this level. This exclusion confines common good considerations. They may be said to "complement" basic justice demands but only in the sense of providing supporting arguments at the level of implementation. What follows seeks to provide grounds for claiming that not only social philosophy but also social economics deserve a place in the pastoral theology dialogue. Neither body of knowledge can play that role in a social justice regime dominated by basic justice imperatives.

III. Understanding Modern Social Economy

WE TURN NOW to the issue posed at the beginning by asking: is the Christian vision in the form urged economically feasible in today's world? What could social economics contribute to a mediation between the possibilities "then" and "now"? The following bears on two themes prominent in the letter: (1) the difficulties surrounding the "true-commonwealth" concept, and (2) the extent to which the biblical vision of full dimensional community living based on love is a feasible norm for organizing economic activity today.

SOME BASICS ABOUT ETHICS, EFFICIENCY AND ECONOMIC DEVELOPMENT

THE BISHOPS ARE justly proud of the consultative process they employed before and since launching the first draft of the letter. However, most of the economic advice given did not relate to the structural reform side of the letter's universe of discourse. Thus the advocated reorganization of economic activity in line with justice-as-participation remains largely unexamined from an economic point of view. Part III addresses this lacuna.

Distinguished economists did offer the predictable — and appropriate — statements about the efficiency or inefficiency of various policy options; they also entered frequent reminders that the choices considered in the letter involve tradeoffs that ought to be faced. Neither the first nor the second draft contains noticeable evidence that these advisory comments touched a responsive nerve.

Something needs to be said at the start about the relevance of these two considerations for theological and ethical approaches to economic reform. Efficiency — better, continued economic productivity growth — has to be taken seriously in social ethics reflection. Two considerations seem compelling in this regard. First and pragmatically, world population growth is not likely to stop short of ten or eleven billion souls less than a century from now. The present figure stands at just under five billion.[53] With much of the population growth concentrated in the poorest regions of the globe, simple redistribution based on the present levels of world production is no solution.

Second, a great many issues call for significant resource commitments if things are to get better. Because of population growth, resources will continue to be scarce. Thus difficult choices among social policy alternatives are going to remain systemic. The fact that a particular subset of objectives is mandated by strong ethical norms does not necessarily tell us what should be done. Among the alternatives that would have to be forgone are bound to be others that are also backed by strong ethical norms. Thus, tradeoffs are unavoidable. They must be considered if action is to be intelligently responsible. This general observation certainly applies to the bundles of demands put forward in the letter.

Concerning the lacuna mentioned: the advocated goal appears to be a form of syndicalism. I suggested at the very beginning that so sweeping a reorganization of socioeconomic life might collide with certain real-world barriers. What are these barriers, and how do they relate to forms of economic organizations?

The question is best approached by reflecting on two observations: the boundedness[54] of individual men and women, physically, mentally, spatially, and in terms of life span, notwithstanding the towering achievements they have brought about in the course of human history. Though the basic point is quite general, we are here interested in economic achievements. We focus, in particular, on the rapid, sustained, and at times turbulent rate of productivity growth and of economic development generally. Until recently, this history is predominantly a dimension of the rise of the West. Today, it is the story of ongoing economic development in the modernizing world.

How were, and are, mere men and women able to mount this performance? The answer has far-reaching ramifications, of course, but one major strand in any supportable explanation is summed up in two concepts: socioeconomic organization, and technological innovation along with technical economic advances. The evidence that the underlying—and interrelated—processes do, in fact, account for the lion's share of observed development rates is overwhelming.

THE LOGIC OF ECONOMIC ORGANIZATION[55]

THE FIRST PROPOSITION is that continued economic performance depends importantly on the ways economic activities—available production techniques assumed constant, for the time being—are organized.

Consider the fact of human boundedness, and how organizational arrangement through which economic activity is carried on can mitigate its consequences. For present purposes, the limitations at issue have their source in three aspects of the human condition: (1) the boundedness of our ability to acquire knowledge, process it analytically, store it, retrieve it, apply it in concrete decisions, learn from observed consequences and so forth (hereafter: information search and processing); (2) related impediments insofar as these affect communicating knowledge to others with different knowledge backgrounds and processing abilities; and (3) the risks associated with behavioral failings in economic contexts, shading from fraudulent claims and deliberate false promises ("opportunism") to taking full advantage of available monopoly leverage, to simply "free riding" on the system.[56]

Information learning, processing, and communicating encounter natural barriers in man's neurophysiological makeup. Consider the requirements of information search and analytic processing. Anyone who has earned a degree in law or engineering or, for that matter, has achieved a carpenter's or machinist's impressive know-how is aware that acquiring the particular "information structure" — the specialized stock of background knowledge — and the corresponding information search and processing skills, amounts to making a long-term investment. The learning process is costly, in time and other resources; it implies forgoing other pursuits, among them most of the other knowledge structures. To the extent useful in economic activity, what is acquired in each case is a specialized form of human capital.

A moment's reflection suggests a further point, namely, that specialized knowledge and information processing capacities are closely related to specialized skills and the ability to exercise them. Although one deals here with a continuum, information processing and skilled task performance are often inseparably linked. This is certainly true of the technical specialties so important in modern production and distribution activities.

Two aspects of this fact deserve emphasis. First, and as just mentioned, mastery in any one field comes at the expense of mastery in others. The effort to acquire a more sophisticated information structure and its skills is purchased by a narrowing of scope. Pursuit of universal understanding is like jacking at many trades: one can do no more than stay near the surface of things. Man's neurophysiological boundedness, alas, confronts us with tradeoffs as well. Second, the narrowness of the specialist is not an unmitigated loss. On the contrary, it is the source of great benefits, *provided the gain in knowledge and skill can be harnessed by organizational means.* The network of markets linked informationally by the pricing system is one prototypical mode of such social organization. Its contribution to productivity growth lies precisely in its capacity to mediate, at low "transactions costs,"[57] the host of specialized production activities and related exchanges.

These matters are left to one side here; they appear as part of the social environment in which the modern business firm, the second prototypical mode of organizing, functions. Reflection on its structural characteristics and the reasons for the shape these take has much to teach about organizational possibilities in other contexts; it bears directly on the feasibility of the "true commonwealth" proposal of the letter.

A revealing way to begin thinking about the modern business firm is to ask how it improves on the boundedness of the one-man or one-woman firm. The answer one comes to is obvious: by organizing a number of functionally specialized persons into one or more sets of cooperative and coordinated activities. Individual and group specialization is a main part of the story; for much of the rest, the firm depends on administrative arrangements and processes. The latter serve within the firm as markets do among them: they mediate the interplay of activities among the persons and groups comprising the company. Needless to say, the mere fact of organizing in this way does not guarantee efficiency. Human organizations mitigate human limitations in particular respects, but only up to a point, as will become clear.

Further thought leads to a second aspect of this question, one which arises from people's limited capacity to communicate clearly, in sufficient detail, etc. As a result, communicating across lines of specialization is difficult and costly. Moreover, the more complex the activity set, the greater and more sophisticated the information flows needed to link the specialized activities. Different information structures and their respective signaling codes must somehow be organized into an information network that allows decision making, cooperation, and coordination to proceed. Here, efficiency gains depend on how well different specialized tasks and corresponding information gathering and processing activities mesh. As the volume of specialized information transmitted mounts, so does the need to abstract from detail and to codify. Both economize on the cost of transmission. However, unless such techniques can be developed and adaptively shaped to the firm's changing needs, man's limited ability to communicate soon exhausts the gains of specialization and large-scale organization.

The third kind of human limitation of interest here manifests itself in lapses from responsible, best-effort contributions to joint undertakings. Consider the well-known problems of this sort in any organization of size and sophistication, especially a modern business firm.[58] Its viability depends on complex micro decision making by specialized persons and groups up and down the line. Good "point" decisions at the top — crucial as sound business strategies are to success or failure — do not suffice. In the uncertain environment in which economic activity takes place, it matters greatly how the many persons and functional groups down the line perform their tasks, how they solve unforeseen problems, whether they take responsibility for innovative moves of their own when "local" opportunities permit, and so on. The quality of such "line" decisions matters a great deal in determining whether "point" decisions go, drift, or fail. Top-down control based on performance monitoring plays a role, but in sophisticated processes, it is a supplementary one. Among other things, it cannot answer the ancient question: *Quis custodiet ipsos custodes?*[59] In such enterprises, a great many people qualify as *custodes*, simply because of the many specialties involved. Individual and subgroup motivation is therefore of signal importance, and not merely to mitigate free riding.

What can be inferred about institutional arrangements from all of the above? Modern business firms are composites of men and women brought to some degree of cooperative, coordinated activity by means of institutional arrangements. Behavioral, information processing, as well as communicating requirements of performing in the uncertainties of economic life make developing such arrangements a major challenge. Viewed strictly in efficiency terms, the problem comes down to mitigating the cost of interpersonal and intergroup "transactions," i.e., the resources expended to enable the interactions that comprise the joint effort. Analytically put, we want to know how different organizational arrangements compare as instrumentalities to limit or reduce transactions costs. The challenge is to minimize transactions costs relative to achievable operating efficiencies.

Space does not allow more than a reflection on the seminal insights of the analysis of this issue in the form developed by Professor Williamson.[60] Consider a short list of basic organizational characteristics. They are widely observed, but we stick to their manifestations in economic activity. The first is that of hierarchy; the second is equality, as in peer group arrangements; the third characteristic is a combination of these two, a mix of hierarchical and peer arrangements functioning within a quasi-constitutional structure of agreed-upon procedural rules.

The ubiquity of hierarchical arrangements has been explained in a great many ways, some unflattering to hierarchs, as we know from the pastoral letter. Efficiency reasons are often neglected in such accounts. That is a serious deficiency. Economic decisions typically call for agreement about what's to be done and how, how much of it, etc., when the information about relevant factors is incomplete and biased in its distribution. In the absence of someone who is in a position to decide, the result, more often than not, is persisting disagreement. How can hierarchical structuring help? Take a simple case. Three members of a firm's engineering department are asked to deal with a case of frequent machine breakdowns. They fail to agree about how best to tackle the problem. All three are equally qualified and no one else in the engineering department knows as much about the problem. Under a hierarchical setup, the chief engineer, although not a specialist, can listen to the three approaches and decide. Under a strict peer arrangement, arriving at a decision is cumbersome because all-member information learning and deciding takes time. The efficiency advantages of getting on with the problem at hand, leaving the others to pursue their specialties, are obvious. Note that the decision reached hierarchically is based on the best available information, incomplete though it obviously is. Good information is requisite to making good decisions. When decisions are instrumental in character, when information is incomplete and unequally distributed among those concerned, hierarchical structuring has significant transactions cost advantages.

This conclusion is easily generalized to include all members of an enterprise. Take a more complex case. A firm's production activity takes place in three stages: (1) the manufacture of basic parts and components, (2) further processing, e.g., procuring of additional components, machining and final assembly into several distinct products, and (3) a final set of operations grouped under "marketing." Organizing the above into a set of efficient processes encounters the same basic problem as the simple case. Uncertain fluctuations in market demands require alert procurement and work-in-process adjustments. Because the firm produces several products, deciding on demand estimates and thus on what subset of responses to initiate is a complex version of the engineering case. The number and variety of experts to be included is much greater, and decisions taken affect, directly or indirectly, more than one of the operating units. If all affected persons were to be consulted, i.e., brought regularly into such decision processes, the firm would sink under the weight of its transactions cost. Our general conclusion is the same as before: *under the widely experienced real conditions described, instrumental decisions require recourse to hierarchical structures.*

The second category of intraorganization relationships is that of equality, as in peer groups. Although this form of organization will not work as the governing principle in operations of any size and complexity, that is not the end of the matter. Return to the example of the three engineers. Would it be efficient—for decision purposes—to rank order the three specialists? They are equally competent insofar as anyone can tell. The fact is, they are peers.

Arranging things in a way that enables them to function as peers has clear efficiency advantages. Situations that allow such arrangements are not exceptional. Business organizations of the type we are discussing are multistage, multiproduct operations. They are also multitiered. From the home office on "down" and "across," various support and service centers are so structured as to supply different intermediate inputs to the respective production and marketing departments. The point is that each of these suborganizations is operated by various specialized groups. Though organized hierarchically as in the engineering case, the resolution of some of their problems can benefit from the operating expertise of those immediately involved. In other cases, the expertise cuts across tasks and production technologies or depends mainly on general experience in the firm. So long as the operations, problems, and opportunities of the subunit as a whole are not too complex and interactive, and provided that it is not too large, issues of the kind indicated will be quite clear to qualified members. Consulting them on such matters is likely to improve problem resolution. True, transactions costs rise with this approach, but the beneficial effects are often well worth the candle. Consulting them also helps improve their performance.

The previous sentence directs attention to the tie-in between behavioral aspects of good task performance and institutional arrangements. When it comes to protecting the joint undertaking from non- or counterproductive conduct, hierarchies resort to formal monitoring systems. Performance monitoring—and experience rating for possible promotion—do encourage good performance. But these incentives tend to direct effort toward the things that carry weight in the evaluation system being used. Formalized monitoring procedures, while useful, cannot fill the entire bill. Responsible best-effort performance has benefits formalization cannot reach.

What is the relation between peer practices and task performance? The value of peer arrangements where conditions warrant them is impressive. Participation in the decision process allows for the exercise not only of the members' specialized backgrounds, but of their intelligence and sense of responsibility as well. The experience of effective involvement, even if only intermittent, is of major importance in motivating best efforts. Furthermore, such involvement helps generate an atmosphere in the particular work place, one that is conducive to team spirit and pride of belonging to the group. We have no space here to go into the sociological and psychological ramifications; suffice it to point out that the associational gains so fostered may also foster performance efficiencies not readily tapped by monitoring and individualized incentive schemes, the next best alternatives in strictly hierarchical settings.

Other benefits could be mentioned. One worth citing here arises from members' daily involvement with one another in the operational technicalities of the unit's function. This provides excellent opportunities for unobtrusive performance monitoring, informal standard setting, and standard "enforcement" as a dimension of work place atmosphere. These manifestations of the unit's solidarity, however, can have counterproductive effects. Whether they do or not depends on the unit's relationship to the larger whole, as we shall see.

Though peer practices and motivations have much to contribute, their usefulness is subject to unavoidable limits. When technical economic factors require larger or more complex functional units, standards setting, monitoring and enforcing tend toward formalization. Thus, hierarchical features tend naturally to dilute the peer-relations content of work life. The point carries beyond monitoring and standard enforcement. Effective "line" decisions and task performance turn importantly on who is assigned to what functional responsibility. Rotating people among positions can work where the needed aptitudes, backgrounds and skills are more or less uniformly distributed among the members or are easily learned. These conditions are not widely met in modern enterprises. On the contrary, for most firms in this category, assigning the right people to the different positions is a matter of survival. Could peer groups deal with the assignment problem? Assume that the members *can* readily agree on all assignments. Although the process of choosing conforms to the peer principle, the outcome does not. Some men or women will fulfill their functions by directing the activities of others, or perhaps by wielding a disproportionate share of influence on decisions. Genetic differences, one's personal history of circumstances and decisions, and so forth are at the root of these widely observed facts.

One loose end remains: how to cope by institutional means with free riding and other such lapses in all those circumstances in which peer arrangements are not appropriate. Hierarchical monitoring, we know, is helpful but insufficient. The problems that remain are well understood; they are ubiquitous in all kinds of large, multi-functional organizations. Hierarchical structures and thus relationships, to prove effective, must find ways of engaging the conscious collaboration and initiative of the various specialists acting in and for the functional units comprising the company. Designing such schemes calls for (1) procedures to search for, attract, and screen candidates with the relevant qualifications and (2) procedures to link employee performance and learning-by-experience with a structure of career ladders whose pay or promotional incentives bear a discernable relationship to performance at each rung. The guiding objective is to engage the long-range, personal, family, and perhaps local pride drives of organization members so as to bring these into closer alignment with the firm's raison d'être. Where operational contexts make free riding and by-the-book performance all but unavoidable, incentives so directed are likely to outperform other feasible arrangements in the present state of production and transactions technology.

To sum up, I would argue, on the basis of considerations well grounded in economic research and in the work of other students of human behavior in large modern institutions, that efficiency requires a mixture of hierarchical and peer arrangements; and that the combinations likely to prove most beneficial depend importantly on considerations of scale and complexity that are not likely to change under modern economic conditions. Note that so far—entirely for ease of exposition—production technology has been assumed to be unchanged. The next section deals with the interrelationships between technical economic and associated organizational innovations. Because efficiency growth is so important, the actual problem is one of finding best combinations consistent with the changing limitations and opportunities so brought about. From that point of view and as a general matter, the search for structural improvements calls for continuing study of, and experimentation with, peer practices as part of the organizational mix, with an eye to benefit gains in comparison to the increasing transactions costs involved.

Unsurprisingly, weak spots remain, and that brings us to the final point of this section. The behavioral nexus between institutional arrangements and systems efficiency is richer and even more problematic than the antecedent argument concedes. In circumstances marked by incomplete information and by biases in its distribution, the process or career-ladder assignments, performance monitoring, and promotion is open to a range of undesirable influences. Thus, certain decisions made hierarchically may be regarded as uninformed, others as unfair or perhaps even as malevolent. Performance might be improved all around if resistance to authoritative determinations in contexts not so transparently justified were to be constrained by agreed-upon rules and corresponding grievance procedures. Such governance structures are widespread, and not only where trade union pressure brought about their acceptance. Modern, well-established companies have developed these arrangements on their own initiative in the belief that they promote responsible best-effort performance.

Recent experience, however, has exposed their limitations. When a firm confronts the need for quick and drastic action to counter survival-threatening developments, the desire for executive, "point"-decision flexibility becomes dominant. Technological change and its economic consequences sometimes demand moves and rearrangements to which more or less formalized governance structures rooted in past experience are poorly attuned. Rather than serve as one of the mechanisms through which operational-structural transformation can be accomplished, they may become barriers whose defense will leave almost everyone worse off.[61]

The problem is crucial; it is the very one that triggered the "true commonwealth" initiative of the letter. The bishops correctly identify the social ethics and social economies issue of our day. Their approach, however, fails to address the dynamics of the problem. Extending decisional and operational rights in multiple directions multiplies attending transactions costs. Its consequence would be to spread systemic rigidity. This can hardly be a workable approach for the United States, while elsewhere in the world the dynamism of new production technologies and economic reorganization continues.

TECHNOLOGY AND EFFICIENT ORGANIZATION

THE ANTECEDENT ACCOUNT of economic organization is obviously incomplete. Technological innovations must somehow be allowed for in explaining the organization-efficiency relation. Sustained productivity growth, largely due to improved production methods and product innovations, has been a prominent characteristic of economic development since the late eighteenth century. In its absence, neither economic nor social forms of organization could have delivered anything like the performance of the past two centuries.[62]

The interrelation between technological change and organization of economic activity is not well understood. A bit of history is essential here. Quantitative research covering the past 150 years or so leaves little doubt that technology-based economic innovations account for the major share of productivity growth and product innovation.[63] Technical development, in turn, can be traced back to a succession of technological innovations consisting in each case, as Professor Rosenberg has shown, of a few ". . . interlocking, mutually reinforcing, technologies . . ."[64] The sequence of complementary clusters began with innovations in steam power, metallurgy (mostly iron and in due course, steel), and a handful of other developments basic for the use of mineral fuels in a number of different applications. Recognizably, the economic opportunities brought about stand at the center of the industrial revolution. A second cluster provided the new knowledge at the core of electrification beginning in the late nineteenth century; the internal combustion engine, a bit later, added to this stream of new developments. Current advances turn on technological innovations in plastics, electronics, and information technology.[65] One should probably add the promise of things to come based on biotechnological research and genetic engineering.

The relationship between the technological knowledge and the process of technical economic advance is neither direct nor obvious, however. It is instructive to think of it as triangular: a cluster of technological innovations forms the apex, the implementation, adaptation, extension, and thus diffusion over a range of applications forms the technical economic advance leg; and the other is formed by the associated organizational arrangements. The triangle image, however, has the disadvantage of appearing stationary and offering a once-and-for-all set of relations. Technical economic advance is an ongoing, experimental process marked by leads and lags, trials and errors, and thus by a complicated research-and-development, learning-by-doing sequence.

A brief comment about the link between the new technological knowledge and the process of technical economic advance can suffice. With rare exceptions, demonstrated feasibility in the form of a laboratory model put together by scientists and engineers conveys but a part of the information and know-how required for actual — and economically successful — use in the plant. Typically, various engineering and maintenance adaptations remain to be worked out. Complementary equipment may pose bottleneck problems calling for entirely different sorts of modification or even inventions. New operating skills have to be learned. And although the problems so indicated are technical, the expected cost of solutions is a key factor in deciding whether to introduce the new equipment now, or to delay until more information is available. If the new equipment is market supplied, an issue may be whether to await likely technical improvements, or price reductions of the machine, or perhaps reductions in the price of some complementary input. Technical advance or price declines in competing equipment are also factors. It goes without saying that expected and actual economic success need not coincide. Forecasting costs and revenues in such situations is fraught with uncertainty.

Let us concentrate on the third side of our triangle, its base, which connects new technology applications and organizational arrangements. We do so because it is the locus of combinations that increase the possibility of enhancing human dignity in the conduct of economic activity. Three kinds of relationships can be distinguished: first, institutional innovations may be required by the new production or distribution technique; second, technical and organizational innovations may develop as a complementary process; and third, the technical innovation may offer opportunities for improving the organization of economic activity by improving the quality of decisions and transactions or by reducing their costs. Representative examples can serve to bring out how these relationships function.

Early railroad development turned on the first kind of relationship. Because the example is a familiar one, suffice it to point out that traditional forms of business organization based on direct management by the proprietor or a very small number of partners could not have brought the railroad to fruition.

Other historical examples illustrate situations in which technical and organizational innovations appear as complementary processes. The last half of the nineteenth century witnessed the introduction of complex, relatively high-cost machines of various kinds, such as sewing machines, harvesters, typewriters, elevators and electrical machinery. With little loss in precision, one can generalize as follows: being new, these products needed demonstration by trained people familiar with their capabilities and operating characteristics. Being complex and but recently introduced, they required expert, speedy service or repair, often in the place where the machines were being employed. And being costly relative to the financial resources of likely buyers, they often required the extension of credit and thus the establishment of a payments collection process. These machines had other features in common. Their manufacture required large fixed capital investments subject to economies of scale. Achieving high production rates as free of sharp interruptions as could be managed had to be a prime objective; scale economies convert quickly into rising costs and prohibitive losses when output levels drop below the break-even mark.

What institutional innovations developed in these areas? How do they link up with the enumerated technical characteristics and their economic consequences? The key economic requirements were large, steady or growing volume and reliable technical as well as financial interface with many customers so as to generate and maintain needed rates of sale. While existing channels via business machine distributors, territorial agents, or even itinerant agents selling through local retailers, etc., were widely practiced, these methods were found inadequate. Demonstrating, selling and coordinating product as well as attendant service and cash flows, and keeping these in step with production rates and inventory decisions, proved unendingly troublesome or even disastrous when handled through traditional channels. In all these instances, the firms in question wound up developing their own distribution organizations. Administrative procedures, it seems, were more efficient in mediating the complex interrelationships than going the market route via middlemen.[66]

The third example, the semiconductor industry, relates directly to the discussion earlier of information processing and communicating. The major concern there was information search and analytical processing in the interests of good decision making throughout the enterprise. That, we said, depends on accurate, speedy communication; information storage and retrieval have an obvious role to play in this. The semiconductor industry fits right in as a source of technical economic innovations that serve to reduce cooperating and coordinating difficulties within firms. The same innovations also facilitate communicating across markets and mixed forms of organization. That the very same electronic devices have a key role in the search for new knowledge and its uses only adds to the attraction. The potential of modern computers and telecommunications equipment is still in its early stages.

It would be tedious to go into detail here. The basic idea is easily illustrated with reference to "networking," as the jargon has it. Existing factory networks, so far only "local" ones for coordinating a number of machine tools working in tandem with each other and with automated materials handling equipment, can be programmed from a single workstation computer. This allows one skilled worker to tell an assembly of sophisticated machines what to do, in what sequence, at what rates, etc., in light of information flows collected from the machines and from other sources. The implicit human dignity advance is obvious. Responsibly contributing to the production process in this manner is a long way from machine tending, 1920s vintage. At the same time, "networking" has an enormous potential for reducing transactions costs.

To appreciate this, as well as the obstacles involved, consider what would be required to coordinate the activities of an entire plant in this way. One would have to link mainframe computers, which process information about work in progress, inventory flows, cost accounting data, etc., the high-powered computers and specialized software used in design and engineering work, and the operating computers employed on the factory floor. The key problem besetting efforts to develop a network of this complexity has been that of inventing — and agreeing upon — a computer language linking the different operating systems software[67] in a way that does not hamstring their operational independence and flexibility. Add the telecommunications interface connecting office and factory, and one has an idea of the transactional advantages promised by automated, trouble-free and consistent communications across the entire range of these information processing machines.

Futurologists are tempted to fantasize about the automated business firm. The argument in this section of the paper is easily extended to suggest that such a vision is utopian. The promise of full network development — major efforts are under way — will be measured by improvements in the quality of task cooperation and coordination, and by reductions in associated transactions cost. Beyond some point, however, remaining informational constraints and rising transactions costs will signal that barriers to further efficiencies along this line are being encountered. That will happen when the men and women whose responsible best efforts are required in the ongoing sequence of "point" and "line" decisions encounter the limitations of their human capacities. The ultimate scarce resource is man's neurophysiological boundedness and his behavioral propensities in economic contexts.

The semiconductor case is well suited to illustrate a second main aspect of the technical-innovation-and-economic-organization nexus. In this industry as in others, the organizational arrangements that have developed are well explained as so many ways to improve the quality of transactions and/or reduce their costs. First of all, the industry is very young. It dates back to a 1940s technological innovation, the transistor, by three research scientists working for Bell Laboratories. By now, the industry consists of firms specialized in the design and manufacture of silicon wafers, as well as others which assemble electronic circuits, its operating controls, etc., install these devices in end products, test them, and so on;[68] still others specialize in producing the machinery and equipment employed by device manufacturers. Initially, electronic component manufacturers developed most of their own equipment; since the 1970s, however, independent companies fulfill this function, ". . . many of them spin-offs from the component manufacturers."[69] Evidently, the economies of scale available by producing this equipment for the market, when combined with the development of information-exchange arrangements between equipment suppliers and their customers, outweighed the transactional advantages of in-house design, production and adaptation, etc., of the equipment.

Then there are the large, integrated device manufacturers such as IBM, Texas Instruments, Japan's NEC, Hitachi, Toshiba, and the Dutch multinational Phillips, to mention some of the major ones. These have succeeded in linking product innovation, manufacture, and distribution with attendant customer service and repair relationships, much as their precursors did beginning in the eighties and nineties of the last century. They follow this organizational strategy for basically the same reasons, a major factor being to save transactions costs.

A final point concerns the mix of market and organizational characteristics of this industry. Professor Flaherty summarizes the evidence by concluding that (1) the engineering staffs of semiconductor companies work closely with selected customer companies in developing better products; (2) production equipment suppliers — as we noted — work with end product manufacturers to keep adapting their products in response to experience in using them and to new consumer needs as these develop; and (3) sustained success as component manufacturers goes hand in glove with close cooperative ties to end-product manufacturers. Such ties are crucial following the introduction of new products again for the purpose of gathering information. Mainly, what is wanted by these specialty firms is the feedback of operating experience which will be helpful in designing improved or new components. Routine trouble shooting is another aspect of this mutually advantageous tie-in between supplier and customer firm. Note that in other respects these firms relate to each other via the market.[70]

Students of Nathan Rosenberg's work on the interactive processes that connect technological innovation and technical economic innovations will not be surprised by any of these findings. His study of interfirm relationships between airframe and jet engine manufacturers on the one hand and commercial airlines on the other conforms to the same pattern. It provides an explanation of the fact that the lion's share of air transport productivity gains over a fifty-year period can be traced to precisely the information exchange Dr. Flaherty described.[71] Students of Oliver Williamson's work will not be surprised, either, knowing the insight with which he has fashioned the transactions-cost approach to organizational forms in markets and businesses into a coherent paradigm.[72]

Joining these two explanatory strands as illustrated in the cases presented throws light on the realistic limitations of proposed structural reform initiatives. Such limitations seem unavoidable in the foreseeable future, and they hamper sociostructural reforms believed desirable on theological or ethical grounds. But taken together, these two strands show us also a hopeful side, precisely in terms of enhancing human dignity. It has been so in the past, as must be apparent to anyone who compares present working conditions and living standards of large majorities in the West and elsewhere in the modern world with the previous conditions for most people as described in Fernand Braudel's *Civilization of Capitalism, 15th to 18th*

Century: The Structure of Every Day Life.[73] Today's technical economic advances and associated organizational forms present us with new possibilities for advancing human dignity, as well as new threats. If the antecedent presentation can help open up theological-philosophical reflections to these considerations as integral to the dialogue about new directions in social ethics, my objective will have been attained.

IV. Concluding Reflections

THE MAIN CONCLUSIONS to be drawn from what has been said must be fairly obvious. First, the "true commonwealth," as a form of social organization which embodies one understanding of the letter's vision of economic life, seems infeasible. No conceivable peer-group arrangement respectful of participation rights wherever relevant could bring to effective and timely coherence the myriad transactions now taking place in firms and via markets. It is neither an accident nor a valid indication of moral turpitude that concrete efforts to institutionalize this ideal on a large scale have ended in bureaucratic centralism[74] or market-oriented forms of organization. The transactions cost implicit in the "true commonwealth" ideal defeat it as a model that is workable in modern social settings.

The second conclusion concerns the possibility of arranging relationships and practices within economic units so as to conform to full-dimensioned community living based on love. As the discussion of peer group procedures in business firms suggests, subunit solidarity based on respect for these possibilities in work life is alive. Nor is that all. Information processing and communication developments are enlarging the scope for peer-like operating modes. But short of something fairly close to full automation across the stages of production, from raw material extraction to final product delivery, economic activity will require men and women with specialized abilities, concentrating on the tasks at hand in responsible best-effort fashion. Only in idealized pastoral or craft-tending settings is full-dimensioned sharing of daily life compatible with productive effectiveness.

I venture the beginning of a third conclusion. Elevating a biblical, and ideological, understanding of basic justice to the status of an architectonic principle risks being interpreted as urging a narrow, populist redistributionalism in the exegetical dialogue to come. With a little vulgarization, the entire question of social order and integration which received so rich and multifaceted an articulation in the

traditional teaching, would seem to be flattened into a simple matter of "power" and "wealth" redistribution. Read in this way, one
might conclude that the letter sees little need for any sort of sophistication about an effective ordering of differentiated social groups and
the integration of their various contributions to the common good.
Participatory processes will take care of what needs to be decided
about such issues.

   This line of reflection leads to familiar issues of political philosophy. They should be extended into the economic dimension as well.
The insufficiency of the distributional approach as socioeconomic organizing principle is most apparent when compared with Heinrich
Pesch's path-breaking work on social economy and social justice. The
reader will recall that central notions of this understanding were summarized in the introduction of this paper. Pesch said that large-scale,
industrializing societies would have to accept, constrain in certain respects, as well as develop economic structures in order to enable the
various persons and professional-occupational groups to play their
differentiated roles. To what end? To enable them to satisfy the
"material" dimensions of common good pursuit.[75] In his view, these
interactions among persons acting in and for their respective groups
is a precondition of ongoing social effectiveness for the greater well-
being of each and all. He saw this effectiveness grounded in human
solidarity as both a fact and an ethical requirement. Equally important, Pesch's "Solidaristic Order" is open to change from two
sources: technological advances and organizational improvements.
Pesch focused on the latter, insisting, of course, that they must be
in keeping with respect for the dignity of work.[76] Thus the structure
of professional, industry branch, etc., groupings would have to be
linked by sound market competition and remain flexibly adaptive.
He warned against the imposition of a particular vocational structure.

   I do not maintain that Pesch's work and thought is the answer
to the bishops' pastoral concern, nor that *Quadragesimo Anno*, though
it strongly reflects his legacy, is all the guide we need today in the
U.S. context. Regarding the encyclical, its economic aspects as these
came to be understood seem indeed too static and thus muscle-
bound for application, or else too much a matter of abstract principle. And Pesch's economic scholarship is now out of date. But his
basic understanding was impressively farsighted. I do maintain that
the modern understanding of economic organization and technical
economic dynamics offers a concrete approach to precisely the issues
Pesch sought to resolve. I also point out, echoing Franz Mueller,[77]
that Pesch's basic understanding took shape within a framework
defined by his Catholic theology and a natural law-based "philosophical sociology." The great strength of this framework derives from

its authentic theological tradition and from its openness to Rahner's conception of theological "philosophizing." Pesch defined this to include the best social economics he could develop. The challenge is to extend Pesch's kind of work and thought in ways that harness modern possibilities, their dynamism and all, for the common good. God is also present in the economic details.

I conclude this paper with an explanation of why elevating distributive justice (in the "basic justice" sense) and demoting the common good principle of social justice (in a Peschian sense) would matter practically. The argument, briefly, is that coming to grips with poverty, a pastoral concern whose urgency the bishops rightly stress, is better approached within a social justice-common good understanding. "Better" is here understood as "more effectively."

Poverty, as variously referred to in the letter, is a composite of situations which differ in complex ways, only some of which belong under the heading of "the poor" as describing those at the margins of economic and/or social life. An important distinction needs to be drawn between persistent poverty associated with bad health, old age, and various other lasting disabilities in relation to economic activity, and other types of poverty deriving from various temporary as well as longer-term factors such as business cycles, job switching upon first entering the labor force, economic disruption due to exhaustion of natural resources, industries in decline for deep-seated competitive reasons, and the like. Let us simplify, pleading expository convenience, by distinguishing between those whose poverty is associated with medical conditions broadly construed, and others whose want is rooted in the malfunctioning of economic institutions.

Responding to the former requires more than mobilizing known health care resources. Redistribution in that sense is, of course, a part of what needs to be done. But the aspects most closely related to justice in economic activity relate primarily to those poor whose disabilities stem from potentially remediable conditions, whether physical, psychological or adversely behavioral in some other sense. Advancing in these respects, insofar as the health sciences and arts can help, depends on continuing research, clinical trials, and thus on learning from failures no less than from successes. At base, it depends on what progress can be made in such specialties as gerontology, abnormal psychology, psychopharmacology, and their underlying disciplines, as well as in certain branches of sociology and social psychology.

The point is this: the "resources" of strategic importance for these poor are not simply "given" and thus available for redistribution. They need continuing reconsideration in light of new evidence, leading to modification or reorientation, or perhaps to being superseded by very different approaches and therapies. Here as elsewhere, resources are defined by the state of knowledge. What is or is not a "resource" for the health sciences and arts undergoes transformations in the knowledge acquisition process.

It follows that continued advance with health-related disabilities is best addressed by policies likely to promote the common good in these respects. Limiting the scope of efforts and the flow of benefits to the poor in questions of health will be counterproductive.

A similar proposition applies in the case of people suffering through spells of poverty because of cyclical swings in economic activity as well as through the more difficult adjustments mentioned. Redistribution by subsidizing activities in danger of losing economic viability on the one hand and establishing widespread participation rights on the other will not solve the underlying problem. *The search for meliorating initiatives must lead to institutional rearrangements that foster the release of innovative energies in complementary directions.* The task of building a correspondingly dynamic social economics for our day is well begun. It is, admittedly, a difficult one because of changing national and international relationships between micro decisions and macro stabilization efforts. Work on these issues deserves the bishops' support because it is the "better" way to approach the very pastoral concern they have espoused.

Here again, the traditional common good approach is to be preferred. It is open to a broader range of efforts, the better to understand and field-test initiatives. Well-directed redistributive efforts, as befits the urgency of particular needs, have a part in this. But designing strategy requires a more inclusive orientation. In the complexities of today's economic interrelationships, long-term, self-sustaining melioration depends importantly on many indirectly functioning factors. Pursuit of the common good gives full weight to these aspects. Our world of growing populations and economic change needs guidance by common good considerations, themselves open to the creativity of God's self-revealing grace in our history. What is needed is a flexible, learning-oriented framework, one suited to the task of effective mediation between the gospel's call and all of the evolving possibilities offered to man's freedom by God's grace.

NOTES

1. I am especially indebted to John Langan, S. J., Bruce Douglass, Gerry Mara, and William Gould for invaluable help on key points. Remaining errors are mine.

2. Cf. Karl Rahner, S. J., "Christianity and the New Earth," *Theology Digest* 16 (February 1968): 71; Rahner comments on *Gaudium et Spes*, J. Gremillion, ed., *The Gospel of Peace and Justice* (Maryknoll, N.Y.: Orbis Books, 1971).

3. National Conference of Catholic Bishops, *Catholic Social Teaching and the U.S. Economy*, second draft (Washington, D.C.: United States Catholic Conference, 1985, chaps. 2 and 4.) Because the third draft had not been issued, corresponding third-draft references are given below in parentheses. All textual and note citations refer to the second draft.

4. Ibid.

5. The most influential voices in this regard were those of Heinrich Pesch, S. J., and his successors. Cf. F. Mueller, *Heinrich Pesch: Sein Leben und Seine Lehre* (Cologne: Verlag J. P. Bachem, 1980); also O. von Nell-Breuning, "Der Koenigswinter Kreis und sein Anteil an 'Quadragesimo anno'," in F. A. Hermens, F. K. Mann and W. Schreiber, eds., *Soziale Verantwrotung: Festschrift fuer Goetz Briefs zum 80. Geburtstag* (Berlin: Duncker & Humblot, 1968); O. von Nell-Breuning, "Octogesimo anno," *Stimmen der Zeit* 17 (no. 5, 1971): 289–96.

6. *Catholic Social Teaching and the U.S. Economy*, nos. 42–44. (nos. 36–38).

7. Ibid., no. 45 (no. 39).

8. Ibid., no. 40 (no. 34).

9. Ibid., no. 47 (no. 54).

10. Ibid., no. 58 (no. 51).

11. Ibid., no. 59 (no. 52).

12. Ibid., nos. 56–59 (nos. 48–52).

13. Ibid., no. 56 (no. 49).

14. Ibid., no. 62 (no. 55).

15. I find it difficult to read this text as saying anything other than that action in behalf of justice by various Christian communities *is* the essential ministry of the universal church, that it *is* evangelization *and* the performance of sacramental acts that confer God's grace. So understood, the language in the text would seem to legitimate a political theology conception of the church's ecclesiology. As such, it would point to a basic kinship between what the bishops choose to include here and the ecclesiological orientation of liberation theology and other variants of political theology. The universal church has not accepted this position. (The language of no. 64 and indeed subsection B, "The Christian Vocation in the World," does not appear in the third draft of the pastoral. Sections 45–55 in the new document deal with the call to discipleship without raising ecclesiological issues. However, an allusion to the proposition that action in pursuit of justice is evangelization remains in no. 60 of the third draft. It is said there that "the concerns of this pastoral ... are integral to the proclamation of the Gospel and part of the vocation of every Christian today.")

16. This formulation is Archbishop Weakland's. Cf. R. Weakland, "The Economic Pastoral: Draft Two," *America* (September 21, 1985): 129–32.

17. *Catholic Social Teaching and the U.S. Economy*, no. 67 (no. 61).

18. Cf. J. Langan, S. J., "The Pastoral: Second Draft, Second Thoughts?" *Woodstock Report* 8 (November 1985): 6.

19. This may well be intentional. The letter necessarily reflects a range of orientations, and is written to build consensus. Also, all parties involved will have been sensitive to the universal church's point of view, even while consciously pursuing an understanding of social ethics believed to be especially geared to the U.S. context. For readings that emphasize the more traditional common-good centered strand in the bishops' message, see the contribution of R. B. Douglass in this volume; and John Langan, S. J., "A Direction for the Future," afterword to *The Catholic Challenge to the American Economy*," in Thomas M. Gannon, S. J., ed., *The Catholic Challenge to the American Economy* (New York: Macmillan Publishing Co.), forthcoming.

20. *Catholic Social Teaching and the U.S. Economy*, no. 73 (no. 68).

21. Ibid., no. 78 (no. 73).

22. Ibid., no. 80 (no. 75).

23. Ibid., no. 81 (no. 76).

24. Cf. Synod of Bishops Second General Assembly, "Justice in the World," in J. Gremillion, ed., *The Gospel of Peace and Justice*, (Maryknoll, N.Y.: Orbis Books, 1971), no 18. (The language of no. 18, cited in the body of the text, has been replaced in the new document by references to no. 10 and no. 16, and to *Octogesima Adveniens*, no. 15. This strengthens the link between basic justice and participatory arrangements; no. 18 of "Justice in the World" is now cited elsewhere, namely, as basis for no. 77 of the third draft; no. 77 is a summary paragraph describing what basic justice demands.)

25. *Catholic Social Teaching and the U.S. Economy* no. 85 (no. 81).

26. Ibid., no. 96 (no. 73).

27. Ibid., (no. 91).

28. Dworkin uses this term to point out that equality of outcome may also violate equality of treatment, as when a participant in a joint project, by reason of personal preferences only, contributes significantly less than others. Here, equal pay for unequal work would imply inequality of treatment. Cf. R. M. Dworkin, "Why Efficiency? A Response to Professors Calabresi and Posner," *Hofstra Law Review* 8 (Spring 1980): 566. As a general matter, deep equality in social relations would require that outcomes are independent of morally irrelevant considerations. Approximating this principle would make more stringent demands than Rawls' maximin modification of equality among participants in social institutions. Cf. John Rawls, "Concepts of Distributional Equity: Some Reasons for the Maximin Criterion," *American Economic Review* 64 (May 1974): 141; also Rawls, "Justice as Fairness," *The Philosophy Review* 47 (April 1958): 164–94.

29. To avoid a misunderstanding here, let me add that the statement in the text reflects observed tendencies. The bishops' position is (1) that government action is able to effect justice in socioeconomic relations; (2) that the urgency of the demand for justice requires stressing action by government over the value of voluntary responses according to the principles of justice; and (3) that government's competence in these respects is limited, although the where and how are obscure in the letter.

30. *Catholic Social Teaching and the U.S. Economy*, no. 129 (nos. 126–128).

31. Ibid., no. 130 (nos. 129, 130).

32. Ibid., nos. 172, 186 (nos. 170, 185).

33. Ibid., nos. 175, 177, 179, 180 (nos. 173, 175–179).

34. Ibid., nos. 145, 146 (nos. 142–144).

35. Ibid., no. 147 (no. 145).

36. Ibid., nos. 152, 149 (nos. 150, 147).

37. Ibid., nos. 166, 167 (nos. 164, 165).

38. Ibid., nos. 181, 183 (nos. 180, 182).

39. Ibid., no. 286 (no. 294).

40. Ibid., (ibid.).

41. Ibid., no. 116 (ibid.).

42. Ibid., no. 117 (ibid.).

43. Ibid., nos. 118 and 119 (ibid.). Italics in the text.

44. Ibid., no. 120 (ibid.).

45. Ibid., no. 301 (no. 309).

46. Ibid., no. 302 (no. 310).

47. Ibid., no. 305 (no. 313). It would be wrong to portray these passages as a summons to central planning of the economy. Central planning as such is explicitly rejected. Cf. *Catholic Social Teaching and the U.S. Economy,* no. 118 (ibid.).

48. Ibid., no. 122 (no. 121).

49. Ibid., nos. 62, 122, 305 and 306 (nos. 54, 55, 66, 121, 313, and 314).

50. Ibid., nos. 253, 280, and 312 (nos. 255, 288, 320).

51. Cf. Henry Briefs, "Solidarity within the Firm: Principles, Concepts and Reflections," *Review of Social Economy* 43 (no. 3, 1984): 295–317.

52. No one has put this point more tellingly than Karl Rahner. He saw that " ... the original event of salvation ... lies 'behind' Scripture, ... is that from which Scripture draws life." Cf. K. Rahner, "Philosophy and Philosophizing in Theology," *Theology Digest* 16 (February 1968): 20. He also saw that God's grace operates in history, that his self-revelation is creative and therefore ongoing. For man, however, God's self-revelation to man is conditioned by all of his understandings, about himself and about the rest of creation. The history of that self-understanding, too, has all along been taking place in the light of God's revealing grace. Thus, what appears to be a merely "quantitative" increase in God's revelation coming to final harvest with Christ's message, actually continues to grow as the potentialities for deeper and more complete understanding present in new knowledge come to be realized. Cf. K. Rahner, "The Historical Dimension in Theology," *Theology Digest* 16 (February 1968): 32–33. Rahner concluded that the task of theology properly seen involves two movements: a movement "backward" to reflection on the events of salvation and revelation, and forward in " ... confrontation with the whole of man's understanding of existence and the world ..." Rahner, op. cit., "Philosophy and Philosophizing." Thus, biblical theology alone cannot suffice for the task of theology, even though it is already "theology." To perform its task in the forward direction, theology cannot avoid "philosophical" reflection. "Theology philosophizes to the extent that man radically confronts the message of faith with his understanding of existence in the world" (ibid., 21). Rahner concluded by saying:

"All of this must be said, not so much and not in the final analysis because there is a light of natural reason, but because the event of salvation, revelation, and faith does not begin with an explicit encounter with Scripture. It precedes this encounter and occurs through self-communication of God in grace. Because of God's universal salvific will, this self-communication takes place always and everywhere at least as an offer to man's freedom, and hence it is prior to one's confrontation with Scripture."

The summary or Rahner's view is taken from H. Briefs, "Catholic Social Teaching Reconsidered: Theological Conceptions and Economic Reality," forthcoming.

53. These figures were obtained from the United Nations, *World Population Prospects as Assessed in 1980*, Population Studies no. 70 (New York: United Nations, 1981); the World Bank, *World Development Report* (Washington, D.C.: the World Bank, 1984).

54. The term is Professor Simon's. He speaks of "bounded rationality" to distinguish the limited kind of best choosing that is possible when information about alternatives is incomplete, and fully rational choosing, given all relevant information. Cf. Herbert Simon, "Rational Decision Making in Business Organizations," *American Economic Review* 69 (September 1979): 493–513.

55. What follows is based on Simon, op. cit.; K. Arrow, *The Limits of Organization* (New York: Norton Press, 1974); O. E. Williamson, *Markets and Hierarchies: Analysis and Antitrust Implications* (New York: Free Press, 1975); O. E. Williamson, "The Modern Corporation: Origins, Evolutions, Attributes," *Journal of Economic Literature* 19 (December 1981): 1537–68.

56. Defined here as ignoring opportunities for assuming responsibility because responding is costly and benefits accrue elsewhere or are too diffuse to observe.

57. Defined as the value of real resources consumed by cooperating, coordinating and exchanging activities via markets and/or within business organizations.

58. We refer here to production and distribution activities carried on by units comprising more than a few persons, many of which contribute specialized, firm-specific skills and information abilities not readily available on competitive terms in external labor markets.

59. Freely translated as, "who is to guard the guardians?"

60. Cf. Williamson, op. cit., *Markets and Hierarchies*, chaps. 3 and 4.

61. For a detailed treatment of this range of issues, see Briefs, op. cit., forthcoming, sec. IV.

62. Economic history and a bit of reasoning support this conclusion. With population increasing at rates even well below those that actually occurred, and with production technologies constant rather than advancing across a lengthening front, organizational efforts to cope with increasing numbers could not have avoided running into diminishing returns. The Malthusian trap is no figment of an otherwise obscure clergyman's speculation. It is, and in the past has been, a component of periodic reality.

63. Cf. M. Abramovitz, "Resource and Output Trends in the United States since 1870," *American Economic Review* 46 (no. 2, May 1956): 5–23;

R. M. Solow, "Technical Change and the Aggregate Production Function," *Review of Economics and Statistics* 39 (August 1957): 312–20; E. F. Denison, *Accounting for United States Economic Growth 1929–1969* (Washington, D.C.: The Brookings Institution, 1974); R. R. Nelson, "Research on Productivity Growth and Productivity Differences," *Journal of Economic Literature* 19 (September 1981): 1029–64.

64. Cf. N. Rosenberg, *Inside the Black Box; Technology and Economics* (Cambridge, England: Cambridge University Press, 1982), 59.

65. Ibid.

66. One should add that these organizational forms evolved as the production techniques underwent further developments, developments largely made possible by the efficiency gains achieved by successive experiments with ways of structuring the exchange relationships comprising the distribution process. In turn, technical design and manufacturing improvements, accompanied by the spread of knowledge about many of these machines, brought about renewed recourse to market channels of distribution. This turn of events, however, proved selective. Whether or not this occurred depended largely on the technical considerations involved.

67. Operating systems software mediates between applications programs, such as those that manipulate particular displays on the screen, and the computer's hardware.

68. Also interesting is the fact that some of these large companies are of recent and exceedingly humble origin: Hewlett-Packard started in a garage in the late 1940s as an instrument inventor and maker. Texas Instruments and Fairchild are post-World War II beginners; they started with an eye for the semiconductor's applications possibilities. Where a new industry's takeoff is based on a new technology, which itself is under active development, bigness or market share seem to matter far less than the comparatively miniscule core of technical entrepreneurs and technicians, and their human capital equipment.

69. Cf. M. Therese Flaherty, "Field Research on the Link between Technological Innovation and Growth: Evidence from the International Semiconductor Industry," *American Economic Review* 74 (May 1984): 68.

70. Another finding was that relative firm size tends to follow from successful technical innovation, but that continuation on that path seems to have been related to maintaining a sufficient share of the market to offset the large and rising costs of plant and equipment acquisition (ibid., p. 69). These interrelationships represent an important part of the challenge to which the large integrated firms are the response. Hence the internalization of the key stages, i.e., end product innovation, manufacture, sales effort, and post-delivery maintenance-repair and follow-up sales.

71. Cf. Rosenberg, op. cit., chap. 8.

72. Cf. Williamson, op. cit., *Market and Hierarchies*; Williamson, op. cit. "The Modern Corporation."

73. Cf. Fernand Braudel, *Civilization and Capitalism, 15th to 18th Century*: vol. 1: *The Structure of Everyday Life* (New York: Harper and Row, 1981).

74. Speaking from the same economic feasibility point of view, one should add that bureaucratic centralism, too, encounters transactional im-

pediments, though it can address coherence and instability problems. The large unsolved problem faced by this form of organization remains that of combining the triad of coherence, stability and efficiency growth. The transactions costs of managing by administrative means the congeries of processes comprising a social economy of sophistication severely limit what might otherwise be rational forms of organizing. As we argued above, beyond some point of scale and complexity, internalization encounters steeply rising transactional diseconomies.

75. Cf. Heinrich Pesch, *Lehrbuch der Nationaloekonomie* (Freiburg, 1924), vol. I, 33.

76. For a textual analysis of Pesch's position in these various respects, see Briefs, op. cit., "Solidarity within the Firm," 296–301; also Mueller, op. cit., *Zweiter Teil*, chaps. III and IV.

77. Cf. F. Mueller, op. cit., *Erster Teil*, also *Zweiter Teil*, chap. V, and "Social Economics: the Perspective of Pesch and Solidarism," *Review of Social Economy* 35 (December 1977).

KEITH A. BRECLAW

From *Rerum Novarum* to the Bishops' Letter: Labor and Ideology in Catholic Social Thought

KEITH BRECLAW is an instructor in
the Department of Government of
Georgetown University. He received his
Ph.D. from Georgetown University in
political science.

I. Introduction

IN THE MODERN ERA, labor and the laborer have become the focal concerns of Catholic social teaching. From the encyclical *Rerum Novarum* through *Quadragesimo Anno* to *Laborem Exercens*, it has been through the condition of labor that the church has confronted industrial production and the mass consumption society that has accompanied it. While the church's official concern came at a rather advanced stage in the history of industrial society, the social doctrines which have developed under its aegis meet the problems of the modern age in an imaginative and not always predictable fashion. Indeed, those doctrines are yet in the process of evolution, a fact that is evident in the bishops' pastoral, *Catholic Social Teaching and the U.S. Economy*.[1]

Although the condition of the laboring class clearly prompted the original concern with labor, the use of labor as the entry point of economic analysis proves especially fruitful because of its broader implications. Labor knits together in itself mundane economic matters and philosophical ones in an unique fashion. For labor, in one aspect, is just one of several factors of production, an *object* in the economic process; yet in another aspect, as one of the encyclicals eloquently insists, labor is also the *subject* of economic activity, both a factor of production and the *end* at which productive activity is aimed. To neglect the latter, of course, amounts to more than a philosophical oversight. As a practical consequence, the existence or well-being of the laborer may be threatened. It is evident that by emphasizing labor-as-subject, some effort is being made to redress the balance between the ordinary demands of economic efficiency and the human requirements of the laborer. But beyond this, the precise nature of that balance has yet to be determined and it has been a matter of imaginative exploration in Catholic social thought.

It is clear from the earliest social encyclicals that the church understands itself to occupy a hostile ideological environment that challenges its most fundamental orientation toward the life of this world and the role of labor in it. This will prove to be a decisive factor in shaping Catholic social doctrine. Both liberalism and socialism are portrayed in the great social encyclicals as variants of an underlying doctrine of materialism that tends to color life in modern society. Both of them deny, overtly or implicitly, the primacy of the spiritual life. In this confrontation, the church is placed at a considerable disadvantage. Socialism and liberalism between them have largely set the terms of discourse within which economic ideas and policies are formulated and debated. They have developed the theoretical foundations on the basis of which explanations of economic behavior can be essayed, forecasts made, goals established and means proposed by which those goals may be attained. The church's social teaching, however, is bereft of such an economic theory and the technical analyses that it can generate. When meeting its opponents, it is not capable of meeting them wholly on their own ground.

Broadly, the church's response to modern economic conditions and their surrounding penumbra of ideas has been conservative in character. The encyclicals reaffirm the place of spiritual values in everyday life and seek to restore a balance between the transcendent impulses in man's nature and his legitimate worldly concerns, a balance that has been lost in the modern era. It is assumed that a spiritual revival along these lines would generate an institutional transformation, bringing social and economic organization into conformity with a revitalized set of Christian values and practice. This much is predictable. But there is the basis for a practical program here as well that also serves to qualify what has just been noted. It is recognized in the encyclicals that proper values can only be cultivated and preserved within a benign institutional setting. A spiritual revival will hardly find encouragement in a materialistic environment. By the same token, institutional reformation alone cannot effect a restoration of values. Spiritual revival and institutional reform, then, are interdependent. In this regard, neither *Rerum Novarum* nor *Quadragesimo Anno* shows reluctance to specify what forms of organization and association are desirable as alternatives to those existing. Nor do they hesitate to distinguish the resources in the present condition that could contribute to their development. Perhaps this is something less than a full-scale blueprint for economic and social reorganization or an economic theory, but it is much more than a mere call for spiritual renewal.

The precise status of papal social teaching is problematic. It is complicated particularly by the church's reason for existence, her spiritual mission. To become an outright partisan of either economic liberalism or socialism, or to compete directly with them as an organized political force, would likely jeopardize the church's authority as universal spiritual leader and perhaps divide her flock into conflicting political groups. But to remain detached also entails difficulties. By attempting to maintain a stance of neutrality in social and economic matters, the church's position may be read as a tacit endorsement of the dominant ideology and its practices; or, equally unacceptable, it may be seen as utterly indifferent to social conditions and their spiritual implications.

The course that the church has adopted is somewhat of a compromise between partisanship and neutrality. In *Quadragesimo Anno*, Pius XI does not refrain from criticism of liberalism and socialism; here he is only following the lead established by Leo XIII. He does, however, attempt to define more clearly the limits of the church's authority in economic matters, and he finds generally that the church cannot address certain matters taken up by other economic doctrines. "Matters of technique" fall outside the ambit of the church's authority, but this should not be understood to exclude her authority "in all things that are connected with the moral law." It is simply mistaken to maintain that the economic and moral order are utterly distinct. The role of "moral science" is to establish the goals to which economic activity should be subordinate; once the legitimate place of that activity within the natural order is grasped, "the particular purposes, both individual and social, that are sought in the economic field will fall in their proper place in the universal order of purposes."[2]

A definite picture emerges from these passages with respect to the relationship of the moral standpoint to economic doctrine: injection of the appropriate moral values into the economic order will transform that order, not by altering the techniques employed — such as reliance upon the market forces to allocate resources — but by infusing them with new purpose and direction. Presumably, then, the church is indifferent as to technique, and it must be so if it is to remain within the bounds of its legitimate authority. No doubt this apparent ability to "piggyback" its values upon techniques developed by competing economic doctrines does lend an air of neutrality to the church's position. And while, for example, the earlier encyclicals might appear to be neutral, though "leaning" toward economic liberalism by virtue of their reaffirmation of the right of private property, *Laborem Exercens* displays a willingness to experiment with forms of ownership, and social ownership is not excluded in principle.

Yet the encyclicals, *Quadragesimo Anno* included, routinely traduce the boundary between moral invocation and the assessment of economic tools and techniques. The papal documents clearly do dabble in matters of technique, although they may not have at their disposal so comprehensive a repertoire of tools and devices as the liberal and socialist economists have. To specify the form of the associational network which is to contain economic activity and direct it toward its rightful goals is already to move significantly beyond a direct and simple call for spiritual regeneration. And such speculation contains an appraisal of the likely effect that a new institutional ordering will have upon the use of specific techniques such as market forces: "free competition, while justified and certainly useful provided it is kept within certain limits, clearly cannot direct economic life — a truth which the outcome of the application in practice of the tenets of this evil individualistic spirit has more than sufficiently demonstrated."[3] Similarly, the basis of property rights is not viewed indifferently. Despite a failure always to distinguish clearly between personal property and productive property or capital, private ownership is considered sacrosanct. Yes, property ought to be used for the common good; no, the state may not enforce that obligation, even when the property right is abused.[4]

It is not my purpose to question the intellectual integrity of the papal documents by pointing out these inconsistencies. Rather, it is to make clear that they are themselves prompted by a genuine dilemma. To say anything meaningful about the economy will involve paying attention to questions of production and distribution as well as to the legal framework behind economic activity, at least on the plane of general principles. That is precisely what these encyclicals are engaged in doing. The reluctance to admit that — evident in the insistence upon the limited authority of the church — undoubtedly reflects the desire to remain above the ideological fray, with the idea in mind of preserving the church's spiritual authority. The choice facing the church appears to be between either making abstract appeals to social justice with the assurance that they will have no appreciable effect, or entering the battle in the marketplace of ideas on a par with the other contestants, endangering its special standing in the process. No wonder that an ambiguous middle position has been cultivated, though no doubt without conscious intent.

However, what the church finally offers in its social teaching is a distinctive alternative to the economics of liberalism or socialism, but not, strictly speaking, at the level of economic theory. In effect, the church presents an *economic philosophy* resting upon radically different assumptions from those which inform the competing economic doctrines. I emphasize that it is philosophy rather than theory due to its relative technical innocence: absent are the staples of economic theorizing such as theories of price, rent, etc. And it aims to be comprehensive; this is not speculation on a set of isolated issues. The ends of economic life and how they are to be integrated into human life as a whole form the subject matter of this economic philosophy, and they are just the questions that have been left behind by modern economics. But such questions, of course, are far from neutral in their implications; indeed, they are the questions of value, the answers to which could have the most profound effect on the organization of economic activity. That much is clear from the suggestions for economic reconstruction to be found in the encyclicals.

It is in times of profound economic change that philosophical matters, long unattended or simply taken for granted, emerge again into the light of day. The great advantage offered by Catholic social teaching is that it has never abandoned these issues. I suggest that the focus on labor and its activity proves to be of particular importance when the role of labor is undergoing such basic alterations as it is today while its future remains so uncertain. The church offers a conservative economic philosophy as the standpoint from which to approach these concerns, an approach which has survived only here; and while the doctrine is by no means complete, the evolution from *Rerum Novarum* to the bishops' letter demonstrates an adaptability that may yet allow it to exert an influence on events.

II.

RERUM NOVARUM AND QUADRAGESIMO ANNO directed their attention
first to the condition of the industrial working class. Not only did
low wages and dangerous working conditions threaten the material
existence of workers, but just as importantly, the workers' spiritual
health was being placed in jeopardy. There was here a direct *political*
connection between the workers' material and spiritual situation that
became the object of particular concern. At its worst, industrial
capitalism was seen as a breeding ground for class hatred and class
warfare. Socialism had elevated class division and antagonism to a
doctrinal principle that frontally challenged the tenets of Christian
charity. For that reason, socialism was to be condemned. Yet the
preoccupation of the socialists with social justice was laudable and
not far removed from the church's own teaching, a point which
Pius XI was willing to admit: "Socialism inclines toward and in a
certain measure approaches the truths which Christian tradition has
always held sacred for it cannot be denied that its demands at times
come very near those that Christian reformers of society justly insist
upon."[5]

The affinity of the socialist message to Christian social thinking made that message all the more dangerous; the legitimate appeal to justice might tempt workers, and others, to compromise their
Christian principles in order to pursue justice under the socialist ban-
ner.[6] The fear was far from misplaced. In the forty years between
Rerum Novarum and *Quadragesimo Anno*, socialist unions in Western
Europe had outdistanced the Christian and liberal unions in recruit-
ing workers, and Catholic workers were not only joining socialist
unions but also voting for socialist political candidates. The socialist
appeal was fortified by changes which had taken place in the industrial economy. In the papal reading of events, the class struggle
had actually *intensified* over that forty-year period as the free market
gave way to economic "dictatorship." The wealth and power of the
economy had come to be concentrated in ever fewer hands and they
had come to regulate virtually the entire economy. Ironically, this
concentration had been effected by the workings of the free market
itself: unrestrained competition had produced monopoly and dictatorship. Conflict became endemic to capitalism under these conditions, being reproduced at all levels and on a pathological scale.
Workers battled the owners of capital, the capitalists were engaged
among themselves in a life-and-death struggle in the marketplace and
for control of the state, and the state itself used economic tools to
gain advantage over other states.[7] Liberalism and socialism emerge
as symbionts in creating the conditions which propagate social confrontation and conflict, a course which can only have a disastrous

end: "Let all remember that Liberalism is the father of this Socialism that is pervading morality and culture and that Bolshevism will be its heir."[8]

The two encyclicals are agreed upon the means that could begin to remedy the situation. Moral regeneration is, of course, the first principle, but as noted above, it is coupled with the recognition that such regeneration can flourish only in an appropriate environment. Leo speaks favorably of both workers' and employers' associations as the means of self-help and mutual assistance that can encourage a sense of community among these social groupings and direct the individual's interest toward the common good. This corporatist theme is repeated, refined, and given even greater emphasis by Pius XI. As he depicts them, these associations are not trade unions organized to further class interests; they are comprehensive organizations, voluntarily organized, that look after their members' material and spiritual needs, binding industrial, professional, and other occupational groups into communities. The English title given to *Quadragesimo Anno*, "On Reconstructing the Social Order," indicates how sweeping an alteration of economic life would be effected by this corporatist scheme. Pius hopes to see established a network of guild-like associations, integrated with those of Catholic Action, that would be intermediate between the individual and the state. Within the boundaries of resuscitated associational life, free competition could be allowed to work, but now safely contained.[9]

Embedded in these two documents is an understanding of the nature of work and its place in the properly ordered human life. Capitalism has reduced labor to a commodity, to a mere factor of production. In that light, the treatment suffered by labor at the hands of capital—and the reaction that it invites—is entirely comprehensible. The task in these encyclicals is to restore sufficiently the dignity and stature of labor to check the abuses it has come to suffer. That is accomplished here by recalling the divinely ordained function of labor, to support human life. There is, however, no intrinsic satisfaction in the laboring activity; its toilsome character is imposed as a result of man's sinfulness: "So far as bodily labor is concerned, man even before the Fall was not destined to be wholly idle; but certainly what his will at that time would have freely embraced to his soul's delight, necessity afterwards forced him to accept, with a feeling of irksomeness, for the expiation of his guilt."[10] Consistent with the function of labor, the demands of the laboring populace ought to be modest. Distributive justice is served when they have a sufficiency of goods to secure a living for themselves and the members of their family, provide for their old age, and leave something for their children. That is what comprises the just wage. There is nothing undignified about working for wages so long as the wage is just. Beyond that, though, the laborers have no rightful claim, whatever disparities of wealth may exist between them and the owners of capital. Between these two classes a sense of order in society is established and that is entirely to the good. At the same time, there is a pragmatic reason for expanding the property ownership of the workers; gross disparities of wealth "establish an unanswerable argument that riches which are so abundantly produced in our age . . . are not rightly distributed and equitably made available to the various classes of people," with the attendant political consequences.[11]

III.

LABOREM EXERCENS takes up the condition of labor fifty years after Pius' reflections, and it represents more than an amplification of the themes of the earlier encyclicals. Most striking is that the sharp political edge of those earlier works has been lost. Less striking, but of equal or greater significance, is the substitution of a new appreciation of work and its meaning.

The sensitivity to the ideological environment persists in this encyclical and in terms that will be familiar to the reader of the earlier documents. As in the past, the economic philosophy of the church confronts those of socialism and liberalism (now renamed economism). But political conditions have significantly altered and they are symptomatic, to a degree, of the altered condition of the working class, if that term is any longer appropriate. Socialism remains a threat but not because socialist unions are drawing Catholics into the class struggle. Certainly, John Paul's silence on this matter amounts to recognition that the course which the labor movement has taken in Western Europe has obviated this particular danger. Socialism threatens elsewhere, in its Marxist form, as the organizer of the political and economic life of particular states. What remains of concern, however, is the underlying materialist orientation of capitalism and socialism that subordinates the laborer to his task and the all-consuming drive for efficiency. Materialism remains the primary threat to man in modern society, but the battle lines between it and the church have been redrawn.

That conclusion is confirmed when the reader searches here for the corporatist recommendations with which we are familiar. They are, in fact, nowhere to be found, nor is their absence noted and explained. But for all of that, the explanation is fairly obvious: social and economic life have evolved decisively away from the organizational framework envisioned by Leo and Pius. Where they see at least a potential for corporatist reconstruction, John Paul surveys a society in which individualism has triumphed. Even the labor unions, in their narrowest construction as adversarial interest groups, have been diminishing in size and power. Increasingly, workers confront the weight of capital and technology without the aid and support of their own organizations. The state performs the welfare functions which had been envisioned for the corporatist network as well as interposing itself, to varying degrees, between labor and capital. This is only evidence that economic liberalism and socialism have, in fact, reached a modus vivendi in the West that is often obscured by rhetoric. The welfare state, in all of its permutations and combinations, is an amalgamation of the operation of market forces and governmental control and direction of the economy, and even where welfare measures run toward the minimal end of the scale, government economic intervention remains.

While this is not explored at any length, the condition of workers in industrial society has changed dramatically even in the last half-century. Leo XIII and Pius XI defined the problem of labor as that of the impoverished industrial proletariat. Poverty was a more general problem and not unique to industrial society. What was striking in the industrial condition was the tremendous productivity of the industrial enterprise and the great wealth produced as against a class of laborers who could barely support themselves despite long and grueling hours of work. The problem of poverty in industrial society remains today but it is *not* primarily the problem of those who work. With respect to work, poverty is a marginal problem, a problem that largely belongs to the unemployed, the underemployed, and the unemployable. That is not to diminish the scale of the problem, nor is it to ignore the connection between unemployment and poverty. It is, rather, to distinguish this problem from the one which preoccupies the early social encyclicals, and, incidentally, the bishops' letter. Affluence has been diffused throughout industrial society and by way of a now highly differentiated working class.

Laborem Exercens uncovers yet another dimension to the problem of labor that reveals itself in this period of late industrialism, and it involves a rethinking of the sources and meaning of the dignity of labor. In fact, John Paul goes back to the biblical text—literally to the very beginning, in Genesis—to weigh the role of labor in human life. While obeisance is payed to the classical encyclicals on the social problem, it cannot be concealed that this document is a new departure in the understanding of labor. "The church finds in the very first pages of the Book of Genesis the source of her conviction that work is a fundamental dimension of human existence on earth";[12] surely this is a contrast to the early social encyclicals on work.

Human work, in John Paul's interpretation, is nothing less than a participation in the divine work of creation. Man's instruction from God to "subdue the earth" was not withdrawn as a consequence of the Fall. Even though toil then becomes an accompaniment of human labor, that fact does not summarize and delimit the meaning of labor. By virtue of his being a participant in creation, the human laborer and his activity acquire a special dignity apart from the function of labor imposed by necessity. John Paul speaks of labor as having an intrinsic value: "Even though it bears the mark of a 'bonum arduum', in the terminology of St. Thomas, this does not take away the fact that, as such, it is a good thing for man. It is not only good in the sense that it is useful or something to enjoy ... Work is a good thing for man because through work man not only transforms nature, adapting it to his own needs, but he also achieves fulfillment as a human being and indeed in a sense becomes 'more a human being'."[13]

By this measure, the problem of labor has become more, not less, pronounced with the advance of industrial society. The enormous role that technology has come to play is a major part of the difficulty, redefining the relationship between capital and labor. On the one hand, technology is a measure of man's collective achievement in subduing nature; on the other hand, the extent of participation by the individual worker in that achievement has actually diminished as he is absorbed into the production process as one factor of production. Human beings have become a small part of the economic mechanism; in the industrial economy, whether capitalist or socialist in organization, human beings in their work are subordinated as mere means to the larger collective purpose of production. As production becomes an end-in-itself which labor only serves, the underlying materialism of industrial society in all of its forms becomes manifest.

In the face of these changes, John Paul seeks to restore what he terms "the priority of labor." Labor, given its role in creation, ought to be the subject of production rather than an economic utensil. Man as laborer is the reason the economic mechanism has been created; he is the "efficient cause" which sets that mechanism in motion. Neither fact is apparent if labor is assessed simply in terms of its contribution to economic output. By that standard, its economic significance will decline and its value will be equivalent to its efficiency. Restoring "the priority of labor" means establishing its dignity, and not simply as an aggregate factor of production. This, as the encyclical stresses, amounts to a "personalist" argument for restoring the status of labor. Each worker must have access to the creative experience which is part of the essential meaning of labor.[14]

That is an enormous task, particularly when one considers that the tendency of industrial production for most of its history has been to run vigorously in the other direction. Indeed, the problem appears to be overwhelming. Leo and Pius could have a mild optimism regarding the likelihood of a corporatist social reconstruction. They, at least, saw evidence of the desired organizations being present if only in a germinal form. Moreover, the solution they were proposing was, on the surface, an appropriate one to the problem as they understood it. It is more difficult to make so charitable a judgment of the response of *Laborem Exercens* to the problem which it poses. John Paul cannot be optimistic and this may account for the somewhat feeble proposals for reform that are presented. The implications of his position on labor for reform are surely radical ones, if not in terms of the pace of change then certainly with regard to the goals against which change is to be measured. At some points there are references to worker ownership as a means of participation. John Paul is aware that mere socialization of the means of production may not lead to the desired participation of the workers, although socialization is not ruled out either.[15] He approves generally of experiments in different forms of worker ownership such as "proposals for the joint ownership of the means of work, sharing by the workers in management and/or profits of business, so-called share-holding by labor, etc."[16] But already this orientation dilutes the theme of the laborer as participant in creation, and that is the direction in which the reforms finally move: "here it must be emphasized in general terms that the person desires not only due remuneration for his work; he also wishes that within the production process provision be made for him to be able to know that in his work, even on something that is owned in common, he is working 'for himself'."[17] That goal is sufficiently vague enough to be reduced to no more than the sense of participation that comes from profit-sharing or holding shares in the company. It is as much as to admit that the problem of labor, as the encyclical conceives it, is all but intractable.

IV.

PAPAL ENCYCLICALS are unlikely to have much direct influence upon economic policy. The first difficulty is simply that of communication; seldom are the ideas behind papal social teachings accurately conveyed to the public. *Laborem Exercens* has suffered just this fate. In the popular press, it is presented as a collection of pronouncements on a wide range of social issues. Or the encyclical is characterized in sweeping terms, the discussion of social ownership and profit-sharing stamping it as "socialist." Perhaps at the highest level of sophistication reached in these popular interpretive efforts, the document is seen as an indecipherable mix of liberal and conservative policies, placing it, albeit uncomfortably, on familiar ideological terrain.

Even if the barriers of communication were overcome, it is doubtful whether there would be much receptivity to the papal message. The sheer strangeness of the ideas presented here—of their unfamiliarity—would be a sufficient impediment to their lodging in the popular consciousness. The profoundly conservative outlook that informs the church's social thought has no counterpart outside of the church itself. This is, of course, especially true of its economic philosophy. No genuinely conservative economics developed alongside the liberal and socialist economic traditions. Modern conservatives who reaffirm the primacy of the spiritual life and insist that social organization should reflect a hierarchy of values, have for all practical purposes made an alliance with liberalism in economic matters. Some are more uneasy with that alliance than others, but at the least, capitalism, however much it may encourage the hedonism and secularism of the modern age, is understood by conservatives as the one effective dike against the even worse excesses of collectivism. This leaves the church and its social teachings, as it were, out in the cold. If the church has an economics, it is one which is all philosophy and no science; and because the philosophy has yet to be tried by events, it persists but in the sketchiest of forms. The church's social teachings, then, represent the residue of a conservative economics that never truly was.

One might conclude from what has been said thus far that the church's social doctrine has long been on the road to obsolescence. Yet this is not the conclusion that I would draw. It is certainly a considerable weakness that the church's economic teachings have had slight opportunity to be put into practice. In spite of that, and of the limited elaboration these ideas have received at the theoretical level, the social teachings have displayed an intellectual vitality that militates against certain atrophy. Within the boundaries of its conservative philosophy, the church has demonstrated an ability to respond to changing circumstances and to do so in a way that draws on novel resources within its own tradition. That much should be evident in the course of development traced from *Rerum Novarum* to

Laborem Exercens. But more than that, I believe that it is the consistent focus upon and concern with labor that comprises its considerable strength and may yet prove to be a source of influence in social and economic life.

Neither of the church's ideological competitors display a similar concern with the meaning and purpose of labor in human life or the effects of work beyond the workplace. They tend, instead, to deprecate the role of labor in one way or another. That is perhaps more apparent in the case of liberalism than of socialism. Going back to Adam Smith, it can be seen that the foundations for treating labor as just another factor of production have already been laid. Labor is identified strictly with toil as illustrated in one version of the labor theory of value presented by Smith: "The real price of everything, what everything really costs to the man who wants to acquire it, is the toil and trouble of acquiring it. What everything is really worth to the man who has acquired it, and who wants to dispose of it or exchange it for something else, is the toil and trouble which it can save to himself, and which it can impose upon other people."[18] The theory of marginal utility, which replaces the labor theory of value as an explanation of price, reinforces the notion of labor as disutility, assuming as it does a primitive utilitarian psychology: economic man is engaged in the rational pursuit and weighing of pleasures, of which labor is not one.[19]

Socialism might appear to offer a more promising assessment of labor but that does not prove to be the case. Marx's thinking reveals a surprising ambivalence toward labor and its potential. At some points in his work, he depicts man as *homo faber*, holding out the promise of making work over, some time in the future, into a source of human fulfillment. At other points, however, fulfillment is defined in terms of leisure, not labor, with the goal of reducing human labor to a minimum. As for socialism in practice, it has become more a strategy for development, of catching up with the capitalist economies or beating them at their own game.

Why shouldn't labor be treated as disutility and as just another factor of production? Setting aside for the moment the moral objections that the church raises, there are other reasons that have arisen from an entirely different source: economic practice in the advanced industrial economies themselves. The business enterprise in the United States is presently undergoing a remarkable transformation. There is no single explanation for it, though undoubtedly the press of foreign competition, the changing mix of goods and services, and alterations in consumer preferences all play a role. And the response has not been uniform nor is it simple to characterize. It is evident, nonetheless, that basic assumptions about the principles of management, labor practices, and the nature of the business enterprise are among the features being reevaluated. Generally, the technocratic assumptions about business activity are the ones being challenged, including a management model built on assumptions of rational behavior, motivation supplied from above, management by numbers, and the conviction that large enterprises are most efficient and best able to take advantage of economies of scale.

Over and against that model has been set a new one with an emphasis on entrepreneurial activity. This is not a mere revival of the figure of the entrepreneur, although some of the literature verges on little more than myth-making, with the heroic figure of the economic innovator as the dynamo of progress.[20] A more reflective part of this literature sees the most successful firms in the new business climate as being pervaded, top to bottom, by the entrepreneurial spirit. Whatever the genius of the founders or leaders of the enterprise, their accomplishment will be short-lived unless management and workers can be drawn into creative participation in the tasks of the firm, and a permanent disposition toward innovation instilled.[21] Traditional forms of hierarchical organization and clear division of functions are displaced by looser forms in which responsibility overlaps, internal competition may be encouraged, and autonomous groups allow for initiative to filter up from the ranks.

Overall, the emphasis is on people and their contribution to the enterprise, a factor that has been neglected to the detriment of American business. That neglect is encouraged by the treatment of labor, at whatever level in the firm, as being on a par with other factors of production. The balance has been redressed somewhat, not due to theoretical insight but rather to the surrounding exigencies of competition. I am not claiming that these developments somehow point toward the conclusions of *Laborem Exercens*, but that, if only for practical reasons, the way of approaching the problem of labor found there is surely not misplaced.

For the moment, there are some indications that economic expediency favors the tendencies that value labor and seek to enhance its status and contribution to production. Less certain is the depth at which those tendencies are anchored: how far will they run into the future and to what extent will they spread in the business community? Robert Reich points to the choice between two differing strategies toward labor that confronts American business—and labor—today. One strategy is to pare labor costs at home and reduce skilled jobs through automation while sending—or threatening to send—capital and jobs overseas. The other strategy: augment the value of labor by retraining, give greater responsibility to workers over production and quality control, and introduce technologies that draw out the creativity and skills of workers. As Reich observes, either strategy can produce short-term profits but the ultimate issue involved is the kind of economy that will emerge in the long run. The first strategy promises to lower skill levels and the standard of living over time, generating hostility between the labor force and management. Yet this may prove to be the easiest route to adopt; the second strategy takes management and labor onto the fickle terrain of innovation, requiring sacrifice of the traditional authority and security each has enjoyed in the past, with no assurance of success.[22] And in a business environment dominated by the quarterly report, organizational experiments will be measured against immediate returns to the firm. What may be required to sustain these experiments is a vision of economic life that holds out to workers and managers the prospect of something more than increases in pay and benefits, that would justify the sacrifices to be made and the burden of new responsibilities to be taken on. A commitment to increasing the quality of labor's contribution to production entails a new attitude toward work itself. The emphasis in *Laborem Exercens* on the dignity of work and its significance in human life could serve as the foundation for that vision, or, at the least, prompt those in the tradition of economic liberalism to search out their own legacy for a new approach to labor.

Looking beyond our immediate condition, exploring the meaning of work has longer term implications of equal or greater importance. We do not know exactly what the future might hold for industrial society, but given its propensity for rapid and thoroughgoing change, the results may be quite unexpected. Keynes, projecting into the future, foresaw a time when the economic problem, for all intents and purposes, would be solved; the tremendous productive capabilities unleashed by capitalism would generate such abundance, and so radically reduce the role of labor, that not only would a sufficiency of goods be available for all, but personal income might actually come to be detached from any objective measure of economic contribution.[23] And there is the prospect for leisure time, and for the great mass of people, to an extent that has not been seen before. Whatever the changes, they need not be confronted as predictions, but to some degree as objects of conscious choice. What choices we make, or if we simply submit to the flow of events, will be conditioned on whether we are aware of the value choices involved and how we answer the questions that they raise. This encyclical, and the tradition on which it rests, raises the kinds of questions we should be asking now: what contribution does work make to human fulfillment? how does one's work affect the rest of one's life? can technology be made more amenable to individual direction and control?

This is an argument for tending the philosophical garden. An economic philosophy organized around labor and its problems could make an immeasurable contribution in guiding the choices that will have to be made in the future, some of which we already face today. To some degree the future can be manufactured, but only when, at those junctures where choices can be made, we are aware of the choices available and appreciate what any one of them will entail. Ideas do have an enormous effect upon history, although their influence is notoriously difficult to trace, and often they produce results that are unintended and unseen by their authors. We do know, however, that our economic universe is bounded presently by a set of ideas that has existed for not much more than two hundred years. Those ideas were startling in their day and particularly when set against the economic ethos of the medieval period. But there is no guarantee that they, too, will not run their course. As economics became increasingly an instrumental science, philosophical matters were left behind; but in an age of revolutionary change, where our instruments can no longer automatically set our goals, philosophizing can become an eminently practical enterprise.

V.

THIS BRINGS ME, at last, to the bishops' pastoral and its standing in relation to the theme of labor as it has evolved in those landmark papal documents. The conclusion I have come to is that the pastoral represents a significant departure, both in form and content, from the philosophical agenda of *Laborem Exercens* and more generally from the traditional concern with labor in papal social teachings.

That may not be evident on the first reading. In Part One of the draft document, the theme of man as an active participant in creation is introduced early on.[24] Also, the work activity itself is reaffirmed as central to a moral examination of economic life.[25] In terms consonant with the message of *Laborem Exercens*, work is understood here to possess a complex significance for ethical life: it contributes to the fulfillment of the person's own life requirements and to the material well-being of others, but work is also "one of the chief ways that human beings seek self-fulfillment," which includes "the spiritual need to express initiative and creativity." This orientation toward

work, taken together with the other normative guidelines of stewardship, distributive justice and community, define the moral envelope
within which American economic life ought to operate.

But the document directs attention away from these matters
in Part Two. Although the bishops maintain that the letter "is not
a technical blueprint for economic reform, but rather an attempt to
foster a serious moral analysis of economic justice,"[26] the discussion of "policy applications," and the large space it occupies in the
pastoral as a whole, suggest otherwise. Whether or not the policy
recommendations, offered in a tentative voice though they are, prove
plausible and consistent, it is they that have drawn the most critical commentary and been most influential in shaping public percep-
tion of the document's content and its ideological orientation. That,
I believe, has proved to be entirely unfortunate as the public per-
ception accurately captures the pastoral's retreat from exploring the
foundations of a comprehensive economic philosophy.

Although the letter opens with a treatment of "the Christian
vision of economic life," there is no clear weighing of the significance
of the norms that emerge from this discussion. What, for example, is
to be done when the requirements of creative endeavor conflict with
those of distributive justice? How significant to human well-being is
a sense of satisfaction in work and to what extent should resources
be allocated to deal with the problem? Missing also, in the leap from
norms to policy applications, is a serious effort to present a portrait
of the American economy, the direction of its present tendencies,
and the possibilities that exist for bringing it into closer conformity
with those norms.

Ultimately, too, the preoccupation with policies obscures such
treatment as there is of those more fundamental issues. It allows
the pastoral to be placed all too neatly within the boundaries of
conventional economic debate: the letter, it is concluded, favors
"socialist" as opposed to "capitalist" policies, "planning" in place
of the "free market." By entering upon the discussion of policy,
the bishops choose the weakest possible ground on which to exert
their influence, that of economic policy. In doing so, they forego the
distinct advantage they would enjoy by confining themselves to the
realm of economic philosophy.

What they have put behind them is the distinctive approach
to economic activity centering upon labor that we have already encountered in the encyclicals. Nowhere does that become more evident than in the bishops' expressed "option for the poor." This
amounts to a moral rather than an analytical imperative, and that
is where its weakness lies. If they are to be taken seriously in

economic matters, the bishops will have to provide analysis guided by moral commitment, and it is not clear to me how the "option for the poor" can accomplish that. Indeed, the bishops are apparently unconcerned about the many specific forms that poverty takes and their sources, yet surely no effective policies can be devised without such an understanding. Poverty comes to exist within the context of a specific economic order that decisively shapes the forms that it takes. Poverty in the South Bronx is not identical in its forms or its origins to poverty in Ethiopia. The point is this: even if it is morally imperative to grant poverty first priority among economic concerns, it must be understood and treated as part of an unique economic order.

In the American economy, work, and not poverty, is the focus of individual experience in economic life. Given the preoccupation with economic activity in this country—and the whole of the industrialized world—it is not so unlikely a hypothesis that how we work, what we make, and the purposes to which we put the products of our endeavor color not only our attitudes toward poverty but toward life generally. I believe that something like this is the working assumption behind the papal reflections on labor. This is not to say that *Laborem Exercens* offers anything near a completed economic philosophy; it does not even present a satisfactory sketch. But that is not what we expect of papal encyclicals on these matters. Rather, it directs attention to the special place of labor in economic life, inviting elaboration on that theme. The bishops' pastoral cannot be expected to be a philosophical document either. But not only does it add nothing to the analysis of labor and the economy, it does much to direct our attention away from it. Rather than establishing a philosophical program, the pastoral pretends that a full-scale Christian economic vision exists, replete with guiding principles, and moves hastily to draw policy applications from them. In fact, the basis for such a vision of the economy has barely been laid; the church's lack of influence in the economic realm testifies to that. The most difficult work has yet to be accomplished, although the traditional focus on labor provides a promising starting point.

NOTES

1. National Conference of Catholic Bishops, *Catholic Social Teaching and the U.S. Economy*, First Draft (Washington, D.C.: United States Catholic Conference, 1984).

2. Pius XI, *Reconstructing the Social Order (Quadragesimo Anno)* (Washington, D.C.: National Catholic Welfare Conference, 1942), 41–43.

3. Ibid., 41–43.

4. Ibid., 47.

5. Ibid., 113.

6. Ibid., 116.

7. Ibid., 105–108.

8. Ibid., 122.

9. Ibid., 88.

10. Leo XIII, *The Condition of Labor (Rerum Novarum)*, (Washington, D.C.: National Catholic Welfare Conference, 1942), 27.

11. *Quadragesimo Anno*, 60.

12. John Paul II, *On Human Work (Laborem Exercens)*, (Washington, D.C.: United States Catholic Conference, 1981), 4.

13. Ibid., 9.

14. Ibid., 15.

15. Ibid., 14.

16. Ibid.

17. Ibid., 15.

18. Adam Smith, *The Wealth of Nations*, ed. Andrew Skinner, (Baltimore, Md.: Penguin Books, 1970), 153.

19. Gunnar Myrdal, *The Political Element in the Development of Economic Thought* (London: Routledge & Kegan Paul, 1953), chap. 2.

20. See, for example, George Gilder, *The Spirit of Enterprise* (New York: Simon & Schuster, 1984).

21. See, for example, Peter F. Drucker, *Innovation and Entrepreneurship* (New York: Harper and Row, 1985).

22. Robert B. Reich, "A Fork in the Road for U.S. Labor," *The New York Times* (Sept. 1, 1985), sec. 4, p. 13.

23. John Maynard Keynes, "Economic Possibilities for Our Grandchildren," in *Essays in Persuasion* (London: Macmillan, 1931).

24. *Catholic Social Teaching and the U.S. Economy*, 31.

25. Ibid., 76.

26. Ibid., 152.

ELIZABETH McKEOWN

The Seamless Garment: The Bishops' Letter in the Light of the American Catholic Pastoral Tradition

ELIZABETH McKEOWN is an Associate
Professor in the Department of Theology
at Georgetown University. She is also
Director of the American Studies
program. She received her Ph.D. from
the University of Chicago.

FOR A LONG TIME in American history the Catholic leadership in the United States was careful to avoid any appearance of being "in politics." From the Act of Toleration in the colony of Maryland in 1649 until American involvement in World War I, the statements and actions of the Catholic clergy and bishops were consistently cautious with regard to the larger issues of public policy. While many bishops were articulate spokesmen in defense of what they perceived to be Catholic rights and interests, all leaders were quite sensitive to the charge of Roman interference in colonial and national life.

In the period from 1919 to the present, this attitude has changed dramatically. The 1984 election and the O'Connor-Cuomo/Ferraro-Malone discussion of American Catholic political and social postures is only the most recent evidence that the Catholic episcopal leadership is a deliberate presence in public policy debates. In the last sixty-six years, the national episcopal conference has pursued a course of increasing involvement in the shaping of American public policy. I will review this growing involvement by way of the recently reissued *Pastoral Letters of the United States Catholic Bishops* in order to establish a context in which to read the current letter on the economy.

The "public issues" that are addressed in the pastoral letters, including war, race, human rights, the economy and the international order, are consistently examined in connection with "family issues," including marriage, divorce, contraception, abortion, the education of children. In developing a public voice, the American bishops have maintained a primary emphasis on the importance of the family and have argued that family is the key to the health of public life. This way of presenting their views would suggest that their sense of authority in regard to family issues is the implicit basis of their claim to be heard in the public forum.

As early as 1919, when the first joint pastoral letter of the newly formed National Catholic Welfare Council was issued, the bishops indicated the central role the family would play. After assessing the impact of the war just concluded, the pastoral moves to a reflection on the difficulties facing the nation in the postwar period by way of an assessment of the importance of the family:

> As the family is the first social group, it is also the center whose influence permeates the entire social body. And since family life takes its rise from the union of husband and wife, the sanctity of marriage and marital relations is of prime importance for the purity of social relations.[1]

Attitudes toward marriage in a society are treated in the letter as an index of the moral level of that society. A lowering of the general estimate of marriage is taken as a "symptom of moral decline." The bishops perceived clear threats to the institution of marriage in the postwar situation: "The demands of industry, of business, and of social intercourse subject the family tie to a strain that becomes more severe as civilization advances."[2]

The nature of these threats becomes clearer as the bishops address the increasing public interest in birth control and family planning. The letter is harshly opposed to the contraceptive campaigns directed by Margaret Sanger and others. It speaks of birth control concerns as a kind of "fraudulent prudence that would improve upon nature by defeating its obvious purpose," and denounces it as a form of "race suicide" and a "crime of individuals for which, eventually, the nation must suffer."[3] Divorce is also seen to have serious "public" implications. The letter calls divorce "our national scandal" and argues that there is an intimate connection between this practice and the health of the nation:

> This degradation of marriage, once considered the holiest of human relations, naturally tends to the injury of other things whose efficacy ought to be secured, not by coercion but by freely given respect of a free people. Public authority, individual rights and even the institutions on which liberty depends, must inevitably weaken.[4]

Family-related issues are clearly central to the fulfillment of the common good, and the restoration of the integrity of family life according to episcopal norms is the natural remedy for threats associated with secularism, materialism and class conflict.

In this context, where the family in effect secures the common good, the bishops' estimate of "woman's influence" is most significant. Echoing a longstanding American sense of the role of woman as sustainer of the "domestic sphere" and the civilizing influence in an essentially uncivil society, the 1919 letter argues that "the influence of woman is potent." The letter notes that "the present tendency in all civilized countries is to give woman a larger share in pursuits and occupations that formerly were reserved to men" and urges women to exercise these new opportunities in a way that preserves the central importance of family life. Anticipating the ratification of the Nineteenth Amendment, the bishops offer the following assessment:

> So far as she may purify and elevate our political life, her use of the franchise will prove an advantage; and this will be greater if it involve no loss of the qualities in which women excels. Such a loss would deprive her of the influence which she wields in the home, and eventually defeat the very purpose for which she has entered the public arena. . . . To reach the hearts of men and take away their bitterness, that they may live henceforth in fellowship one with another—this is woman's vocation in respect of public affairs, and the service which she by nature is best fitted to render.[5]

Thus a woman's primary responsibility with respect to public affairs is to create a climate of nurture in the home so that her husband and children may be good citizens. And when she appears in public life, she is urged to replicate that familial nurturing influence.

The pastoral letters and statements of the 1930s and 1940s continue to emphasize the family and family-related moral issues as the key to the common good. The bishops responded to the economic disaster that developed in the 1930s, and in "Present Crisis" (1933) note its impact on the family: "the destruction or serious impairment of home life [by the Depression] has brought about a menacing decline in the birth rate" and has "helped to promote the godless, selfish, and inhuman propaganda of birth prevention."[6] They argue that, while economic conditions are cited as a justification of the use of birth control, the use of contraception is in fact evidence of "a criminal marital life" and is a result of "the new paganism of our day."[7] The letter calls for a "restoration of the social order" that will encourage an increase in the birth rate and "will enable parents to make ample provision for the larger family."[8]

By November 1933, the bishops announced strong support for the Roosevelt administration, urging a spirit of "friendly cooperation" with the President and his programs. The bishops' own recommendations were significantly more sweeping than the New Deal proposals. They emphasize moral renewal as the key to economic reform:

> The plague spots in our financial centers that destroyed business integrity and debased business methods must be made amenable to justice and decency; the pesthole that infects the entire country with its obscene and lascivious moving pictures must be cleansed and disinfected; the multitudinous agencies that are employed in disseminating pornographic literature must be suppressed, and all those forces and influences that bring starvation to the bodies of men and poison to their souls must be utterly destroyed.[9]

Ten years later, in November 1943, the bishops responded to the crisis of World War II with a statement outlining "The Essentials of a Good Peace." Here they develop a new emphasis on the notion of the common good in an international context and extend their programmatic use of the family to refer broadly to the "family of nations." But their family focus remained primarily on the literal level, and they stress that "in God's plan the family is a social institution with its own rights and dignity," and that its "stability, unity and sanctity are as necessary to a right social order as the proper constitution of government itself." A good peace includes economic as well as political considerations, and the bishops argue that "political authority which earnestly seeks the common good of all citizens will not fail to lend itself to the establishment of a just family wage, in order that family income may be commensurate with the discharge of family duties."[10] Their interest in "a good peace" led the bishops to a further comment on the role of women. The letter calls for "prudent political leadership" to perpetuate a very traditional role for women. It instructs political leaders to take it upon themselves to warn women against the "false economy of our times, which turns her mind and heart away from the home, thereby depriving the family, state, and Church of her proper contribution to the common welfare."[11] The corollary comment on birth control condemns again the "propaganda of so-called planned parenthood, which violates the moral law, robs the family of its nobility and high social purpose, and weakens the moral fiber of a nation."[12]

Virtually the same themes were repeated later in the decade in a "Statement on Secularism" (1947) in which predictably the family is presented as both the central means to the reconstruction of society after the war and the primary measure of the success of those efforts. Again there is the call for an adequate income for families, and again there is an attempt to establish a connection between proper family life and the well-being of the national and international community. (Ironically, here the bishops find it appropriate to introduce the language of family planning with the claim that "God planned the human family.") This use of a family to refer to the international context is increasingly a factor in episcopal statements from this point forward. The "Statement on Secularism" goes on to reiterate that "artificial family planning on the basis of contraceptive immorality, cynical disregard of the nobel purposes of sex, a sixtyfold increase in our divorce rate during the last century, and the widespread failure of the family to discharge its educational functions are terrible evils which secularism has brought to our country."[13]

In their November 1949, statement on "The Christian Family," the bishops made the connection between family concerns and public policy even more specific. Claiming that "any attack of the state on family life is suicidal," they insist here that the state must respect the rights of families, that it must not fail "to provide opportunities for the adequate housing of families, for the requisite education of children, for the use of the common benefits supplied through the taxing of citizens."[14] They call for "a just measure of economic security" for families and point out what they consider to be an imbalance in public policy initiatives:

When, in a wealthy and prospering nation, diligent and willing parents are forced to live in grinding poverty; when parents have no opportunity of owning their own home; when the aid of government is extended to those who raise crops or build machines, but not to those who rear children; there exists a condition of inequity and even of injustice. Social legislation and social action must concur to improve man's economic opportunity, to enable him to marry early, to free him from the peril of unnaturally limiting his family, and to afford him some certainty of sufficiently gainful employment and some assurance that death or accident will not reduce his dependents to the status of public charges.[15]

This episcopal support for the initiatives of the welfare state in the light of its familial ethic was supplemented in the 1951 statement "God's Law and the Measure of Man's Conduct," by the inclusion of themes drawn from natural law theory. In this statement, the bishops put forth an outline of the scholastic notion of natural law which is accessible to the individual through the use of right reason. They suggest that the human use of right reason reveals certain basic elements of the natural law. These include a particular conception of the family: "Out of the inherent demands of human nature arises the family as the fundamental unit of human society, based on a permanent and exclusive union of man and woman in marriage." The bishops insist here that the principles of natural law are perennial and unchanging, and that the application of the natural law to social questions will make clear the necessary structure of the family as well as its importance in society. There is no indication that cultural context and social change are regarded by the bishops as relevant to their normative teaching.

By 1959, the bishops began to be influenced by claims of a worldwide population problem, and they confronted this challenge in the statement "Explosion or Backfire?" Calling the phrase "population explosion" a "terror technique phrase," the bishops suggested that recent attention to the problem of population growth constituted a "smokescreen behind which a moral evil may be foisted on the public." They responded to a perceived claim that "birth prevention within the married state is gradually becoming acceptable even within the Catholic Church" by issuing a categorical denial, and they insisted that "United States Catholics believe that the promotion of artificial birth prevention is a morally, humanly, psychologically, and politically disastrous approach to the population problem."[16] Using the natural law framework, they argued that the position of American

Catholics with regard to the population question was itself "a realistic one which is grounded in the natural law . . . and in respect for the human person, his origin, freedom, responsibility and destiny."

The issue of artificial contraception continued to be a central focus for the bishops in their efforts to articulate a consistent viewpoint both for their pastoral duties and for their public policy stances. A most telling expression of this is to be found in the American response to the encyclical letter *Humanae Vitae* of Paul VI, issued in 1968. In that letter, Paul addressed the issue of contraception directly and reflected on it in the context of the family and of what he termed "rapid demographic development."[17] Declaring that the use of artificial methods of birth control constituted a morally unacceptable response to population pressures "even when the intention is to safeguard or promote individual, family or social well-being," Paul called for another type of action from public authorities:

> To rulers, who are those principally responsible for the common good, and who can do so much to safeguard moral customs, We say: Do not allow the morality of your peoples to be degraded; do not permit that by legal means practices contrary to the natural and divine law be introduced into that fundamental cell, the family. Quite other is the way in which public authorities can and must contribute to the solution of the demographic problem: namely, the way of a provident policy for the family, of a wise education of peoples in respect of the moral law and the liberty of citizens.[18]

Paul went on to make the connection between "a provident policy for the family" and "social justice" based on social and economic progress. This connection sets his condemnation of birth control squarely in the context of the pursuit of social justice and solidarity which he developed in his 1967 encyclical *Populorum Progressio.*

The broad dissent among Catholics from the conclusions of Paul with regard to contraception have been widely discussed and documented.[19] Most observers recognized that the dissent constituted a serious problem for the teaching authority and external credibility of the church. In their response, however, the American bishops chose to affirm the authority of the papacy in this matter and called upon American Catholics to study Paul's statement and to "form their consciences in its light."[20] The response does not linger on the theological and ethical issues involved in the encyclical; it turns instead to policy implications. While taking time to note some of the cultural changes that were making an impact on the family, the American bishops argue that there has been a "national failure to adopt comprehensive and realistic family-centered policies during the course of this century."[21] Specifically scoring the "consequences of poverty and racist attitudes," the bishops call for better food and housing programs and criticize current "welfare" policies as inadequate to the needs of the family in its role as the concrete expression of a social order conducive to the achievement of the common good.

The implications of this call for a domestic social policy based on the needs of the family are then extended to a discussion of international policy. In this portion of the response, reference is made once again to the "family of nations," and a question is raised whether "the present policy of maintaining nuclear superiority is meaningful for security."[22] The bishops criticize what they call "the fickleness of public interest in and Congressional support of foreign aid" and "the lack of a stable, persevering, national concern for the promotion of the international common good."[23] Most significantly, the bishops conclude their response to *Humanae Vitae* with their first strong statement of concern about the American military involvement in Vietnam. In a 1966 statement "Peace and Vietnam," the bishops had declared that "while we do not claim to be able to resolve these issues authoritatively, in the light of the facts as they are known to us, it is reasonable to argue that our presence in Vietnam is justified."[24] But in 1969 they adopted a more critical nuanced tone:

> In assessing our country's involvement in Vietnam we must ask: Have we already reached, or passed, the point where the principle of proportionality becomes decisive? How much more of our resources in men and money should we commit to this struggle, assuming an acceptable cause or intention: Has the conflict in Vietnam provoked inhuman dimensions of suffering? Would not an untimely withdrawal be equally disastrous?[25]

They went on to recommend a modification of the Selective Service Act to permit selective conscientious objection and in the process offered a strong apology for the rights of conscience. The letter concluded by referring again to the church's "defense of human life in our day" and by calling for "conversion" and a "renewed spirituality" which will "reaffirm the sacred character of married love through which life is begun, the dignity of the family within which love brings life to maturity, and the blessed vision of peace in which life is shared by men and nations in a world community of love."[26]

Immediately after this statement of support for papal teaching on contraception which linked opposition to birth control to other issues, however, the argument took a new direction. Statements issued by the American hierarchy began to shift the emphasis from contraception to abortion. While it is true that the issue of abortion was gaining more public attention in the late 1960s and early 1970s, it is also true that American Catholics in large numbers dissented from the papal teaching on artificial contraception, and there was a corresponding erosion of regard for the leadership of the church.

In April 1969, six months after their response on the contraception issue, the United States Catholic Conference issued a "Statement on Abortion," setting the question of abortion in the context of the war in Vietnam by suggesting that the war created a "crisis of conscience" over the dignity of human life. Citing the "widespread effort to 'liberalize' the present laws that generally prohibit abortion," it concluded that "we are now facing a determined effort to repeal totally all abortion laws — thereby resulting in abortion on demand."[27] This is the first of more than a dozen statements directly addressing the abortion question in the decade of the 1970s.

The *Roe v. Wade* decision of the Supreme Court in 1973 resulted in a series of five responses from the American hierarchy in that year alone. Cardinal John Krol of Philadelphia, then president of the National Conference of Catholic Bishops, called the decision "an unspeakable tragedy for this nation."[28] A month later, the Administrative Committee of the NCCB issued a fuller analysis of the decision and its implications, declaring that the Supreme Court failed to "protect the most basic human right — the right of life," and went on to "reject this decision of the Court because, as John XXIII says, 'If any government does not acknowledge the rights of man or violates them, . . . its orders completely lack juridical force'."[29] The bishops concluded their response by calling for the creation of a "pro-life atmosphere" in which the value of human life would be recognized and sustained, and they asked for persistent effort to bring about a reversal of the Supreme Court decision.

In addition to the number of anti-abortion statements and the specific injunctions against abortion in their "Pastoral Guidelines for Catholic Hospitals and Catholic Health Care Personnel," the bishops issued a "Pastoral Plan for Pro-Life Activities" in November 1975. The plan contained an outline whose purpose it was to "activate the pastoral resources of the Church" in a public information effort in support of its pro-life stance and in "a public information effort directed toward the legislative, judicial and administrative areas so as to insure effective legal protection for the right to life."[30] The plan also called for a pastoral effort "addressed to the specific needs of women with problems related to pregnancy and to those who have had or have taken part in an abortion."

For the purpose of this account, it is the effort to influence public policy featured in the bishops' plan that is of greatest interest. For here clearly the American hierarchy seeks to achieve a "deliberate presence in public policy debates" in an unprecedented manner. The plan calls for the passage of a constitutional amendment which would protect the unborn and for the passage of federal and state laws and the adoption of administrative policies which would restrict the practice of abortion. It exhibits a marked sophistication with regard to political strategy and explicitly calls for "appropriate political action to achieve these legislative goals."[31] The plan details the need for state coordinating committees, diocesan and parish pro-life committees and the "development in each congressional district of an identifiable, tightly-knit, and well-organized pro-life unit" which would organize in support of the constitutional amendment. Among other objectives, the bishops instruct congressional district pro-life groups to "maintain an informational file on the pro-life position of every elected official and potential candidate" and "to work for qualified candidates who will vote for a constitutional amendment and other pro-life issues."[32] The diocesan pro-life committees are likewise instructed to maintain communication with the National Committee for a Human Life Amendment with regard to "federal activity" in order to "provide instantaneous information concerning local senators and representatives."[33]

By September 1976, during the presidential campaign, statements of the American bishops had clarified the relationship between their aggressive political involvement on the abortion issue and their other concerns. Having met with both Gerald Ford and Jimmy Carter at the invitation of the candidates, the bishops issued a statement which did not endorse either candidate but instead put the abortion question at the center of their public policy agenda:

> Abortion and the need for a constitutional amendment to protect the unborn are among our concerns. So are the issues of unemployment, adequate educational opportunity for all, an equitable food policy, both domestic and worldwide, the right to a decent home and health care, human rights across the globe, intelligent arms limitation and many other social justice issues.[34]

In contrast to the broadly negative response to the Vatican-American position on the question of contraception, the bishops noted a strong measure of support from Catholics and other Americans for their initiative against abortion, and suggested that "a profound spiritual renewal is now taking place among many American Catholics" in which "ethical and moral abuses, such as legally sanctioned permissiveness concerning abortion, have helped create a renewed sense of unity among concerned Catholics and have awakened them to their responsibility to be a positive force for good in the nation's life."[35]

On the strength of their convictions with regard to the issue of abortion and their developing sense of the implications for public policy of a "pro-life" stance, the bishops offered an account of their views on the political responsibilities of Catholics in anticipation of the 1980 election. Claiming that "current popular reactions against the government and government programs reveal an excessive individualism and a decline in our commitment to the common good" as a nation, they urge Catholics to "take stands on the candidates and the issues."[36] As the bishops elaborate on the role of the church in the political order in this statement, they make it clear that political involvement has become a central element in their view of the church's ministry and mission. The church must relate positively to the political order, they argue, since social injustice and the denial of human rights can often be remedied only through governmental action. In today's world, concern for social justice and human development necessarily requires persons and organizations to participate in the political process in accordance with their own responsibilities and roles.[37]

The list of issues drawn up in this statement begins with abortion and includes a reflection on family life, and these concerns established the context for analyses of the more conventional "public" issues of arms control, the economy, agriculture and health care. The remarks on the family in this statement, however, reveal a new emphasis in the thinking of the bishops in the documents of the late 1970s. As advocates of the "critical values of human rights and social justice," the bishops have begun to use the language of "participation." In the case of the family, the bishops argue that "comprehensive decisions of a national or regional scope must take into account their impact on family life. Families . . . must be allowed their rightful input in those decisions which affect their daily lives."[38] This echoes verbatim a 1978 statement in which the bishops called for "a family governmental policy based on the principles of Christian social justice" and noted that the "delicate, yet decisive, relationship between society and the family demands careful study, and where destructive influences on family are apparent, society ought to be challenged in support of the rights of families."[39] The bishops make clear their determination to "extend the impact made by Christian families on the formation of public policy and social legislation."[40]

This familial index to American Catholic social teaching and public policy initiatives is maintained even in the technical and widely argued pastoral letter of May 1983 on nuclear policy. That letter states that

> the fundamental premise of world order in Catholic teaching is a theological truth: the unity of the human family—rooted in common creation, destined for the kingdom, and united by moral bonds of rights and duties. This basic truth about the unity of the human family pervades the entire teaching on war and peace: for the pacifist position, it is one of the reasons why life cannot be taken, while for the just-war position, even in a justified conflict bonds of responsibility remain in spite of the conflict.[41]

And the bishops tell parents "your role, in our eyes, is unsurpassed by any other; the foundation of society is the family."[42] Again, the deliberate connection to abortion dominates the episcopal reflection on the appropriate "response" to the demands of the nuclear issue. Stressing the need for "a disarmament of the human heart," the letter cites the use of abortion as the particular form of violence which "blunts a sense of the sacredness of human life." The bishops draw a contrast between a situation in which a defense may have the unintended consequence of claiming innocent victims—"This is tragic, but may conceivably be proportionate to the values defended"—and the practice of abortion, which they call "a direct attack on human life:"

> We must ask how long a nation willing to extend a constitutional guarantee to the "right" to kill defenseless human beings by abortion is likely to refrain from adopting strategic warfare policies deliberately designed to kill millions of defenseless human beings, if adopting them should come to seem "expedient."[43]

It is evident that the family-centered approach to public policy involvement on the part of the bishops has been consistent throughout the existence of the national episcopal conference. It is indeed their "seamless garment." Furthermore, it is clear that out of this orientation certain issues have come to be treated with special emphasis. Foremost among these are the issues of artificial contraception and abortion. In the case of contraception, the bishops have voiced continuing opposition throughout the period to contraceptive practices, both on the part of individuals and as a feature of American foreign aid initiatives. However, after 1969 the issue of contraception was greatly overshadowed by the attention given by the hierarchy to abortion. This latter issue has proven a much more successful focus for the bishops in terms of the popularity of their leadership in American public life. They have enjoyed strong support from both Catholics and non-Catholics for their views on abortion and have used the abortion issue to enter a wedge in public policy discussions for a broad range of other issues.

WITH THIS PATTERN IN MIND, it is instructive to turn to the larger tradition of Catholic social teaching as it has emerged from papal and conciliar reflections in the last century. A review of the key documents embodying this teaching shows that the American pastoral statements have accurately reflected the wider tradition. The family was a theme of central importance for Leo XIII and for all of his successors as they reflected on the "social question." In both his encyclical on marriage (*Arcanum Divinae Sapientiae*, 1880) and his "labor encyclical" *Rerum Novarum* (1891), Leo places the family at the center of his teaching on economic justice and the common good. The family anchors his discussion of the right to private property and the right to a just wage for the worker. And it is the concrete point of reference for his discussion of the common good.

Pius XI continued the Leonine linkage of the family to broader social questions in both *Casti Connubii* (1930) and *Quadragesimo Anno* (1931). In the former, he presents a view of Christian marriage, stressing its value to society:

> For experience has taught that unassailable stability in matrimony is a fruitful source of virtuous life and of habits of integrity. Where this order of things obtains, the happiness and well being of the nation is safely guarded; what the families and individuals are, so also is the State, for a body is determined by its parts.[44]

In *Quadragesimo Anno*, he reaffirms the teachings of Leo XIII on the right to private property and a just wage based on the assumption that the worker is a family man, and he uses the family to insist on the role of charity in "the reconstruction of the social order:"

> For justice alone can, if faithfully observed, remove the causes of social conflict but can never bring about union of minds and hearts. Indeed all the institutions for the establishment of peace and the promotion of mutual help among men, however perfect these may seem, have the principal foundation of their stability

in the mutual bond of minds and hearts whereby the members are united with one another.... then only will true cooperation be possible for a single common good when the constituent parts of society deeply feel themselves members of one great family and children of the same Heavenly Father ...[45]

The central importance of the family is implied in Pius XI's discussion of subsidiarity. The family is the prototype of the voluntary association which stands between the individual and the state. It concretely expresses the notions of organic interdependence and hierarchical order that are the hallmarks of Pius's teaching on the principle of subsidiarity and the common good.

Pius XII and John XXIII reiterated these themes during their respective pontificates, and John particularly stressed the connection between the "human family" and what he called the "universal common good." In his famous "Signs of the Times" discussion in the encyclical *Pacem in Terris* (1963), he reflects on the "inadequacy of modern states to ensure the universal common good" and calls for the development of more effective transnational forms of public authority. This reflection is couched in familial terms:

No era will ever succeed in destroying the unity of the human family, for it consists of men who are all equal by virtue of their natural dignity. Hence there will always be an imperative need—born of man's very nature—to promote in sufficient measure the universal common good; the good, that is, of the whole human family.[46]

John's use of the family to articulate a vision which would extend the understanding of the common good to the international context was developed extensively by the bishops of Vatican II in the conciliar document *Gaudium et Spes* (1965). The bishops rely heavily on the family as a basis for their reflections on the universal common good. The concept of family is used here as a symbol of human unity and solidarity in the midst of what they see as the pluralism and cultural complexity of modern life. Their reflection proceeds on two distinct levels. Individual families are regarded as the primary source of the moral qualities that make possible the achievement of the common good in society. They are "a kind of deeper school of humanity" and the "foundation of society" in which "the various generations come together and help one another to grow wiser and to harmonize personal rights with the other requirements of social life."[47] A close reading of the document shows that the Council fathers have in mind here a quite specific notion of how the family should function. They think of the family as monogamous, fecund, hierarchically organized, faithful to assigned roles, and committed to both the development of the person and the good of the whole. Central to this concept is the assumption that parents are willing recipients of the church's moral and social teaching and that, as such, they will serve as primary transmitters of that tradition to their children. Everything that the bishops have to say about human dignity, solidarity, and freedom, as realized in the family, is grounded on their assumptions about matrimony and even more specifically on their understanding of "conjugal love." The relationship between married spouses is the basis on which this model of family and, in turn, the derivative social teaching of this document rest, and it is clear that the bishops have in mind a quite specific notion of how it should be ordered:

> Hence ... the true practice of conjugal love, and the whole meaning of the family life which results from it, have this aim: that the couple be ready with stout hearts to cooperate with the love of the Creator and Savior, who through them will enlarge and enrich His own family day by day.[48]

When the primacy of the conjugal relationship in the social teaching of the church is thus emphasized in a document as important as *Gaudium et Spes* has turned out to be, the use of family by the American hierarchy is not surprising. Neither is their preoccupation with questions of contraception and abortion. The intimate behavior of married persons has been and continues to be a substantive as well as a strategic element in the modern presentation of the church's social teaching.

The other way in which the concept of family figures in *Gaudium et Spes* has to do with the international context, and in this setting it has two functions. It is used to express the Council's conviction about the unity of all humanity in the midst of acknowledged cultural diversity, and it is also used to identify the church as "the family of God's sons." The "family" of the church shares the characteristics of individual families. These include fidelity, fecundity (the church is "composed of members of the earthly city who have a call to form the family of God's children during the present history of the human race, and to keep increasing it until the Lord returns"), hierarchical ordering, and the interdependence of members. In this view, the church "serves as a leaven and as a kind of soul for human society as it is to be renewed in Christ and transformed into God's family."[49]

Thus the document identifies the church as integral to the formation of family and the family as both the source and the standard of the common good from the local level to that of the entire "human family." Subsequent social pronouncements of the magisterium, both papal and episcopal, show that this conception remains integral, but there are various shades of emphasis. In the encyclical *Octogesima Adveniens* (May 1971), for example, Paul VI seems to make the family subordinate to a larger context which he calls "politics." He speaks of the need "to pass from economics to politics" as Christians seek effective involvement in social questions. In this context, "political power" is personified and identified as the proximate source of the common good, and the family is given a subordinate position:

> Political power, which is the natural and necessary link for ensuring the cohesion of the social body, must have as its aim the achievement of the common good. While respecting the legitimate liberties of individuals, families and subsidiary groups, it acts in such a way as to create, effectively and for the well-being of all, the conditions required for attaining man's true and complete good, including his spiritual end.[50]

However, in the document *Justice in the World* (November 1971), in which the world Synod of Bishops took up Paul's theme of political activism, the family appears again in a central role. It is both the primary source of "education for justice" and the sign of human solidarity which must be seriously affirmed as a prologue to political action.[51]

John Paul II, in turn, has made the family the mainstay of his program. The pattern he has outlined in his apostolic exhortation *Familiaris Consortio* (1981) reiterates and reinforces the pattern we have been pursuing throughout this essay. That document presents an analysis of the situation of the family in the modern world and outlines "the plan of God for marriage and the family." It places "conjugal communion" again at the center of the discussion and goes on to show the relationship between the family properly understood and the international order. It is significant, however, that the exhortation prefers to speak of the political responsibilities of Christian families and of the rights of families, however, rather than of the "human family" building the common good through political action.[52]

The conclusion to be drawn from this review of the larger body of church teaching is that the American episcopal emphasis on the family is very much in keeping with the social thinking of the magisterium in the last century. The church fathers have consistently taken family as the index of a well-ordered society and have extended it to address contemporary problems of international economics and political justice. The family is thus not only the basis of the American hierarchy's presence in American policy discussions, it is also a reflection of its agreement with the larger body of Catholic social teaching.

Given the case as outlined above, the obvious question is whether the family, as both an institution and metaphor, should bear the burden which modern Catholic teaching imposes upon it. One can well understand the appeal of the concept on both levels. The idea of the family has an obvious relevance to the themes the church seeks to address in its social teaching. This relevance is based on the importance of the family in the nurture of individuals and on the connection between that nurture and what goes on in wider forms of human association. Much of Catholic teaching rests, moreover, on the ideal of organic interdependence of human beings in a hierarchically arranged society, and the monogamous nuclear family obviously conforms well to that ideal. In addition, the family as it is understood in these documents is a microcosm of what the church has said over the centuries about its own identity. It understands itself to be an organic society based on a hierarchical order, and it seeks to create a unity among the faithful analogous to what is supposed, at least, to be the unity of the members of the nuclear family. Finally, there is also the fact that in recent public life the fate of the family has become an important political issue, and almost all serious contenders for political power in the last decade have felt the need to address "family" concerns. By speaking to these concerns, the American hierarchy in particular has been able to establish an active and influential presence in public life, and the particular way in which the concept of the family has been treated in Catholic teaching has meant that the hierarchy has been able to do this without allying itself simply or neatly with either the left or the right.

On the other hand, the ideal of the family that is consistently assumed in all of this discussion is one that is static and in increasing tension with the realities of life in rapidly changing societies. Sooner or later, papal and episcopal understanding of the family must deal with cultural pluralism and begin to take account of the fact that, while the monogamous and fecund family dedicated to the nurturing of children continues to be a prominent feature of social life, this form of intimate human social organization is but one among many. Even within the family properly so-called, a diversity of form is increasingly evident. John Paul II alludes to this, for instance, in his condemnation of polygamy in *Familiaris Consortio*. But a more thorough reflection on the bases of the current pluralism might indicate that there is more that needs to be said. The understanding of the family that leads to John Paul's judgment here is simply too univocal. To do justice to the situation we now face, a good deal more subtlety and flexibility is necessary.

Much work remains to be done in this context if Catholic social teaching is to be adapted successfully to modern conditions. Assuming that such work can in fact be done, two other problems with the continued use of family as so central a theme suggest themselves. First of all, the pattern of anchoring the discussion of family in claims about "conjugal communion" leaves church leaders in a vulnerable position as major dissent persists among Catholics over papal directives on contraception and divorce. Because significant numbers of Catholics question the specifics of church teaching on these and other issues, the model itself loses some of its force. And second, the attitudes and behavior of women have very direct implications for the familial basis of Catholic social teaching. The assumptions that anchor the bishops' pastoral leadership and public policy presence require the support of women, and because the relationship between the church hierarchy and women is increasingly fragile, the familial model as basis for Catholic teaching is correspondingly vulnerable.

The situation can be summarized in the following way. In principle, the notion of the common good as it has been developed in Catholic teaching may be of great value in American public policy discussions, as well as in the international effort to develop more adequate structures for the pursuit of justice and peace. The concept of the family is, in turn, integral to what the church has had to say in this regard. But there is very little evidence to suggest that this use of family has been undertaken in a critically self-conscious manner, or that the hierarchy has begun to understand how problematic the assumptions that they make about the family are in relation to contemporary conditions. Insofar as they are serious about pursuing a significant public role for the church, this uncritical use of the family must change. Either they must develop a more complex and nuanced concept of the family, or they must seek another foundation for their teaching.

There are indications that the authors of the current pastoral on the economy are aware of at least some of this. They make, for example, the predictable references to the face of the family as a measure of economic justice and to the metaphor of the human family as a way of addressing the international issues they want to raise. But at the same time, there is less explicit and focused reliance on the nuclear family as the basis of social order, and the communal themes are not nearly so directly tied to familial images as has been true in the past. The first draft, at least, suggests other ways of considering the common good. It stresses the notion of "communities of memory" and of "communal solidarity" without specific invocation of the family itself. The language of rights and of "participation" also appears in a central way in the document, and this may indicate, among other things, a decision to consider persons as individuals as well as members of family units. The cost, of course, is that such language tends to be a good deal more vague and abstract. It may therefore seem less appropriate as a means of evoking the images of solidarity and cooperation that the letter has attempted to call forth. For this and for other reasons, the bishops may be persuaded to return to the mode of discourse which is more familiar to them. If they choose to do this, they may well gain more appreciation in the short run for what they have to say, at least in some quarters. But in the long run they will almost certainly lose. For the way of treating the family that has been characteristic of Catholic teaching in the past simply will not suffice, not least for Catholics themselves. The longer the magisterium persists in speaking in this fashion, the less credibility it is likely to have. To the extent that the present letter represents a change in this regard, however limited, it is to be applauded. Viewed retrospectively, this could well turn out to be one of its most important contributions.

NOTES

1. "Pastoral Letter Issued by the Roman Catholic Hierarchy of the United States, September 26, 1919," in Hugh J. Nolan, ed., *Pastoral Letters of the United States Catholic Bishops* (Washington, D.C.: U.S. Catholic Conference, 1985) vol. I, 309.

2. Ibid., 311.

3. Ibid., 310.

4. Ibid., 312.

5. Ibid., 314.

6. "Present Crisis: Issued with the Authorization of the American Hierarchy, April 25, 1933," in Nolan, vol. I, 384.

7. Ibid.

8. Ibid.

9. Ibid.

10. "The Essentials of a Good Peace: A Statement Issued by the NCWC Administrative Board in the Name of the Bishops of the United States, November 11, 1943," in Nolan, vol. II: 1941–1961, 47.

11. Ibid.

12. Ibid., 48.

13. "Statement on Secularism: A Statement Issued by the NCWC Administrative Board in the Name of the Bishops of the United States, November 14, 1947," in Nolan, vol. II, 76.

14. "The Christian Family: A Statement Issued by the Catholic Bishops of the United States, November 21, 1949," in Nolan, vol. II, 93.

15. Ibid., 94.

16. "Explosion or Backfire?: A Statement Issued by the Catholic Bishops of the United States, November 19, 1959," in Nolan, vol. II, 222.

17. Paul VI, *Humanae Vitae (On the Regulation of Birth)*, July 25, 1968, in Joseph Gremillion, *The Gospel of Justice and Peace: Catholic Teaching since Pope John* (Maryknoll, N.Y.: Orbis Books, 1976), 427–44.

18. Ibid., 439.

19. See, for example, the survey data presented by Andrew Greeley in *The American Catholic: A Social Portrait*, (New York: Basic Books, 1977).

20. "Human Life in Our Day: A Statement Issued by the National Conference of Catholic Bishops, November 15, 1968," in Nolan, vol. III, 170 ff.

21. Ibid., 178.

22. Ibid., 187.

23. Ibid., 189.

24. "Peace and Vietnam: A Statement Issued by the National Conference of Catholic Bishops, November 18, 1966," in Nolan, vol. III, 76.

25. "Human Life in Our Day," in Nolan, vol. III, 191.

26. Ibid., 194.

27. "Statement on Abortion: A Statement Issued by the United States Catholic Conference, April 17, 1969," in Nolan, vol. III, 194.

28. "Statement on Abortion: A Statement Issued by the President of the National Conference of Catholic Bishops, January 22, 1973," in Nolan, vol. III, 366.

29. "Pastoral Message on Abortion: A Pastoral Issued by the Administrative Committee of the National Conference of Catholic Bishops, February 13, 1973," in Nolan, vol. III, 367.

30. "Pastoral Plan for Pro-Life Activities: A Statement Issued by the National Conference of Catholic Bishops, November 20, 1975," in Nolan, vol. IV, 82.

31. Ibid., 87.

32. Ibid., 90.

33. Ibid., 88.

34. "Resolution of the Administrative Committee: A Resolution Passed by the NCCB Administrative Committee, September 16, 1976," in Nolan, vol. IV, 157.

35. "A Review of the Principal Trends in the Life of the Catholic Church in the United States: A Statement Approved by the National Conference of Catholic Bishops, June 15, 1974," in Nolan, vol. III, 462.

36. "Political Responsibility: Choices for the 1980s: A Statement Issued by the Administrative Board of the United States Catholic Conference, October 26, 1979," in Nolan, vol. IV, 319.

37. Ibid., 320.

38. Ibid., 325.

39. "The Plan of Pastoral Action for Family Ministry: A Vision and a Strategy: A Statement Issued by the National Conference of Catholic Bishops, May 1978," in Nolan, vol. IV, 260.

40. "To Do the Work of Justice: A Statement Issued by the National Conference of Catholic Bishops, May 4, 1978," in Nolan, vol. IV, 247.

41. "The Challenge of Peace: God's Promise and Our Response: A Pastoral Letter Issued by the National Conference of Catholic Bishops, May 3, 1983," in Nolan, vol. IV, 556.

42. Ibid., 573.

43. Ibid., 569.

44. Pius XI, *Casti Connubii (On Christian Marriage)*, December 31, 1930, in Claudia Carlen, I.H.M., *The Papal Encyclicals*, vol. 2, 1903–1939 (Washington, D.C.: McGrath Publishing Company, 1981), 397, para. 37.

45. Pius XI, *Quadragesimo Anno (On the Reconstruction of the Social Order)*, May 15, 1931, in Carlen, 437, para. 137.

46. John XXIII, *Pacem in Terris (Peace on Earth)*, April 1963, in Carlen, 121, para. 132.

47. *Gaudium et Spes (The Pastoral Constitution on the Church in the Modern World* (Second Vatican Council, December 7, 1965), in Joseph Gremillion, ed., *The Gospel of Justice and Peace: Catholic Teaching since Pope John* (Maryknoll, N.Y.: Orbis Books, 1976), 289.

48. Ibid., 286.

49. Ibid., 274–75.

50. *Octogesima Adveniens (The Eightieth Anniversary of Rerum Novarum)*, May 14, 1971, in Gremillion, op. cit., 507.

51. *Justice in the World*, Synod of Bishops, Second General Assembly, November 30, 1971, in Gremillion, op. cit., 524.

52. "Apostolic Exhortation *Familiaris Consortio* of His Holiness Pope John Paul II to the Episcopate, to the Clergy, and to the Faithful of the Whole Catholic Church Regarding the Role of the Christian Family in the Modern World," December 15, 1981 (Washington, D.C.: United States Catholic Conference, 1982).

VICTOR FERKISS

The Bishops' Letter and the Future

VICTOR FERKISS is a Professor in
the Department of Government at
Georgetown University. He received
his Ph.D. in political science from the
University of Chicago. He also holds
an M.A. in political science from Yale
University.

THE BISHOPS' LETTER on the American economy has been attacked from many sides.[1] Most of the critics have argued that it is primarily a rehash of ideas left over from the New Deal and the Great Society. These critics are to a great extent correct, but for the wrong reasons. What is most problematic about the letter's approach is that it is an attempt to treat a dynamic situation as if it were a static one, with the result that it pays insufficient attention to change and to the uncertainty of our future. The bishops are clearly aware of the complexities of our situation. "High interest rates, the federal budget deficit, the growing international trade deficit and the problems besetting U.S. agriculture and industry are interrelated problems that call for hard choices," they write.[2] But while they note that "The causes of our national economic problems and their possible solutions are the subject of vigorous debate today,"[3] they are content to say that "our approach to analyzing the U.S. economy is pragmatic and evolutionary in nature,"[4] and when they address the special topics they choose to concentrate on — employment, poverty, food and agriculture, and international economics — they note that "the treatment of these issues does not constitute a comprehensive analysis of the U.S. economy."[5] But failing such a comprehensive analysis, what confidence can we have that their judgments take account of all relevant factors?

"If it ain't broke, don't fix it" is an old and honored maxim. Many of the bishops' critics argue that the American economy is not nearly so defective as the letter implies, and hence does not need fixing. But surely this is not time for complacency. What if the economy is in fact breaking down, or at least altering its structure so that it seems to be? What if, to shift the metaphor, the signs of illness that we see around us are in fact signs of physiological change attendant on maturity, or even incipient senility? To prescribe for an illness, you must first be able to diagnose it properly. While the bishops refer to many symptoms in passing, they eschew a really systematic analysis, as we have noted, and their regimen may be based on an implicit partial diagnosis that is erroneous. I would argue that our real economic problem as a nation is that we lack the systematic analysis any diagnosis presupposes, that we don't really know whether the patient is sick or not, and if so, exactly what the illness is. Obviously, some of the symptoms we see are uncomfortable. But are they signs of approaching collapse or simply of movement toward a new stage of life? Certainly, the bishops deserve credit for calling attention to many of our problems and for challenging us to engage in Christian reflection upon them. They are surely right to refuse to allow us to accept the existing order as divinely inspired and guided. The only question is whether or not the questions asked and the answers proposed successfully accomplish the task they have set themselves and us.

Part of the problem, of course, is that all social change is painful in some sense, and there are always victims. Part of the bishops' difficulty is that while they sometimes advert to the fact of change, they do not clearly recognize that change — however painful to some — is one of the hallmarks of a modern industrial society, whether "liberal" or not. Where they do perceive change, they object to the fact that the pain it causes is being inflicted on the already disadvantaged poor, running counter to their basic moral precept that "The fundamental moral criterion for all economic decisions, policies and institutions is this: They must be at the service of *all people, especially the poor.*"[6]

What are the symptoms of change which we see all around us? What kind of diagnosis of our condition can be derived from them? What, if anything, can persons of good will do to relieve the inevitable sufferings which change causes? These, in my opinion, are the key questions which the bishops' letter fails to address adequately. This failure stems from several causes. One is the already mentioned unwillingness of the bishops to undertake a systematic analysis of the American economy. Another is the fact that the bishops' letter is inevitably heir to a long tradition of analysis and criticism of industrial capitalism. Perhaps most important, no one yet really has the complete answers to the factual questions upon which moral judgment must rest.

The first set of questions has to do with the structure of the American economy. The bishops refer several times in passing to technological change and robotics, but never treat them systematically, saying, in justification, that "The 'signs of the times' noted here are not a complete portrait of the economy."[7] But what if the "signs of the times" are, in fact, basically dependent upon forces such as technological change which are not discussed? Even the average citizen is aware that something seems to be happening to alter the shape of the American economy. Old-fashioned heavy manufacturing—the smokestack industries of the "frost belt," now sometimes called the "rust belt"—apparently is being replaced in our economy by the "high tech" glamor industries associated with the computer. This has occasioned not only bitter wrangling among members of Congress along regional lines, but much learned debate among economists and others about the "deindustrialization" and "reindustrialization" of America as well.[8] Anticipating a theme that has been recently taken up by mainstream thinkers, some of my fellow futurists have written at length for many years about the coming of an "information society," in which primary production in the old sense would be increasingly replaced by the processing of information, variously defined.[9]

No question exists but that many people in older industries have been displaced, and that Silicon Valley was once a great place in which to work. But it is very difficult to define "high tech" and even more difficult to get a fix on its significance for the future of the economy. While many older industries are rapidly reorganizing their work processes to use computers and automation, direct employment in the computer industry as such is a very minor economic factor (and much computer manufacture and use can take place abroad anyway, something that is increasingly happening), and the extent of the change is much exaggerated. It is, indeed, highly likely that traditional manufacturing will remain a major component of the American economy for at least the next generation, just as agriculture has remained important despite the rise of manufacturing. Much the same thing applies to the move toward the "service industry" which is undoubtedly taking place on a massive scale and is duly noted by the bishops.[10] Service industry, after all, does not mean simply restaurants and boutiques; it also includes such things as computer programming, banking, tax preparation, and a myriad of other related "business services."

How one assesses the impact of change largely depends, moreover, on the criterion: is the importance of an industry a matter of how many people it employs or its gross product? Despite the fact that fewer people work on farms every year, agriculture remains a major factor in American economic life, especially in our international balance of payments. The fact that more people are employed by McDonalds than by the entire American steel industry (and this has been true for many years) does not mean by any stretch of the imagination that the former is a more important actor in the economy. Thus in the last analysis this argument, like so many others, turns not simply on what the statistics say but also on what one thinks they mean. But after all is said and done, the preponderance of evidence does suggest that a major change is, in fact, taking place in the structure of the American economy. Moreover, the evidence also suggests strongly that in the not too distant future the computer and robotics will radically alter the future of employment, one of the bishops' four major concerns, destroying far more jobs than they create, with yet unpredictable consequences for the very nature of work.[11]

This same uncertainty conditions discussions of the nature of work and the shape of the American class structure, both obviously closely related to the questions we have just been considering. The bishops' letter spends much moral energy in exalting work as a fundamental human need on a number of levels. Indeed, for them, it is actually a duty: "all who are able to work are obligated to do so."[12] Their treatment follows the example set by Pope John Paul II in his encyclical *Laborem Exercens*.[13] Yet what exactly is work in our present economy? Though the bishops consciously or otherwise muddy the waters somewhat by referring to the activity of "homemakers" and others as work,[14] work in the modern American economy is essentially anything which the market will pay you for doing, as arbitrary a concept as the related one of the Gross National Product, which measures the total amount of all goods and services involved in the market. But much of what people are paid to do may be socially useless, and many socially useful tasks, such as housework, are ordinarily not compensated monetarily. In a capitalist economy, people are rewarded only if they do work in a form that results in market exchange. The bishops clearly do not accept this principle, but they confuse the issue by going on to insist that in addition to deserving support by society simply in virtue of being human, people are also entitled to the opportunity for meaningful work. They compound the confusion by speaking of unmet social needs which should be filled by creating new jobs. "It is both good common sense and sound economics to create jobs directly" for this purpose, they say.[15] Perhaps, but not within the logic of capitalist economics.

But work in this sense is a moral abstraction. More directly measurable—in theory, at least—is whether or not the American class structure is changing. Many analysts suggest that what has been happening in recent years is that well paid blue collar jobs have been disappearing while jobs in the less well paid service industries (such as McDonalds) have been increasing, and that the result on a national scale has been a dimunition in the size of the middle class. Though the bishops note this phenomenon and say that "the changing industrial and occupational mix in the U.S. economy could result in a shift toward lower-paying and lower-skilled jobs,"[16] they do not attempt to look at this in terms of a possibly changing American class structure.

Despite conflicting reports, such a change seems to be happening. An influential recent study concludes that the middle class, measured in income terms, has not in fact been shrinking.[17] But the study fails to go beyond income to take into account some of the subtler aspects of the issue such as the security and status various jobs provide, and thus it does not deal with the insecurities generated by change in the minds of many "middle class" Americans. The issue is by no means merely academic. How one interprets the evidence determines to a great extent the conclusions to be drawn not only about the viability but also about the moral status of the current American economy. The bishops make much of the issue of economic marginality, and rightly so. But the emerging problem may, in fact, be far more severe than they perceive. What if the country is destined to become increasingly polarized between rich and poor? As they rightly note, in speaking at the level of moral principles, Catholic social teaching not only challenges "economic arrangements that leave large numbers of people impoverished. Further, it sees extreme inequality as a threat to the solidarity of the human community, for great disparities lead to deep social divisions and conflict."[18] The civil strife based on rampant class inequality which wracks many Latin American nations could possibly threaten the United States at some future date if present trends continue.

Though an intelligent jury could still remain out on the question of whether the American work force is changing all that much in terms of income levels or job status, there is no question but that important changes are taking place in its sociological composition. The major one—indeed, so major as to be discussed even by President Reagan in terms of unemployment rates during the recent recession—is the entry of women into the paid work force in a massive way. Women have, of course, always worked outside the home, but in recent years their presence in the work force has increased so much that it has taken on the character of a major new economic reality. Indeed, the labor participation rate of women is on many indices higher than that of men. One thing which clearly made a difference in softening the hardship caused by the recession of the early 1980s, for example, was that while many men lost their factory jobs, their wives still had work, largely in service industries. One should note that the bishops' letter is equivocal on this subject. While not rejecting the presence of women in the work force and the changing structure of the American family which it both reflects and helps cause, they still cling to the idea that a single wage should be adequate to support a family, an interesting reaffirmation of the long-standing tendency in Catholic social thought to make the primacy of the family unit a principal feature of social justice.[19] Here, too, one senses an inability on the part of the bishops' letter to come to grips with the reality of change.

At the same time that there has been a change in the gender composition of the work force, there have been changes in its ethnic composition. There seems to be an increasingly significant "underclass" arising in America, composed of people who for one reason or another are not needed in the economy—not for reliable, ongoing employment at a living wage, at least. Younger black males form a major component of this underclass. At the same time, there has been a large, unprecedented, and economically very significant recent immigration to the United States, legal and illegal, largely of Hispanics but also of Asians and people from the Caribbean, for whom the nation seems to be able to provide jobs, though often at substandard wages. The extent and meaning of this development is, of course, a major subject of controversy among observers, to say nothing of what if anything can or should be done about it. Though many immigrants work at substandard wages, American organized labor, at least in industry, is increasingly tolerant of this in the justified fear that if this labor pool did not exist, the work they do would be exported to other countries, leaving all worse off. The bishops deplore racial discrimination and the idea that anyone's labor might be rejected, and they note the increasing presence of aliens—which they have on other occasions welcomed in terms of immigration policy; but they do not attempt to relate these changes in the nature of the work force to the surface economic problems of poverty and employment which they address.

Another factor of change, referred to only in passing in the bishops' letter, has been internal migration in the United States, of both industries and workers, generally from colder to warmer climes. This, of course, reflects not only the fact that for various physical reasons the newly expanding industries have located in the "Sunbelt," but also the fact that this is an area where in the past organized labor has been weakest, usually with the approval of local public opinion. Finally, there is the increasingly salient fact that the American population is aging—despite immigration—and there is a growing problem of how, even leaving aside escalating medical costs, a relatively smaller work force can bear the burden of supporting the politically potent elderly.[20] One solution, of course, would be to reverse the trend toward earlier retirement and allow people to work longer, but this would only exacerbate unemployment problems.

Another major economic problem—perhaps our greatest—which the bishops do not even mention is that of declining American productivity per worker. Economists argue about its cause, but is an undeniable fact. It is not, of course, entirely unrelated to the changing composition of the work force. It should be noted, ironically, that many European countries with far more generous welfare programs have, over the past several decades, been leading the United States in increased productivity per worker.

What is true of the nature of the work force, and its relationship to the probable structural changes taking place in the American economy, is true also of the nature of poverty. It too is a matter of debate. Poverty is, of course, a central concept for the bishops, and its theological meaning is beyond our concern here. But certain aspects of poverty are amenable to discussion on a factual level.[21] Here, the bishops are more closely on target than elsewhere. First of all, as they point out, we must disabuse ourselves of the widely held notion that all of the poor are poor because of some physical or social disability such as age, health, or unemployment. Many American workers, the bishops note, still receive wages which place them below the poverty line as individuals, and many of the working poor are not in a position to pool their wages with other family members in order to survive. The bishops quite rightly weigh in on the side of the poor who are the objects of an increasingly niggardly treatment on the part of American governments at all levels, especially in the federal, in various ways. The bishops clearly disagree with the implicit (and in the past, often explicit) American belief that to be on welfare is degrading and should clearly be so labelled. This belief stems from the fact that an economy based on growth and exchange has a difficult time tolerating the possibility that people should live well materially and do nothing in return by way of "work"—unless, of course, such people are well off financially, which implies past "accomplishment" by them or by their ancestors.

But in the bishops' letter there is, despite their rather loosely defined attacks on "material display," "a consumerist society," "luxury consumer goods" and "greed," and their avowal that "great wealth is a constant danger,"[22] a tendency to equate standards of living with monetary income. Even leaving aside the complicated empirical question of the extent to which transfer payments (aid to dependent children, for example) alter any calculations of income distribution based solely on tax returns, there is an increasing debate in the nation, and indeed in the Western world generally, about the soundness of this equation.[23] Many would argue that as our income as Americans has been rising, our standards of living—as measured by such things as housing size, for example—have been going down. One may argue that the hardships of those newly not so affluent as their parents are not to be taken all that seriously, as in some "objective" sense they probably are not. This malaise is not simply the "insecurity" about economics that bishops attribute to the "lower middle class"[24] and "moderate-income" Americans who have lost their jobs.[25] It is far more basic. Psychologically, at least, a feeling that one can no longer count on being "better off" than one's parents is a radically new departure in American life, and those who have this feeling are not at all likely to be responsive to appeals for any redistributive measures advocated by clerical groups. Much of the widespread American hostility to the "welfare class" is not simply meanmindedness (though some of it undoubtedly is), but is also a product of resentment at a perceived loss of status and affluence on the part of many. One can dispute many things that are popularly asserted about current trends in America's economy and society, but one thing that seems to be beyond dispute is a growing competitiveness among the young, generally expressed in material terms.

It is extremely important to understand this sentiment as well as to judge it. It springs, I believe, from a concern not only with affluence, but with security as well. If, as polls indicate, the young no longer have faith in the Social Security system, if even beginning employees are concerned about pension plans and about Individual Retirement Accounts (IRAs) of their own, these attitudes tell us something about our nation. The insecurity they reflect means that no matter how affluent the majority may seem to be, they will not be easily moved by concern for those who are less well off. This is especially true if—as surely is the case—high living standards are based on an unprecedented level of borrowing. As the Lay Letter (written by Michael Novak and associates as a preemptive strike against the bishops) correctly implies, there is no necessary logical connection between an entrepreneurial society based on risk and change, and the absence of a social "safety net."[26] But what is true logically is not necessarily true psychologically. Thus, even many whom we might regard as well off may still feel very insecure and for this reason be less inclined to help the truly needy at the risk of their own long-term well being. Security, it can be argued, is just as basic a human need as an adequate standard of living, and no attempt to address distributional issues in this society which ignores this fact can be taken seriously. The spectre of a generational war over Social Security is one which troubles many Americans. The bishops' emphasis on community as opposed to liberal individualism would have relevance to this issue, presumably, but their failure to address it directly is a major weakness in their economic analysis.

Central to the failure of the bishops' letter to take note of the changes taking place in our economy is the key question of America's role in the world. Throughout the letter are the conventional assumptions of the past, the era when the United States dominated the world economy and to a large extent could frame its domestic policies with little concern for what was happening in other nations, except perhaps insofar as our actions might affect them. That era has passed forever.

Consider the following facts. Today the United States has a budget deficit unprecedented in history, one which is having the paradoxical effect of enabling us to continue economic growth while Europe (though not, of course, Japan) is stagnating. This situation comes about largely because the strength of the dollar and high interest rates (which are directly related) draw capital from foreign nations to our shores. Though our political stability is a contributing factor, there seems to be a general consensus that the superior profit possibilities of investment in the American economy allow us to continue to function at a high level, despite the appeals of other nations to change our policies so as to give them more room for maneuver. But this entails a tremendous risk. If for any reason foreign investors should decide to change their policies, the United States would face a major economic downturn, perhaps even a catastrophic depression. This vulnerability is exacerbated by the fact that for the first time in generations (since World War I) the United States is a debtor nation in international terms.

This whole problem, of course, is a major source of controversy among economists and politicians, but it is not inconceivable that sometime in the near future we could witness a situation in which we can no longer finance our deficit by foreign borrowing and are forced to lower our standard of living by curtailing imports and radically increasing exports in order to pay off or even service our international debt. But could we increase our exports sufficiently? Is the strong dollar, as some claim, the only culprit in our international balance of payments problem? The United States, once a world leader in most forms of manufacturing, has long since lost that lead, and now imports automobiles, steel, and all kinds of consumer goods. Only in computers—and here we are under severe challenge from Japan— and in a few other hightech areas such as aircraft and some biological products, are we still competitive.

This condition decreases our capacity to establish control over our own economy. It is no accident that trade is emerging as one of our most important political and economic issues. Arguing that "Catholic economic teaching on the international economic order recognizes this complexity but does not provide specific solutions,"[27] the bishops do not directly address the question of protectionism, despite the fact that the relative inefficiency of many American industries (Japan far surpasses us in the use of industrial robots, for example) means that in a competitive world market many American firms will have to cut their wage bills drastically merely to survive. Some economists such as Lester Thurow suggest that it may be possible for the United States to compete effectively in world markets, at least as the economy is currently structured, without drastic decreases in the living standard of the American worker.[28] Many industries have already been pushing for (and getting) "givebacks" from unions in their contracts and adopting a "two-tier" system of wages in which newer employees are paid less than older ones.

Not all of this, of course, is due to foreign competition. Much of it stems from domestic deregulation, as in the case of the airlines, and it has been the occasion of an increasing number of labor disputes. But the handwriting is clearly on the wall. In many areas the United States is fighting for its economic survival. How do the bishops think we should spread the burdens of a possible decline in our standard of living? They seem to make the conventional liberal assumption

that continued economic growth will solve all problems of distribution, since as the pie gets larger the absolute size of the slices will
grow as well, even though their shape has not been altered. But if
that assumption proves to be no longer applicable, the distributive
problems must be confronted much more directly, and in a form
which the present letter does not begin, unfortunately, to address.
Nor does the letter reflect much appreciation of the possibility that
large-scale growth may be ecologically or environmentally unsound
or simply not possible, though the bishops do note that continued
population growth is a real problem.[29]

What all of this change adds up to is problematical. Some argue
that the future of the United States can be seen in the economy of
Great Britain, still faltering despite years of Prime Minister Thatcher's
attempts to make it more competitive through austerity. According
to economist Mancur Olson, it is inevitable that nations which have
long enjoyed economic predominance become sclerotic as interest
groups entrench themselves and newer competitors, with less of
a development history, come to the fore.[30] The recent economic
success of some of the nations of the Far East (South Korea, Taiwan,
Singapore) lends credence to his views. In any event, the United
States no longer has the free hand it once had in ordering its domestic
priorities with scant attention to the power and intentions of others.
This is no longer the 1930s. Yet the bishops letter shows little sign
of recognizing this. Its implicit premise is that the United States
is a rich nation in a world of the poor, and that even if we take
measures to reduce what the bishops rightly consider the scandalous
(and perhaps unnecessary, in terms of economic competitiveness)
gap between the wealthier part of our population (there are now
more than one million millionaires in the nation) and the poor at
home, we still have an open-ended obligation to help the needy
abroad.

In this connection, foreign aid appears high on the bishops'
agenda — in principle, rightly so. As they note, the United States
gives less to foreign aid per capita than virtually any other developed
nation, and when one discounts the amounts given in quasimilitary
aid to politically favored nations such as Israel and Egypt, the gap
is even larger. But here again there is a tendency for the letter to
slip into what can only be regarded as pious rhetoric. The plain fact,
which the bishops ignore, is that most foreign aid does not help the
poor in the nations to which it is directed, as Francis Moore Lappe of
Food First pointed out in a critique of the letter's first draft.[31] Indeed,
there seems to be a general rule of thumb that as national GNPs
increase, so also does the Gini index (which measures inequality

within nations) increase as well. How to avoid this unfortunate consequence is a difficult question. Basically, the problem is that the nations to which we send aid are all under the domination of small elites, which are unlikely to welcome or even permit anything which might upset their local patterns of economic and political power. The American aid program was well described many years ago by a member of Congress, who referred to it as a system whereby money was taken from the American poor (by means of a tax system regressive even then) and given to the rich of other nations.

The bishops say that "we want a world that works fairly for all. Effective action toward this end requires a definition of political community that goes beyond national sovereignty."[32] But their treatment of foreign aid lacks not only economic but political sophistication as well, in that it does not directly address the role which national sovereignty plays in complicating the problem. The current frustration of foreign aid donors with the Ethiopian government's policies regarding its starving subjects vividly illustrates the difficulty of providing for the basic human right to an adequate diet if governments object, just as the South African government's denial of the basic political rights of its black subjects illustrates the impotence of the international community to help them.

It is simply impossible to discuss the American economy without discussing its current trends and possible future, and these can only be adequately considered in an international context. This is true not only of international economics as conventionally understood, but also of foreign and military policy as well. "War is the health of the state," wrote dissident Randolph Bourne during World War I, and it is in its role as a possible wager of war that the federal government most massively confronts us. This is especially true in light of the budget priorities of the Reagan administration. The bishops have made a good start toward analyzing the international military problems of the nation and the world in their hotly debated pastoral on nuclear warfare, and there has been some suggestion that the new letter on economics be integrated with it. Though there are a few references to the problem,[33] the letter on the economy desperately needs to devote more attention to the impact of military spending and thinking on the economy. Indeed, it can even be maintained that most of our serious economic problems could be solved by a reordering of our foreign and military policies. This is not simply a question of how many hungry children could be fed for the cost of an MX missile, though this is an issue. Nor is it even a matter of noting that Japan, our major economic competitor, has a miniscule defense budget. Beyond such particular considerations, a good case can be made that the great attention that the United States has given to armaments in the broadest sense since at least the Korean war has fundamentally distorted our economy in terms of the training and work experience of management, the directions of research, and similar matters, and that nothing less than a major reorientation of our view of the world and our role in it can ever enable us to attain any of the goals which the bishops and others of good will desire in the economic realm.   To put it in plain terms, the real obstacle to reform may be the "military industrial complex" of which the late President Eisenhower warned.

If, as I have contended, we are becoming a different kind of economy with a different kind of work force and a different class structure, with perhaps intractable problems of foreign and internal debt, a very different attitude toward economic possibility and personal security and a radically different position in the world economy, and if our economic problems are inextricably tied to our political problems, then most of the practical solutions put forth by the bishops are really not very useful, however desirable the ends they are intended to serve may be. What is really required is a fundamental change of attitude, toward which the bishops' letter does not clearly point.

How can a change take place, even leaving aside considerations about the exact forms such a reorientation might take? Here we come to the essence of the weakness of the bishops' letter. The letter as written is addressed to Catholics primarily and to persons of good will generally. It stands foursquare in an old American tradition of political action through proclamation of ideals. It is an exercise in persuasion, and implicitly assumes that once citizens have made up their minds to do something, then that something—in a democratic system—will be done. But what if it is not that simple? What if changing deep-seated economic patterns is not like bringing back old Coke?

Economics and politics are inseparable in any society. Power is power is power. The bishops' letter fails to address the question of power directly. Throughout the letter, there are references to the "empowerment" of the poor, at home and abroad—stemming, it would appear, from the rhetoric of liberation theology in the broadest sense. But the fact remains that in the contemporary United States the poor have little power. This is true at two levels. The first level is that of the immediate (local, if you will) institutions in which they are involved. Being on welfare is demeaning—often made deliberately so—and local institutions for economic self-help are almost nonexistent, as the bishops are aware. One reason why they do not exist is that at the second level, the larger society, there is no demand for them, to say the least. Political participation of any kind is in inverse relation to wealth in all nations, but among modern legally democratic nations, in some ways especially and increasingly so in the United States. Most of those who do not vote in elections are poor, and save in special cases little is done to motivate and mobilize them, even, paradoxically, among party organizations dependent largely on their support.[34] Some of this nonparticipation is due to social causes particular to the nature of the American poor. But much of it is due to the fact that the rest of the population is not interested in having the poor participate in politics.

Throughout history, democracy has been spurred by the fact that in most nations the poor were the majority and the rich the minority. However, in many modern industrial societies, notably the contemporary United States, this is no longer quite true. Most Americans do not consider themselves poor—no matter how insecure they may be—and do not identify with the poor. We now have the spectacle of a society in which the minority does not, at least not openly, oppress the majority, but the other way around. For this, formal democratic institutions offer no cure. As long as most Americans remain convinced that the present economic system is just and desirable, it will remain in place, unaltered.

It is crucial to any reform, therefore, to convince the vast majority of middle class Americans (whether they really are a majority or not is beside the point, since they consider themselves to be such) that the present system of political and economic power is unjust and/or simply does not work. Whether such a system deserves to be called liberalism in the classic sense does not matter. A good case can be made that despite the rhetoric of competition (intensified by ideology and even by legislation in recent years) what we have in America today is an established corporate order, in which power is divided among the major interest groups, in a shifting balance that now even more than normally is severely tilted against those groups based on the poor and disadvantaged, and in which such things as the system of government subsidies and contracts and tax codes at various levels are the important arenas of adjustment. The only way to break through this curtain of confusion is by a long-term and precise enlightenment of the citizenry, and—leaving aside the extent to which the economically privileged control the channels of communication—there is a real question of how much enlightenment the American public really wants or can endure. Certainly, public opinion, especially the opinion of policy elites, plays a great role in our society; but on many issues, particularly the fundamental premises of our contemporary economic order, basic perceptions and familiar belief systems are too firmly entrenched to be changed save by a major obvious catastrophe, such as another Great Depression or a disastrous war.

What has been said about the letter as a whole — its failure to look at developing trends and try to assess them in systemic and realistic terms — is not quite applicable to one of its major parts. The section on food and agriculture is superior in most respects to the rest of the letter. It was originally drafted by a small committee of bishops from farm areas and later incorporated in the letter, and betrays its origins in its special merits which, based on first-hand knowledge of agriculture and its problems, include stress on the trend toward disappearance of the family farm (which they deplore on various grounds, including its greater efficiency compared to giant agribusiness) and the related importance of stewardship of the environment (which they rightly think will decline as agribusiness takes over the American land).

While the second draft of the bishops' letter is not written in stone, it is unlikely that any further major changes will be made. That is probably a pity, because as it stands, it is a flawed document. Yet it still has purposes. Even if the future is as uncertain as I have tried to indicate that it is, responsible human beings must act upon their best estimates of what it holds, ever alert to alter their beliefs and actions as new information unfolds. That the bishops have not done as well as they might to spot current trends and alert us to future possibilities, is a major practical weakness of the letter, but while they may fail to address systematically and adequately trends developing in our economy, the bishops deserve major applause for calling our attention to the broad problems, reminding us of the primacy of the poor, insisting that the existing American system is not God-given, and asking us to place it under the judgment of principles derived from the Gospel.

Notes

1. For a particularly hostile attack, alleging that the bishops are the prisoners of their staffs, see Dinesh D'Souza, "The Bishops as Pawns," *Policy Review* (Fall 1985): 50–56.

2. National Conference of Catholic Bishops, *Catholic Social Teaching and the U.S. Economy*, second draft (Washington, D.C.: United States Catholic Conference, 1985), 16.

3. *Catholic Social Teaching and the U.S. Economy*, 300.

4. Ibid., 129.

5. Ibid., 131.

6. Ibid., 28.

7. Ibid., 25.

8. See, for example, Barry Bluestone and Bennett Harrison, *The Deindustrialization of America: Plant Closings, Community Abandonment, and the Dismantling of Basic Industries* (New York: Basic Books, 1982).

9. See Edward Cornish, ed., *Communications Tomorrow: The Coming of the Information Society* (Washington: World Future Society, 1981); Wilson P. Dizard, Jr., *The Coming Information Age: An Overview of Technology, Economics, and Social Policy* (New York: Longman, 1982); and Yoneji Masuda, *The Information Society as Post-Industrial Society* (Washington: World Future Society, 1981).

10. *Catholic Social Teaching and the U.S. Economy*, 144.

11. Roger Draper, "The Golden Arm," *New York Review of Books*, XXXII (October 24, 1985): 46–52.

12. *Catholic Social Teaching and the U.S. Economy*, 101.

13. It should be noted in passing that, as one theologian has pointed out, Pope John Paul II, despite his aversion to some aspects of liberation theology, has in this encyclical in effect explicitly accepted the Marxist definition of man as first of all a producing rather than a rational animal. Gregory Baum, "Marxism on his Mind," *National Catholic Reporter*, March 29, 1985.

14. *Catholic Social Teaching and the U.S. Economy*, 99.

15. Ibid., 164.

16. Ibid., 144.

17. Spencer Rich, "Middle Class Jobs Remaining Stable," *Washington Post*, April 21, 1985.

18. *Catholic Social Teaching and the U.S. Economy*, 78.

19. Ibid., 102.

20. See Phillip Longman, "Justice Between Generations," *Atlantic Monthly* 225 (June 1985): 73–81.

21. For a summary of data on contemporary American poverty, see Christopher Jencks, "How Poor Are the Poor?," *New York Review of Books* XXXII (May 9, 1985): 41–48.

22. *Catholic Social Teaching and the U.S. Economy*, 56.

23. Robert Pear, " 'Living Standards' Can Be Confusing," *The New York Times*, April 28, 1985.

24. *Catholic Social Teaching and the U.S. Economy*, 87.

25. Ibid., 171.

26. Lay Commission on Catholic School Teaching, *Toward The Future: Catholic Social Thought and the U.S. Economy* (New York: American Catholic Committee, 1984), 32–33, 62.

27. *Catholic Social Teaching and the U.S. Economy*, 253.

28. Lester Thurow, "Losing the Economic Race," *New York Review of Books*, XXXI (September 27, 1984): 29–31.

29. *Catholic Social Teaching and the U.S. Economy*, 274.

30. Mancur Olson, *The Rise and Decline of Nations* (New Haven: Yale University Press, 1982).

31. *Food First News*, no. 20 (Winter 1985): 2.

32. *Catholic Social Teaching and the U.S. Economy*, 250.

33. Ibid., 130, 167, 308 for examples.

34. Frances Fox Piven and Richard A. Cloward, "Prospects for Voter Registration Reform: A Report of the Experiences of the Human SERVE Campaign", *PS* XXVIII (1985): 582–93.

GERALD M. MARA

Poverty and Justice: The Bishops and Contemporary Liberalism

GERALD MARA is Associate Dean for Research in the Graduate School at Georgetown University. He received his Ph.D. in political science from Bryn Mawr College.

I. Introduction

IN THEIR RECENTLY ISSUED draft pastoral letter, *Catholic Social Teaching and the U.S. Economy*, the U.S. Catholic Bishops have identified a "preferential option for the poor" as the cornerstone principle of a just society. A concern for those afflicted with poverty, hunger, or homelessness should, according to the bishops, be reflected in the fundamental purposes and concrete programs of the American economy and, by extension, of all those similarly situated. Accomplishing this is not simply a matter of constructing new social programs or creating more or different elements of the governmental bureaucracy, but one of "framing a new rational consensus that *all*

157

persons have rights in the economic sphere and that society has a moral obligation to take the necessary steps to ensure that no one among us is hungry, homeless, unemployed or otherwise denied what is necessary to live with dignity" (emphasis in text).[1]

On the surface, the political contours of this position seem reasonably clear. The bishops' urgings resemble far more those of Mario Cuomo and John Kenneth Galbraith than they do those of Jack Kemp and Milton Friedman. And for this reason, they have been accused by more than one critic of simply baptizing the liberal agenda. But does this charge stand closer scrutiny? Once we penetrate the surface, as the bishops say we must, and ask how these recommendations relate to a general teaching on the nature and value of economic life, do we find simply a restatement or refinement of contemporary liberalism?

This question is complicated substantially by the fact that both sides of the familiar liberal/conservative debate in American politics endorse important dimensions of philosophical (as opposed to partisan) liberalism. Neither Cuomo nor Kemp, Galbraith nor Friedman would dispute the claim that politics should limit itself to the protection of individuals' rights to pursue their own dreams and build their own lives. Nor would any of them allow the state to intrude inappropriately on the personal activities of citizens. That they disagree significantly over the implications of these requirements should not obscure the fact that there is as much consensus as conflict in their assessments of the nature and purpose of political institutions. This argument-within-agreement suggests that much of what passes for debate about principles in American politics is really an intramural contest between what Douglas MacLean and Claudia Mills have called two "strands of thought within the liberal traditions."[2] While liberals are committed to "equal respect for persons," they differ over what this commitment, in fact, means. One possibility is urged by the Harvard philosopher Robert Nozick who, in his influential book *Anarchy, State and Utopia* offers consummate praise of individual *freedom*. In Nozick's eyes, individual rights are so absolute as to condemn any active governmental efforts to redistribute the products of free enterprise as the bureaucratic equivalent of slave labor.[3] Alternatively, writers such as John Rawls, whose book, *A Theory of Justice*, has exerted enormous influence over the last fifteen years, urge us to interpret "equal respect" as demanding that each individual have, at a minimum, an equal chance to develop his own talents and realize his own ends. Thus, desirable political structures are not those which avoid at all costs crossing the boundaries set by individual freedom, but those which are most capable of supporting (through "activist" policies, if necessary) liberal *egalitarian* social arrangements.

By endorsing a preference for the poor and urging activist governmental policies, the bishops appear to side squarely not only with Cuomo and Galbraith, but also with the egalitarian strand of liberal theory. There is much to favor this assessment. The bishops themselves note a strong similarity between their position and Rawls's second principle of justice, which tolerates social and economic inequalities only if they work to the advantage of the least favored.[4] More generally, it seems obvious that, to some degree at least, the bishops' intention is to support the contemporary liberal position with respect to the issue of poverty. But this is hardly all they are trying to accomplish.

The real drift of their argument, I would suggest, is to encourage us to move far beyond the bounds of philosophical liberalism. Several commentators have emphasized that the bishops' specific endorsement of individual rights occurs within a broader recognition of communal interdependence. Accordingly, the rights which they champion cannot be — as they are in liberalism — those of isolated, self-interested egoists who are locked, if not in mortal combat, at least in impersonal competition. Predictably, commentators have responded to this in differing ways. For some, the bishops' discovery of community is a welcome rejection of the potentially heartless self-centeredness which they see infecting unrestrained liberalism.[5] For many critics, however, the bishops' emphasis on community represents a disappointing and damaging inclination toward socialism.[6] Other observers who recognize that the rights "strand" is as crucial to the bishops' presentation as the "community" strand, often conclude that the bishops have chosen an unsatisfactory, perhaps even incoherent, compromise for reasons that are more related to political pressures than to political principles.[7]

Whatever one's response to the logic of the argument and however one wishes to explain its genesis, it is clear that the bishops place themselves well outside the theoretical and practical parameters of liberalism. While they support many of the specific policies endorsed by egalitarian liberals, at key philosophical junctures they appear to be antagonistic to liberal principles. Yet the bishops' alternative does not amount to the simple affirmation of communal solidarity. While appealing to the natural liberal attraction to individual rights, they seek to place the notion of rights in a context which offers a more comprehensive vision of social and political life. To construct that vision, they appeal ultimately neither to rights nor to community, but to the idea of personal salvation.

But while this appeal allows the bishops to avoid siding exclusively with either liberal individualists or united communitarians,
it has the very serious drawback of appearing to be relevant only to
the community of the faithful. While the bishops admit that religious
convictions must be confirmed by human wisdom and experience,
their admission is not followed by any account of the good which
is defensible or accessible in purely human terms. However, such
an account would appear to be available within an important secular
alternative to both liberalism and communitarianism, an alternative
which has important connections with the tradition which implicitly
supports the bishops' own claims. This, at least, is what I propose
to argue in what follows.

II. Poverty and Liberalism

LIBERAL POLITICAL THOUGHT is rooted, above all, in a respect for individual choices. In the eyes of one of the earliest and most important
figures in the development of liberalism, John Locke, "to understand
political power right and derive it from its original, we must consider
what state men are naturally in, and that is a state of perfect freedom
to order their actions, and dispose of their possessions and persons
as they think fit, within the bounds of the law of nature without
asking leave, or depending upon the will of any other man."[8] The
primary function of government is, then, to protect freedom as much
as possible and to provide the conditions necessary for individuality
to flourish.

Of course, the activities of Locke's free individuals are not in-
determinate. They are guided by the universal desires, first, for
survival and, subsequently, for the material benefits and resources
which make life worthwhile. Both of these needs can be satisfied by
human labor, which enables men to acquire "those things as nature
affords for their subsistence" and those benefits able to contribute to
"the support and comfort of their being."[9] The central consequence
of Locke's focus on labor is the primacy of economic or productive activity. Material needs are met and the human condition is advanced
through the creation of poverty, the natural outcome of laboring.
Thus, Locke's glorification of labor and property is neither venal nor
philistine; admirable or excellent human beings are precisely those
who employ their productivity for their own well-being and, by extension, for the potential benefit of their fellows.

Although Locke's emphasis on the right to property has a contemporary echo in Nozick's work, most liberal theorists today reject

this focus as too confining. Instead, they see true freedom as the fulfillment of the potential for self-development. According to this perspective, the satisfaction of economic needs is a necessary but not a sufficient condition for a fully human existence. Although human beings cannot develop their expressive talents until their physical survival is secure, the unlimited pursuit of material gratification is viewed as a serious misordering of priorities, indicative of a stunted or immature personality (Howard Hughes?). This hierarchical perspective on individuality underlies Rawls's distinction between what he characterizes as "thin" and "full" theories of the good[10] and finds further support in the theories of psychological development of Abraham Maslow and Lawrence Kohlberg. In their eyes, praiseworthy human conduct is not simply productivity while playing by the rules; it is the construction and fulfillment of a multidimensional life-plan which, by definition, entails a variety of practices. One who lives thus resists the temptation to pursue a dominant end "to which all other ends are subordinate."[11] This theory of self-actualization likewise confines the legitimate activities of government to ensuring security; an activist government is dangerous not simply because of its threats to the rights of liberty and property but also because paternalism stultifies mature individuality.

It is important to realize that this praise of individual self-development refines rather than eliminates Locke's way of understanding human well-being. From the perspective of a free human life, the pursuit of economic goals, narrowly understood, must be integrated into a more complete life-plan. But this is not carried to the point of stipulating particular goals. Beyond the observation that a well-rounded development of one's talents is desirable, no attempt is made to say what specific content a fulfilled life should have. The accent is on individual freedom of choice and the individualistic character of personal life-plans means that human rationality is essentially instrumental. The reasonableness of a certain course of action depends on its effectiveness in achieving personal goals, rather than on its pursuing goals of a particular kind.

This avowed value neutrality cannot, however, be maintained, for it is necessarily in tension with the attachment to multidimensional life plans. The claim that multivariance is always more praiseworthy than single-mindedness must be defended rather than assumed. Any defense of multidimensionality would, however, necessarily depart from the cornerstone liberal principle that rational life plans are not subject to critical scrutiny.[12] And once liberals admit that there *are* better and worse ways of living, there is no good reason for focusing exclusively on breadth in assessments of relative quality. It is remarkable, for example, that Rawls's praise of inclusive as opposed to dominant ends pay so little attention to the *kinds* of dominant ends involved. Compared with the inclusive life, *any* plan shaped by a dominant end is "inhuman," "irrational," "mad" and self-disfiguring. But while the condemnation of single-minded misers or rakes is noncontroversial, the same can hardly be said of committed saints or heroes.[13] What results is a (paradoxically) single-minded evaluative perspective on human life: the extreme glorification of scope at the almost complete expense of substance.[14]

It should be clear that neither the protection of economic freedom nor the call to self-actualization particularly supports a preference for the poor. According to the Lockean perspective, the exercise of individual economic rights is bound only by a prohibition against violating others' rights. Given the dispersal of the capacity to labor among all reasonably healthy individuals, wealth and poverty are assumed to be largely matters of individual choice and responsibility. Moreover, Locke's portrait of the remarkable progress of historical labor assures the personally industrious that their own prosperity has the de facto consequence of increasing the common stock of benefits available to mankind. In a seventeenth century version of trickle-down economics, Locke proudly observes that even the most wretched day laborer in England is better off materially than a king in the primitive Americas, owing to the superior productivity of civilized economies.[15]

The fuller liberal praise of the actualized life avoids this narrow glorification of material goods. But it limits acquisition not in the name of charity or generosity but for the sake of a well-rounded personality. While nothing prevents a commitment to fight poverty from being included among personal satisfactions, there is nothing about self-fulfillment which would make that commitment essential to the fully developed life. The contrast between this position and that adopted by the bishops could hardly be more stark; whereas the bishops treat concern for the poor as morally obligatory, the liberal theory of self-development makes it optional—literally one alternative among many.

Both versions of liberal individualism thus consign the fate of the least advantaged to the contingent decisions of the admittedly self-gratifying or self-centered. Whatever we may think of Locke's optimism at the dawn of the industrial age, recent experience in even the most progressive democracies must make us suspicious of the likely social consequences of banking on egoistic individualism in this manner. Another school of liberal thought would appear to share that concern. Although utilitarianism is often thought to be synonymous with maximizing the most venal personal gratifications, the actual intention of those who created it was to develop general, rather than private or selfish, criteria for evaluating moral decisions.

While there are important differences among the utilitarian principles of such philosophers as Jeremy Bentham, Adam Smith, and John Stuart Mill, all agree that truly moral choices are those which maximize happiness for the largest number of persons involved in a particular interpersonal situation. To proceed on the basis of even the most enlightened *self*-interest is to distort seriously the nature of morality. Utilitarians do, however, disagree significantly over the nature and indicia of the greatest happiness to be pursued. Smith bases his economic utility almost solely on societal productivity. For Bentham, happiness is measured by the greatest possible excess of pleasure over pain. Mill's conception of utility challenges Bentham's refusal to make qualitative distinctions among pleasures. Instead, utility must be "utility in the largest sense, grounded in the permanent interests of man as a progressive being."[16] Attention to permanence and progressivity means that utility seeks the dominance of better desires and higher pleasures within the human community.

Mill's attempt to establish a hierarchy of pleasures may initially appear as simply an effort to avoid the most embarrassing consequences of an uninhibited hedonism. But its importance within utilitarianism strikes me as much more than that. All utilitarians must explain why a concern for the greatest happiness of the greatest number should effectively motivate the actions of individuals who are concerned primarily with maximizing their personal advantage. The only reasonable answer seems to be that benevolence can be personally rewarding or pleasurable. And this insight requires a psychology which recognizes more elevated motivations than the desires for acquisition or egoistic gratification. In a sense, Mills' permanent and progressive being is the only kind of person willing to act in accordance with the principle of utility. Thus, the pleasures of Mill's progressive being must presuppose developed sympathies and an elevated sense of what it means to be human.[17]

But in spite of the emphasis on benevolence which lies at the heart of utility at its best, there are serious difficulties in the way in which it, too, deals with the fate of the least favored, for there is no reason why the interests of the poor must coincide with the greatest public happiness (however defined). In many circumstances that are easily imagined, meeting the needs of the poor would, in fact, impair or diminish the welfare of society at large. In the opinion of some contemporary conservative economists, for example, expensive social programs feed inflation, which undermines general economic stability. Even when the greatest happiness is measured by standards other than purchasing power, policies designed to alleviate misery could be far less effective in furthering the *general* welfare than alternative strategies. For example, ameliorating the dismal educational or medical situations of the very poor might absorb resources which, if used in other ways, would greatly improve general levels of education or health care.[18]

Mill would certainly reject the empirical likelihood of a conflict between general welfare and concern for the least favored; his confidence in progress foresees technical advances that will overcome natural scarcity and social advances that will dissolve class conflicts. Thus, the disappearance of poverty is envisaged as one victory within the decisive human conquest of prejudice and ignorance.[19] In the late twentieth century, however, one can be allowed a greater degree of skepticism about the benevolence of the domination of nature by technology and about the solubility of human problems simply through rational care and effort. The experiences of the past century do not necessarily confound utilitarianism's intent to foster general happiness. But they do expose the naiveté of believing that all social interest can be accommodated without pain or deprivation. They underscore the likelihood of potential conflicts between the pursuit of the general good and the preference for the poor.

Neither individualism nor utilitarianism, then, seems capable of clarifying or justifying an option for the poor. For some, this conclusion simply underscores a sad but incontrovertible reality. However, liberalism's critics argue that the vulnerability of the poor to talented or aggressive individuals or to skilled architects of the general welfare is an indictment of the liberal framework itself. For poverty is not an ineradicable feature of the human condition but, rather a predictable consequence of a social system which fosters individuality and accumulation at the expense of fellow-feeling and generosity.

According to many of these critics, liberalism is flawed by at least two major theoretical deficiencies which contribute to its objectionable callousness toward the problems of the poor. The first, noted especially by proponents of a "communitarian" political theory, is its highly artificial portrait of social life. According to Jean Elshtain and Michael McGrath, liberalism views society as nothing more than a series of exchange relations among randomly interacting persons with no essential concern for one another's pursuits or welfare. But this portrait of individuals seriously distorts the ways in which cooperative practices shape, indeed create, personal goals and choices.[20] Individual pursuits and opinions, to say nothing of benefits and opportunities, are really products of concrete social environments. For communitarians, liberalism's artificial focus on separable individuals masks the fact that problems such as poverty are truly *social*, not only in their manifestations or consequences, but also in their primary causes.

A second major structural criticism concerns liberalism's implications for moral philosophy. Just as a distorting focus on individuals ignores the social causes of poverty, so liberalism's relatively undemanding treatment of the nature of moral obligation forecloses a number of possible solutions. According to this objection, any psychology whose premise is that "nature has placed mankind under the governance of two sovereign masters, pain and pleasure,"[21] is not well equipped to offer a moral teaching which challenges that which would be comfortable, gratifying or safe to do. Thus, Michael Novak, who has sought to build a theology of economic life on principles borrowed from liberal individualism, faces the very difficult task of supporting his calls for generosity with a psychology which admits that men are not angels and which proceeds on the basis of "ordinary and statistically more frequent motivations."[22] Of course, no relevant moral philosophy can rest on the assumption of widespread human angelicism. But it seems equally extreme to confess the inevitable sovereignty of pleasure and pain and, therein, to reject any possibility of an appeal to motivations beyond the statistically most frequent. Such a strategy threatens, among other things, to interpret clear instances of difficult, dangerous or self-sacrificing moral acts as exceptional rather than exemplary. It is to emphasize, that is, the conduct of Ray Kroc while minimizing the significance of Mother Teresa.[23]

III. A Theory of Justice

JOHN RAWLS'S VERSION of the liberal theory of justice clearly recognizes the difficulties attending both rights-based and utilitarian liberalism. Thus, his intent is to establish principles of justice which both recognize liberal premises *and* ensure that the needs of the least advantaged are effectively met. But is this really possible?

Rawls contends that the adoption of his two principles of justice is compelling for those who place themselves in what he calls the original position. That is, rational, mutually disinterested individuals concerned to further their own life plans but uncertain (shrouded in a "veil of ignorance") about all the particular details of their identities would naturally seek conditions favorable to the least advantaged. Now it seems clear that Rawls's psychological assumptions are generally congenial to mainstream liberalism. But he cannot award priority to the needs of the least favored without making significant alternations within some of the more problematic elements of liberal theory. Thus, while Rawls does not adopt the strong communitarian position that individual needs and practices are constituted by social structures, he recognizes the importance and inevitability of an "idea of social union" within truly just societies. Moreover, even though he believes that one of the key advantages of his theory is that it can be supported by relatively weak motivational suppositions, he nonetheless recognizes that a willingness to reason about moral questions as if we were shrouded in a veil of ignorance requires some degree of liberation from the desire for personal advancement.

If successful, Rawls's effort would seem to rescue liberal theory from the practical and theoretical problems which beset its treatment of the disadvantaged. But I want to suggest that it flounders, not because of oft-noted difficulties within the logic of his derivation of principles,[24] but because of problems directly connected with the centrality of a concern for the least favored in his most just society. In this context, one can quarrel particularly with the abstract character of his second principle of justice and with the inadequacy of his moral psychology. I think these problems emerge with particular clarity when we compare Rawls's strategy with that of the bishops.

For the bishops, a personal and societal concern for the poor is an integral part of the biblical teaching on justice. This teaching confronts men of good will directly in the words of Scripture, the prophets and the church. Although Rawls begins his treatise on social justice with a recognition of our "intuitive conviction of the primacy of justice," he proceeds to clarify and support that intuition through a "thought experiment" in which self-interested individuals plagued by uncertainty prudently decide to minimize the worst that could happen.

The variation between these two approaches is not simply traceable to differences between religious and secular orientations. Rather, it concerns the initiating question of those confronting the words of Scripture on the one hand and the choice under uncertainty on the other. For Rawls, the choice of the second principle of justice is contingent on the answer given to the question: how shall I fare? For the bishops, the demand that the lives of the poor be improved is a significant part of the answer to a quite different question: what should I do? The difference is fundamental. The bishops assume the necessity of appealing to the moral, as distinct from narrowly prudential, interests, and make no pretense of trying to derive the former from the latter.

This difference over motivational assumptions is connected in turn to another difference—over what the definition of poverty is. For Rawls, poverty is operationally defined as the occupation of the least favored position in a society. It is a relative designation; short of conditions of complete equality, any society, no matter what its character, includes some who are *least* favored. This conception of poverty follows directly from Rawls's reliance on the priorities and decisions of rational contractors. His assumptions about the motivations of the partners in the original position suggest that it is rational for them to choose those principles whose worst outcomes would be least damaging. Accordingly, the uncertain architects of the just society would prudently imagine themselves as occupying its least favored position and having done so, take into account the interests of persons thus situated. For the bishops, however, poverty is defined much more objectively or categorically; what they have in mind is a lack of the most basic physical resources, such as food, shelter, and clothing.

A final and related difference between the way in which Rawls conceives of the problem of justice and that of the bishops concerns the role of a preferential option for the poor as a principle for evaluating the relative justice or injustice of existing societies. Rawls believes that the applicability of the two principles of justice can be waived only in situations of severe underdevelopment. The principles adopted by the partners in his hypothetical choice situation thus apply in a simple and straightforward manner to any society except the most backward (where the resources to pursue justice in Rawls's sense will almost surely be lacking). But the bishops, while supporting the preferential option for the poor with what they take to be universally valid theological principles, also insist that its application in particular cases depends heavily on contextual considerations (the "signs of the times"). Thus, the demand to remedy economic inequality is contingent on the level of absolute poverty which exists in a given community at a given historical period.

I believe that this comparison reveals significant shortcomings in Rawls's attempt to make a concern for the least favored *the* dominant social principle. While this principle has been outlined much earlier, let me now repeat it in its most fully developed form in Rawls's own words. "Social and economic inequalities shall be arranged so that they are both:

(a) to the greatest benefit of the least advantaged ... and

(b) attached to offices and positions open to all under conditions of fair equality of opportunity."

Both principles of justice can be summarized by a general conception which states: "All social primary goods—liberty and opportunity, income and wealth, and the bases for self-respect—are to be distributed equally unless an unequal distribution of any or all of these goods is to the advantage of the least favored."[25]

My initial reservations about Rawls's second principle relate to its categorical character. As many critics have observed, a strict enforcement of the second principle would require that even very important improvements in the general welfare be foregone if they would result in even the smallest disadvantage to the least favored.[26] This implication is particularly unsettling once we remember that Rawls insists on defining poverty in relative terms. His argument applies just as much to the least favored in wealthy as in poor societies. Although Rawls's priorities do recognize the severity of many relative deprivations, it seem anomalous, to say the least, to ignore the implications of different levels of wealth among developed societies in the construction of principles of justice. While Rawls rightly objects that utilitarianism does not do justice to questions of distribution, his fixation on distribution to the exclusion of considerations of need threatens to excise all attention to the common good from his theory of justice.

One of the most significant but least appreciated advantages of the bishops' position is that it resists the temptation to impose the preferential option for the poor as an abstract principle prior to an interpretation of existing social and historical circumstances. Their substantive definition of poverty prevents the immediate subordination of other important goods to the needs of the least favored in cases where the latter may not, in fact, merit priority. The bishops' concern with the changing contours of empirical circumstances is, in fact, likely to produce a more resolute opposition than Rawls's theory to existing instances of extreme want. A potential dark side to Rawls's commitment to generality is abstraction from the most visible features of actual economic deprivation. Because his principles are designed to combat inequality, rather than poverty per se, they lack the urgency of the bishops' demands. His principles of justice seem too universal to address particular distributive problems occurring among identifiable groups or individuals at particular times.[27] For the bishops, though, particulars constitute the field of application for moral action; hence their admirable concern to differentiate among the responsibilities of various economic and political agents.

However, the most important contrast between Rawls's position and that endorsed by the bishops concerns moral psychology. What is required to elicit support for the preference for the poor? What is required to make it effective motivationally? Rawls deliberately avoids appealing to anything other than self-interest to prevent his principles of justice from resting on an unrealistic assumption of general altruism.[28] But he is forced to replace the seemingly problematic inclination to benevolence with a series of motivational and cognitive stipulations which, while perhaps unobjectionable in themselves, combine to paint a highly contrived portrait of human beings. Ultimately, Rawls faces the same problem as Kant in explaining why individuals who are committed primarily to furthering their own life-plans can be motivated to participate in the uncertain "choice game" of the original position. In light of this and other significant ambiguities, Rawls's dismissal of benevolence as hopelessly complicated and unrealistic strikes me as being itself ultimately unrealistic — and arbitrary. He does not appear to appreciate fully the limits or exclusiveness of his own psychological assumptions.

We touch here on a fundamental problem of liberal theory which is by no means unique to Rawls. It is not nearly so easy as Rawls believes to derive relatively demanding principles of justice and morality from relatively undemanding motivational principles. Rawls's theory of morality is heavily influenced by the premise that rational individuals put first things (the fulfillment of their life-plans) first. Obviously, this perspective on human motivation can support a number of moral demands. But it is difficult to believe that it can serve as the basis for all of the actions that would be encompassed by even a *relatively* demanding moral philosophy. In Rawls's eyes, a moral act advances another's good at minimal risk to the agent. Where the risk to the agent is more than minimal, such an action can be classified as supererogatory — admirable and praiseworthy, but not binding or required. Much the same applies to acts to benefit the least advantaged of the sort that Rawls says are required if we are to be just. But our obligation to be just in this instance is limited to that behavior which would be consistent with our personal definition of our self-interest. This raises the obvious question of why we should be just in the first place. And it takes more than the appeal to something like the hypothetical original position to provide a convincing reply.

The bishops implicitly reject the notion that our way of thinking about these issues must be constrained by the inevitable influence of the needs for personal gratification and security. Instead, they seek to appeal directly to certain values and principles which are capable of shaping our personal satisfactions. The "dignity of the human person" which is "the criterion against which all aspects of economic life must be measured" demands that individuals conduct themselves in partial recognition, at least, of what is needed to respect that dignity.[29] In David Norton's secular language, the bishops believe that ideals can legitimately influence the development and articulation of interests.[30] The fulfillment of one's own life-plan is not an unalterable given which precedes the discovery and pursuit of what is required for moral action. Rather, life-plans can and should include the insights supplied by the demands to act well in certain definite ways.

IV. Beyond Liberalism

THE DEFICIENCIES OF Rawls's position, as highlighted in comparison with that of the bishops, raise serious doubts as to whether an effective preferential option for the poor can be coherently defended even within an extensively revised version of philosophical liberalism. Liberalism's avowed neutrality about the worth of alternative life plans means that it must be, to say the least, modest in its expectations for other-regarding behavior. Thus, Rawls's thin theory of the good, which stipulates that human beings generally desire more rather than less of those resources (such as wealth, power and liberty) which allow them to reach their highest level of personal satisfaction, effectively justifies Michael Novak's decision to focus on "statistically more frequent motivations" in the articulation of a morality of economic life. That such motivations are inadequate to generate a truly effective concern for the poor is increasingly obvious once contemporary liberals begin to address the issue. One can acquire such concern only by rejecting or forgetting (as Rawls does, I think) some of the most significant features of liberal psychology. That some individuals do, in fact, amend liberalism in this way says nothing, however, about the character of liberalism per se.

Thus, while the bishops' statement is presented in a language of rights that is easily confused with liberal egalitarianism, it rests, in reality, upon a significant departure from some of liberalism's most fundamental tenets. According to the bishops, an adequate understanding of human life recognizes its inherent sociability. "To be human is to hear the call to community."[31] Economic and social institutions do not simply referee independent interactions; they do things for and to people and thus can be legitimately examined and altered to maximize benefits and to minimize damage. Moreover, while the bishops are not blind to human imperfections, they nonetheless "insist" that the gifts of God involve corresponding responsibilities, which are not limited by but are challenges to our self-interest and personal advancement. Economic justice does not rest on ordinary psychological motivations but on a demand that we act upon "a sense of what is right or should happen."[32]

However, while the bishops' sense of the need to depart from liberal principles is penetrating, their success in offering clear alternatives is problematic. Two key deficiencies within the bishops' position emerge if we return to the "dialogue" between the draft pastoral and *A Theory of Justice*.

As noted, the bishops resist a Rawlsian elevation of the abstract second principle of justice to dominant status in favor of a more context-dependent sensitivity to the needs of the objectively destitute in definite social and historical environments. But the other side of this sensitivity to context is that what the bishops have to say is insufficiently general to serve as a comprehensive principle of social justice. While the existence of "poor, hungry and homeless people in our midst" leads to the very radical condemnation of *any* inequalities in income and wealth,[33] the bishops are almost completely silent on the criteria to be used for determining just distributions of wealth and power should the signs of the times improve. From what is said in the letter, the bishops vision of the just society recognizes only "the minimal conditions for community." While they appropriately resist the Rawlsian mania for universality, their reluctance to employ biblical principles for substantially more than a vigorous denunciation of existing injustice is a serious deficiency within their avowed purpose of articulating a Christian vision of economic life.

Moreover, while the bishops rightly insist that moral principles rise above the common and the comfortable, Rawls's suspicion of assumptions of general benevolence is neither sinister nor absurd. The bishops' rejection of a moral psychology limited by narrow self-interest must be followed by a positively stated and humanly accessible alternative. Without it, their position would be vulnerable to the "realist" objection that their moral injunctions are not simply demanding but imaginary. To their credit, the bishops avoid suggesting that the preferential option for the poor is simply a prima facie duty which compels performance apart from any reference to human motivations and possibilities. From the bishops' perspective, George Kateb's judgment that our duty to remedy the misery of others is both absolute in its demand and intuitively obvious in its justification needs to be defended in light of a fuller account of the human good.[34] Moreover, a coherent *human* standard is a necessary condition for the coherent *social* standard which is not completely presented in the draft pastoral. To what extent is that standard expressed or implied in the pages of the draft pastoral?

V. Community, Salvation and Flourishing

THE BISHOPS' CLEAREST DEPARTURE from the psychology of contemporary liberalism is, of course, their recognition of the human tendency to community. Relationships to and solidarity with others are not simply benefits of which free individuals *may* avail themselves. Rather they are constitutive of or essential to human life. Politically, the pursuit of common benefits not only requires but also involves an active political community whose legitimate functions extend far beyond protection. Consistent with their community orientation, the bishops picture this activism in participationist rather than bureaucratic terms. The "principle of subsidiarity" which "states that government should undertake only those initiatives necessary for protecting basic justice which exceed the capacity of individuals or private groups independently" makes the bishops as opposed to unnecessary centralization as is the staunchest libertarian.[35] However, their alternative to overarching control is not free-floating individualism but, rather, a local self-reliance characterized by the creative and critical participation of all individuals united by a common enterprise or problem.

In these psychological and political pronouncements, then, the bishops seem to reject individualism and the night watchman state in favor of a cooperative and participationist pursuit of the common good. However, the bishops' particular version of the common good orientation is not simply equivalent to that espoused in communitarian political theory.[36] "Community" itself is a notoriously ambiguous concept which is often defined less by what it offers than by what it rejects. For example, "community" may affirm the presence of a common procedure through which all members interactively create binding norms or goals for a society. As Mark Roelofs has shown, however, there is nothing to prevent a community, thus understood, from establishing a privatistic acquisitiveness as the dominant behavioral norm.[37] Even if we agree that a society's goals, and not simply its procedures, should reflect men's essential commonality, historical experience gives us a bewilderingly diverse range of authentically common goals to choose from. It goes without saying that at least some of these common pursuits may do considerably more damage to the human condition than uninhibited individualism.[38] It is, of course, unlikely that a well-integrated community could allow vast discrepancies of wealth among its members. But I doubt that the bishops are any more willing than thoughtful secular commentators to praise a community solely on the grounds that it avoids economic injustice. The solution to the problems attending liberal freedom cannot be completely supplied by the discovery of community. By implication, then, the bishops reject the tendency present in much of contemporary political thinking to require exclusive choices between individual freedom and common welfare or solidarity.[39] Rather, the bishops seem to maintain a respect for both goals—they recognize that all individuals have *rights* in the economic sphere *and* that human life is essentially communitarian—within a more comprehensive vision.

In theological terms, this vision is the message of salvation. While essentially intertwined with Christian eschatology, the idea of salvation is extended by the bishops to include the demand that "Christians . . . embody in their lives the ethos of the new creation while they labor under the weight of the old," and that they not only recognize but also live up to "the dignity of the human person."[40] As a religious formulation, however, this standard may serve as a moral appeal only to members of the community of the faithful or to that much smaller group of people who order their lives in accordance with religious principles. Moreover, Scripture, like secular moral philosophy, recognizes that ought implies can. And what human beings can and cannot reasonably be expected to do is not a clear premise from which scriptural interpretation can confidently proceed. For example, differences over human psychology allow the bishops and Novak to interpret the scriptural teaching on economic life in dramatically different ways.

The bishops' failure to provide a precise elaboration, much less a convincing defense, of the psychology which underlies their exhortations is perhaps the most damaging theoretical shortcoming of their effort. This is especially true in light of their avowed intention to provide a theology of economic life and their clear recognition that religious teachings must be confirmed by human wisdom and experience.[41] This deficiency in the pastoral requires us to search for a plausible account of the human good which might be consistent with the bishops' position. I want to suggest that such an account is available within a closely related tradition of moral and political theory.

The tradition I have in mind is the Aristotelian perspective on human flourishing or excellence. Like the challenge to salvation, the call to excellence recognizes that any defensible option for the poor requires a prior description of the value and limitations of economic goods within the broader panoply of human goods. In Book One of Aristotle's *Politics*, for example, *oikonomikē*, the art of managing the household (*oikos*), is not the efficient accumulation of as many material possessions as possible. Rather, the practitioner of that art, the manager or ruler of the household, the *oikonomikos*, aims at ensuring the highest quality of life possible within the limits of the institution for all of the household's members.[42] It is this purpose which limits the practice of the art of acquisition (*Chrēmatistikē*) to supplying the resources needed for the household's broader activities.[43] Even when understood solely in terms of its own horizon, then, *oikonomikē* is not narrowly selfish or materialistic. Moreover, the household itself is not the most excellent of human associations. The city (*polis*) is its superior, both for providing the guidance necessary for the household's completing its own task and for offering a peculiar good or value not available through the household. This political good is moral virtue (*aretē ēthikē*), the quality of character which allows a person to be praised and emulated.[44]

The morally virtuous person's attitude toward material accumulation will reflect the decidedly partial or subordinate character of economic goods. The proper attitude toward material things is neither greed nor asceticism, but a certain kind of moderation as regards one's own needs and a certain kind of magnanimity or generosity toward others.[45] Thus, governmental policies to alleviate misery are not understood simply as social engineering, but also as part of the city's overall efforts to assist in the development of a morally virtuous character.[46]

It is important to note that this praise of moderation and magnanimity does not, in Aristotle's view, require us to assume unrealistically that human beings are altruistic or benevolent. Aristotle builds upon the common opinion that material goods or acquisitions are subordinate to the broader goals pursued within the household. Upon reflection, the goods of the household appear to be limited or partial, although they point beyond themselves to those benefits which are, in the best of circumstances, available exclusively in the city. The fact that the moral excellences are pursued or encouraged only infrequently and imperfectly does not, then, compromise their appropriateness for human behavior at its best. Aristotle's account of human virtue or flourishing rests, for him, on a view of human possibility which is at once natural or "realistic" and resolutely normative and challenging. It takes human nature very seriously, but at the same time is not content to take what is "statistically most frequent" as the last word.[47]

IV. Charity and Virtue

WITHIN A CHALLENGING VIEW of human perfection along the order of that articulated by Aristotle, a concern for the poor might well be, in this day and age, an essential component. Such an attachment to human excellence can perhaps explain and deepen Ronald Dworkin's conviction that the citizens of a truly just society should categorically reject any urge to purchase a materially stable future by ignoring current needs of the poor as an insult to human integrity.[48] What Dworkin identifies as *the* characteristic mark of liberal societies cannot be accounted for without moving beyond liberal principles. Nonetheless, a contemporary discussion of excellence informed by Aristotelian principles will be reluctant to *define* human virtue simply as the concern to alleviate misery. Just as the concentration on freedom outshines questions about how we use our freedom, so the consummate praise of charity ignores too many other activities (such as intellectual accomplishment, personal integrity and the practice of a kind of justice which goes beyond the commitment to a fair distribution of resources) which must be part of an excellent or complete human existence. From the perspective of human excellence, then, any concern for distribution within moral and political thought, be it Catholic, liberal or socialist, must always be defensible in terms of a more inclusive account of the human good.[49]

The bishops' own position on this question is, as I have suggested, disappointingly vague. But if they are even half right about what is required for us today in ordering our economic life, this account must, even if it confirms the relative desirability of many partisan liberal policies, depart significantly from the philosophical liberal framework. In short, the bishops seem thoroughly justified in their ambition to forge a new vision of economic life. That they succeed only partially is undeniable. But in demanding a more responsive and elevating view of economic activity, the bishops make a substantial and innovative contribution to debates critically affecting the public interest. And by making that demand in a letter addressed to persons of good will, the bishops help to extend a broadly philosophic search beyond the narrowly philosophic bounds of the academy. This is not the least of the services rendered by a document whose obvious flaws should not blind us to its considerable significance.

Notes

1. National Conference of Catholic Bishops, *Catholic Social Teaching and the U.S. Economy*, first draft (Washington, D.C.: United States Catholic Conference, 1984), 338.

2. Douglas MacLean and Claudia Mills, eds., *Liberalism Reconsidered* (Totowa, N.J.: Rowman and Allanheld, 1983), ix–x.

3. Robert Nozick, *Anarchy, State, and Utopia* (New York: Basic Books, 1974), 169.

4. John Rawls, *A Theory of Justice* (Cambridge: Harvard University Press, 1971), 75.

5. For two measured and different defenses of the bishops' endorsement of a kind of community, see R. Bruce Douglass, "At the Heart of the Letter," and Nancy S. Barrett, "The Case for Collaboration," *Commonweal* 112 (1985): 357–67.

6. Michael Novak never refers to the bishops' letter explicitly. But the timing of the publication of *Toward the Future* strongly suggests its responsive and critical posture vis-à-vis the bishops' presentation. Novak is, of course, intensely concerned to defend the virtues of liberal capitalism against unidentified contemporary socialist onslaughts. Cf. Michael Novak, *Toward the Future: Catholic Social Thought and the U.S. Economy* (New York: American Catholic Committee, 1984), 48.

7. This can, of course, be interpreted positively as a respect for pluralism and a recognition of the incredible complexity of the social and technical issues involved or negatively as bordering on a kind of intellectual dishonesty. For a generally favorable assessment of the multiplicity of the bishops' concerns, see John P. Langan, S. J., "The Bishops and the Bottom Line," *Commonweal* 111 (1984): 586–92. A much more critical posture is taken by Andrew M. Greeley, "The Bishops and the Economy: A 'Radical' Dissent," *America* (Jan. 12, 1985): 19–24.

8. John Locke, *Second Treatise of Government*, sec. 4.

9. *Second Treatise*, sec. 26.

10. *A Theory of Justice*, 395–99.

11. Ibid., 552.

12. So, Brian Barry admits that a coherent liberalism must rest "on the proposition that some ways of life, some types of character are more admirable than others." See *The Liberal Theory of Justice* (New York: Oxford University Press, 1973), 126–27.

13. For an expanded statement of this criticism, see Victor Gourevitch, "Rawls on Justice," *Review of Metaphysics* 28 (1975): 485–510 at 499–501.

14. It can be argued, of course, that Mill's glorification of scope is itself a substantial affirmation. Thus, in spite of his express intentions, Mill may offer a definitive teaching on the content of the best life. As such, this teaching can be interrogated and challenged. Mill himself seems to experience some discomfort at the thought of preferring versatility, simply, to any sort of narrowness. While it is better to be Pericles than either John Knox or Alcibiades, the narrow morality of Knox is preferable to the spectacular fluidity of the opportunistic Alcibiades. (Cf. *On Liberty*, chap. 3, par. 8).

15. *Second Treatise*, sec. 41.

16. *On Liberty*, chap. 1, par. 11.

17. Cf. *Utilitarianism*, chap. 2, par. 6; chap. 5, par. 20.

18. Cf. John C. Harsanyi, "Can the Maximin Principle Serve as the Basis for Morality?" *American Political Science Review* 69 (1975): 594–606 at 596–97.

19. *Utilitarianism*, chap. 2, par. 14.

20. Cf. Jean Bethke Elshtain, "Liberal Heresies: Existentialism and Repressive Feminism"; Michael J. G. McGrath, "On Radical Individualism and

Social Justice: A Critique of Robert Nozick's Political Theory," in McGrath, ed., *Liberalism and the Modern Polity* (New York: M. Dekker, 1979), 33–61 and 273–97, respectively.

21. Jeremy Bentham, *The Principles of Morals and Legislation*, chap. 1.

22. *Toward the Future*, 23–24.

23. Ibid., 41.

24. Cf. *The Liberal Theory of Justice*.

25. *A Theory of Justice*, 302–303.

26. Cf. Harsanyi, "Can the Maximin Principle Serve as a Basis for Morality?" 596–97.

27. This is, of course, in part due to Rawls's specific intention to avoid recommending "distributions of particular goods to particular individuals who may be identified by their proper names." Rawls's alternative, rather, is to proceed from the point of view of "representative persons holding the various social positions." *A Theory of Justice*, 64.

28. *A Theory of Justice*, 437–39.

29. *Catholic Social Teaching and the U.S. Economy*, 343.

30. David Norton, "Can Fanaticism Be Distinguished from Moral Idealism?" *Review of Metaphysics* 30 (1977): 497–507.

31. *Catholic Social Teaching and the U.S. Economy*, 343.

32. Ibid., 346.

33. Ibid., 352. This claim is softened somewhat in the Second Draft, which "calls into question extreme inequities of income and consumption when so many lack basic necessities." Cf. *Catholic Social Teaching and the U.S. Economy*, second draft (Washington, D.C.; United States Catholic Conference: 1985), 266.

34. George Kateb, "The Night Watchman State," *The American Scholar* (Winter 1975–76): 816–26 at 824.

35. *Catholic Social Teaching and the U.S. Economy*, first draft, 355.

36. For a clear and concise discussion of communitarian principles, especially as they relate to the various strands of liberalism, see especially, Michael J. Sandel, "Morality and the Liberal Ideal," *The New Republic*, May 1984. The classic affirmation of the splendor of communitarian politics is, however, to be found in the work of Hannah Arendt, especially *The Human Condition* (Chicago: University of Chicago Press, 1958) and "What is Freedom?" in *Between Past and Future* (New York: Viking, 1968).

37. H. Mark Roelofs, "Hobbes, Liberalism and America," in Michael J. G. McGrath, ed., *Liberalism and the Modern Polity*, 119–42.

38. As the bishops clearly recognize in their second draft, "(e)fforts to achieve social solidarity that do not take into account (the) limits on knowledge and love may only end by suppressing human freedom and degenerating into oppression." *Catholic Social Teaching and the U.S. Economy*, Second Draft, 265.

39. Cf. Philip Abbot, "The Tyranny of Fraternity in McWilliams' America," *Political Theory* 2 (1974): 169–95. For Stephen Salkever ("Freedom, Participation, and Happiness," *Political Theory* (5), 1977: 391–413), these are, of course, not the only alternatives. Salkever believes that an Aristotelian focus on happiness can allow the adoption of what is best in both the

liberty and the community paradigms while avoiding victimization by the shortcomings of either.

40. *Catholic Social Teaching and the U.S. Economy*, first draft, 345.

41. Ibid., 343. This admission is, if anything, stronger in the Second Draft. Cf. *Catholic Social Teaching and the U.S. Economy*, second draft, 265.

42. *Politics*, 1259b.

43. *Politics*, 1257b.

44. *Nicomachean Ethics*, 1101b.

45. *Nicomachean Ethics*, 1122a – 1123a.

46. *Politics*, 1267a.

47. This conclusion supports contemporary efforts to understand moral and political problems from a perspective informed by Aristotelian principles. See G. E. M. Anscombe, "Modern Moral Philosophy," reprinted in W. E. Hudson, ed. *The Is-Ought Question* (London: Macmillan and Co., Ltd., 1969) 175–95; Henry B. Veatch, "The Rational Justification of Moral Principles: Can There Be Such a Thing?" *Review of Metaphysics* 29 (1975): 217–38; Salkever, "Freedom, Participation, and Happiness"; "Who Knows Whether It's Rational to Vote?" *Ethics* 90 (1980): 203–217.

48. Ronald Dworkin, "Neutrality, Equality and Liberalism," in McLean and Mills, ed., *Liberalism Reconsidered*, 1–11 at 11.

49. So, in the *Politics* Aristotle rejects the suggestion of Phaleas of Chalcedon that economic problems be solved through radical egalitarianism or property. What is needed instead is character development which makes unlimited acquisition and covetousness undesirable. Cf. *Politics*, 1266b–1267b.

Diane Yeager

The Bishops and the Kingdom

DIANE YEAGER is an Assistant Professor
in the Department of Theology at
Georgetown University. She received her
Ph.D. in religion from Duke University.

I. Introduction

MOST DISCUSSIONS OF the pastoral letter on the economy recently released by the U.S. bishops are founded on the assumption that the letter shows the substantive influence of Latin American liberation theology in both its conceptual grounding and its policy recommendations. There is, to be sure, a certain superficial resemblance. Drawing heavily on biblical resources, the bishops criticize consumer capitalism, calling for greater frugality and simplicity; they emphasize community and solidarity; and they employ treatment of the poor and the marginated as the index of social justice, bringing forward and endorsing the preferential option for the poor. Whether this resemblance is anything more than superficial is a question that deserves more careful examination than it has ordinarily received. While the social agenda and phrasing are suggestive of similarity, at deeper levels of approach and conceptualization the relationship of the pastoral letter to the work of the Latin American theologians proves more problematic. The study of this question is relevant, of course, to an accurate assessment of what the bishops have undertaken and accomplished in this document. Its greater importance, however, resides in its capacity to bring to light the degree to which the governing theological paradigm of Latin American liberation theology varies from the theological paradigm that has traditionally shaped Roman Catholic reflection on the relation of the church and the world.

As a means of moving to this deeper level of analysis, it is appropriate and helpful to set *Catholic Social Teaching and the U.S. Economy* against the historical background provided by the two-volume study *The Social Teaching of the Christian Churches* by Ernst Troeltsch. Though more than three-quarters of a century old, this work remains the most systematic available assessment of the worldly activities of the Christian churches, and what elevates it to the level of a classic text is the author's determination to discover and display the way in which fundamental theological principles cooperate with the complexity of particular historical situations to produce differing conceptions of the relations that ought to obtain between Christianity and culture. Both a sociologist and a theologian, Troeltsch traces the development of the self-understanding of Christian social groups from the earliest scattered gentile communities through the rise of the sacramental church as an institution to the "ascetic protestantism" of the eighteenth century.

In the course of this survey, he offers a provocative and extended analysis of the theoretical difficulties that attend Christian efforts to define the role of the individual Christian and of the institutional church in a fallen world. On the basis of that analysis, Troeltsch then argues the thesis that only twice in the first eighteen hundred years of its existence did the Christian community develop a viable paradigm by means of which some sort of integral connection could be conceived to obtain between religious and social responsibilities. The first of these was the hierarchical ordering of the nature and the supernatural achieved by St. Thomas Aquinas through his appropriation of the idea of "relative natural law" from the Stoics. The second was the theocratic conception of a Christian social order developed by John Calvin.

Troeltsch's reasons for undertaking this comprehensive task are instructive. Like so many Christians of his time, he was deeply concerned about the human misery arising as a consequence of the industrialization of Western culture, and it was with some enthusiasm that he accepted an invitation to write a review of *The Cooperation of the Church in the Solution of the Social Problem* by Nathusius. He judged it to be a "miserable book" that provided no sound foundation for its emotional call to action; moreover, Troeltsch discovered "that there were no books in existence which could serve as a basis for the study of such a question, and then I began to try to lay the foundation for such a study myself."[1] Though he ends his study with a section titled "Developments in Christian Social Doctrine since the Eighteenth Century," he is not able to describe the paradigm that will succeed that of "ascetic protestantism" and be matched to the sociological situation of the modern industrial state. He brings his study to a close with the assertion that "If the present social situation is to be controlled by Christian principles, thoughts will be necessary which have not yet been thought, and which will correspond to this new situation as the older forms met the need of the social situation of earlier ages."[2]

II.

TROELTSCH IS QUITE EXPLICIT in describing the difficulty Christians have experienced in their periodic efforts to connect the Christian religious program with the project of social reform. The roots of the problem are to be found in the apocalyptic character of the teachings of Jesus, reinforced by the paradoxes of Pauline theology, in which

> the duty of the recognition and use of social phenomena as organizations and institutions — which did not come into existence without God's permission and which contain an element of good — mingled with a spirit of inner detachment and independence, since, after all, these things belong to a perishing world and are everywhere steeped in paganism.[3]

Thus, while theologians have always held that one of the principal characteristics of the Christian religion is an organic union of religion with morality and theology with ethics, this union has generally been conceived in terms of "the sanctification of the individual in all his moral activity for the sake of God, or that 'purity of heart' which, when the Kingdom has actually come, will enable a man to 'see God'."[4] Thus, the Gospel ethic, "marked by emphasis on purity of intention and a greatly intensified reverence for all moral

commands, without any allowance for conflicting motives or for expediency,"[5] produced a social group which has always had difficulty
defining its proper relationship to the political order and its proper
attitude toward the non-Christian communities with which it shares
a common social context. With the erosion of agrarian culture and
the rise of a money economy, the relation of the Christian community
to the institutions and practices of the prevailing economic order became similarly problematic.

Repudiation of "the world, the flesh, and the devil" is one solution. Ascetic disregard for physical and social concerns has func-
tioned in most ages as a measure of holiness. The history of Christianity is rich with monastic movements and religious sects which turn
in upon themselves in the creation of isolated, coherent religious
communities dedicated to the internal practice of the gospel ethic
but indifferent to the reform of the political, social, and economic
habits of the surrounding society. Jesus, of course, taught neither
asceticism nor isolation. As Troeltsch points out, "The ethic of Jesus
is heroic rather than ascetic."[6] Moreover,

> In the eyes of Jesus the ordinary life of humanity, in spite of
> its sin, was full of traces of the Divine goodness, and He recog-
> nized the naive and natural accents of piety in children, sin-
> ners, and Samaritans; to Him the dividing-line was not drawn
> between the world and the Church, but between the present
> and the future.[7]

World-denying activities must be read, therefore, not as disciplined
response to the mandate of Scripture, but rather as a reasoned, if
not wholly satisfactory, solution to the experience of conflict which
began to emerge as early as the second century. The persistence of
time and the growth of the Christian communities complicated the
simple, pure project of the original religious fellowship of love.

The source of the conflict can be found in the shifting and uncertain Christian understanding of the significance of history and the
value of life in time in the economy of redemption. Practically speaking, this vacillation results from the struggle of the Christian community to bring the teachings of Jesus to bear on a history stretch-
ing out far longer than Jesus apparently expected. Theologically,
the vacillation results from fundamental and probably unresolvable
ambiguities arising from the doctrinal dialectic by means of which
Christian systematic theology has sought to hold together as complementary truths claims that otherwise are held to be contradictory.
Christians confess both the transcendence and the immanence of

God, the simultaneity of freedom and dependency, the injustice of the created world and the justice of its Creator. Most importantly for present purposes, Christians affirm both that human beings are created in the image of God, godlike in freedom and moral responsibility, and that human beings are afflicted with sin which compromises that freedom and infects all human activity.

Aside from paradoxes intrinsic to the teachings, the conflict was made more acute by sociological changes in the early church. While the first communities had been made up primarily of slaves, freemen, laborers, and artisans who exercised little economic or political power, later converts came increasingly from among the educated and wealthy; these Christians struggled with the question of whether the gospel ethic which governed the Christian fellowship was meant for broader application. Moreover, as the Christian fellowship itself became larger, more widely dispersed, and more diverse, it developed its own internal requirements for organization, regularization, and hierarchical governance. In response to this need, the complex sociological reality of the patriarchal sacramental church took shape. Troeltsch notes, "the term 'the world' came to be regarded as a synonym for all those social institutions of life outside the Church."[8]

Christians are a people who live in hope, but it is not at all clear that Christian hope pertains to *this* world. Neither scriptural exegesis nor the theological tradition can define authoritatively the correct posture of a Christian with respect to the sinful world. Thus, except for the two cultural and religious achievements identified by Troeltsch, Christian communities for eighteen hundred years adopted an ironically Pilate-like posture of washed hands.

This detached attitude, amounting to a refusal of responsibility for conditions in the world, did not, however, prevent Christians from influencing the course of worldly events. Apparent indifference to temporal affairs was, for example, considerably moderated by the Christian commitment to the personal service of the individual "neighbor." Thus, while the church took no interest in affairs of state or social reform, its personal and organized ministry to those who suffer ensured its active involvement and influence in those spheres of worldly events that it otherwise refused to inhabit. In addition, as Troeltsch rightly notices, the Christian ethic, however apparently careless it may be of politics and society, can actually exert "revolutionary influence" through its shaping of individual lives. Thus, "in spite of all its submissiveness, Christianity did destroy the Roman State by alienating souls from its ideals."[9] The social and political effects of the practices of transformed individuals is no small force in the rise and fall of secular powers:

that spirit of Christian submission and adaptation to circumstances will always stop short at the borders of the values of the inner life, of the religious-ethical world of ideals, and of the ecclesiastical organization which supports these ideals. In actual fact it will exercise a very profound transforming influence, and will venture on the most searching interference with the social order; it will do this sometimes by indifference to existing conditions, sometimes by submitting existing conditions to the only valid test, the test of its own ideals and of its transcendent values; thus, without any deliberately revolutionary intent, it will succeed in destroying and breaking down evil institutions and in inaugurating new ones.[10]

However, Troeltsch, like most of us, believes that it is possible and necessary for Christianity to define a posture toward the world that authorizes a more direct commitment to social reform. For that reason he analyzes at great length and with great care the Christian civilization of the high Middle Ages and the theocracies created by Calvinist communities in Geneva, Scotland, and the New England colonies. Both attempts to bring all facets of society under the domain of the authentically Christian community represent high achievements of Christian culture and have much to teach us in our present efforts. However, both attempts at unity were battered to pieces by subsequent forces of dissolution. Neither, Troeltsch makes plain, is a workable solution for this perennial problem as it presents itself in our own times.

The task of defining the appropriate Christian attitude toward life in time became acute in the wake of Enlightenment thought, which began as anticlerical and ended as antireligious. Outspoken critics of Christianity have attacked religion explicitly on the grounds of its otherworldly bias and its indifference to issues of social justice. Over and over, in the works of such figures as Feuerbach, Nietzsche, Marx, and Freud, we find the argument that while the religious illusion arose to enable the mass of men to cope with the experience of suffering and injustice, in fact it functions viciously to ensure the perpetuation of such misery. By placing the resolution of the problem in the afterlife, Christianity rendered the problem insoluble in this life. The intense concern with social justice which typically accompanied this argument led, in turn, to the conviction that it was necessary to repudiate Christianity and to the hope that once social justice was realized, the need for such a "religious illusion" would naturally evaporate.

Even as these voices were being raised outside the community of the faithful, a curiously sympathetic argument was emerging within it. For reasons too complex to be fairly described here, we find in nineteenth-century European Protestant theology a new and quite distinctive accent on the theme of the kingdom of God. From this impetus arose an aggressively worldly theology which drew heavily upon the synoptic Gospels, especially the teachings of Jesus, and self-consciously sought to purge Christian theology of the dualistic influences of Neoplatonism. It elevated the authority of the Hebrew Scriptures, particularly the prophetic books, and focused attention on the motifs of community and covenant in the pre-Christian tradition within which Jesus taught. The theology of the kingdom of God was probably most notable for its attack on the tendency to treat salvation in highly individualized terms and to image redemption as spatial passage from one world to another. Kingdom theology sought to replace the prevalent hope of individual escape from an irredeemably fallen world ruled by powers of darkness with a transformative vision of communal salvation and the redemption of life in time. This revised eschatology brought with it major changes in the definition of Christian moral responsibilities in the world. It thereby established the basis for a new approach to that coincidence of piety and social responsibility which Troeltsch believes to have been achieved only twice before in the history of Christianity. Kingdom theology summoned the church as an institution as well as all individual Christians to the work of building the kingdom of God within the frame of history. The gospel is a social gospel with direct implications for social policy; the "good news" that is preached is not the promise of the escape of worthy persons from the "mass of damnation," but is rather the message that through the grace of God the world itself may be transformed.

Since its inception this school of theology, variously described in the early part of this century as liberal Protestantism, cultural Protestantism, and (especially in the United States) the social gospel movement, has been sharply criticized on the grounds that it reduces faith to an ethical program, collapses the distinction between God's purposes and human purposes, and fails to take sin seriously, suggesting that we can look forward to the unimpeded progress of humanity toward perfection. While none of these criticisms is groundless and while all of them do probably apply to the more popularized versions of kingdom theology, the best examples of this theology, especially when read in their dialectical context, cannot be dismissed on these grounds. The announcement in the 1930s and 1940s of the demise of the movement has obviously proved to be premature.

After a period of vital dogmatic renewal in the Christian church between the wars, a period during which theology focused its conversation on the internal life of the church rather than its relations with
culture, kingdom theology has reasserted itself with renewed vigor in
the rise of the predominantly Protestant theology of hope in Europe
and the Roman Catholic theology of liberation in the Americas. Whatever final judgment history may pass on the theological adequacy
of the various forms of kingdom theology, they constitute a powerful and challenging development in Christian theology: a movement reflecting a distinctively post-Enlightenment anthropology and
a movement authentically grounded in the cultural situation of the
modern West. The fact that kingdom theology represents the most
exciting theological conversation of the current period arises from its
stature as the most promising contemporary attempt to develop a
viable theology and ethics for the church in the world.

The question to be addressed is whether the bishops' letter on
the economy is actually informed in any significant way by this new
accent and this revised conception of the relationship of the church
and the world or whether, on the contrary, it represents a reversion
to the paradigm of thought which Troeltsch argues to be a permanent
and defining feature of all Roman Catholic social teaching—and a
mark of its inability to speak effectively to the complexities of the
modern situation.

III.

THERE IS A GREAT DEAL of evidence that the bishops do believe themselves to be working toward a solution to the problem defined by
Troeltsch. At the same time, there is also evidence that they are
determined to distance themselves from the strategies and commitments that characterize liberation theology, especially in Latin America. The fact that the letter is grounded in the language and convictions of traditional liberal/rational rights theory places it at some
distance from the precise assumptions of kingdom theology. The
casting of the letter in the language of rights may be a strategy
designed to insure implementation, and, of course, we must keep in
mind that kingdom theology is not indifferent to individual rights.
Nonetheless, the language and approach of the bishops' letter tend
to reflect the paradigm that Troeltsch describes as the compromise
solution constructed by the medieval church.

In order to understand the thinking which lies behind the letter, it is important to examine not only the letter itself, but also the

various pronouncements on the themes it addresses that have been made in recent years by various members of the American hierarchy. I have in mind in particular the reflections of Cardinal Joseph Bernardin, who has been quite explicit in describing the agenda of the United States Conference of Bishops. Consider, for example, the address which Cardinal Bernardin delivered on the subject of "Religion and Politics" at Georgetown University, under the auspices of the Woodstock Theological Center, in the midst of the 1984 presidential campaign. He made very clear the conviction that it is the responsibility of church leaders to articulate and promote a moral vision that can adequately inform public policy decisions. These "religiously rooted positions must somehow be translated into language, arguments and categories which a religiously pluralistic society can agree on as the moral foundation of key policy positions."[11] In elaborating this theme, he returned to and developed the idea of the "seamless garment" of a consistent moral philosophy which he had introduced in a lecture at Fordham University a year earlier. He advanced "concern for human life in diverse situations"[12] as the warp across which the threads of many issues might be woven, and he paired "the duty to protect human life" with "the responsibility of promoting the dignity of each human person."[13] Speaking three months later, in January 1985, at The Catholic University of America, he argued that the letter on the economy, like the earlier peace pastoral and like the American hierarchy's position on abortion, represents a further elaboration of this "consistent moral philosophy."[14]

The introductory outline of the first draft of the pastoral letter on the economy opens with the claim, "The theme of human dignity is central to Catholic social thought and forms the basis for our perspectives and recommendations in this letter."[15] This opening reflects almost word for word the position advocated by Cardinal Bernardin in a major address given in 1983 as the keynote speech of a symposium sponsored by the newly established Center for Church/State Studies at DePaul University. Speaking on the subject of "The Role of the Religious Leader in the Development of Public Policy," Cardinal Bernardin argued vigorously that "Religious values are *not* limited to personal morality and religion." On the contrary:

> Religious values include recognition of the dignity and worth of all people under God *and* the responsibilities of a social morality that flow from this belief. Catholic social doctrine is based on two truths about the human person: human life is both sacred and social. Because we esteem human life as sacred, we have a duty to protect and foster it at all stages of development from

conception to death and in all circumstances. Because we acknowledge that human life is also social, we must develop the kind of social environment that protects and fosters its development.[16]

To read the letter on the economy in this light is most revealing. Like the earlier peace pastoral, it is part of the campaign, to which the U.S. bishops are now committed, to take an active part in the creation of a social environment that will ensure human flourishing. To be sure, they continue to be concerned with the spiritual state of the individuals in their charge; thus, the bishops are explicit in defining two of their purposes as (1) the formation of conscience of individual Christians on matters of economic justice and (2) the effort to help individual Christians arrive at some understanding of the religious dimension and meaning of all the hours of their lives that they invest in labor inside and outside their homes. However, it is also clear that the letter purposes something more than the address of the shepherds to their flocks regarding appropriate behavior and attitudes within the fold. The legitimacy and success of the letter ought to be evaluated in terms of this larger project of establishing a moral consensus that will command the respect, allegiance, and energy not simply of Roman Catholics, and not even simply of Christians, but of an entire diverse nation. Late in the letter we find an interesting and revealing characterization of the United States as "a nation founded on Judeo-Christian principles,"[17] implying that it thus bears a special burden and is subject to a special calling which presumably can best be made clear by the religious leaders. The authors of the letter, like Cardinal Bernardin, seem to be trying to weave from the special resources of the religious vision a public philosophy according to which institutions may be shaped and policy decisions made— not simply by the coercive vote of the majority but by reason of a recovered moral consensus.

They do not trouble to give the grounds upon which they proceed with this project; perhaps they believe the grounds to be self-evident. If we looked to the letter itself, we might say that scriptural revelation is the justification that is offered. The letter begins with what some have remarked to be an uncharacteristically firm emphasis on the rootage of their moral prescriptions in the Christian Gospels. They offer the program that they offer because it is the program compelled by careful attention to the teachings of Jesus, as those teachings have been preserved in the synoptic Gospels. It is Jesus' special concern for the poor that authorizes the bishops to present the preference for the poor as a moral imperative. However, the bishops do not limit themselves to reflection on the example and explicit teachings of Jesus. From their scrutiny of Scripture, they draw out the motifs of "Creation, Covenant and Community" as the foundation for their "reflection on issues of economic and social justice."[18] These, in their turn, provide the justification for "the criterion against which all aspects of economic life must be measured": "the dignity of the human person."[19]

The difficulty, of course, that attends this grounding of public policy pronouncements in Christian Scripture is that only certain segments of our society are disposed to recognize those Scriptures as reliable guides to truth. Accordingly, even if they are, in fact, reliable revelations of truth leading to effective and benevolent social policies, not everyone will recognize their authority. In a pluralistic society, such reliance on revelation is almost sure to be a source of conflict rather than of consensus. Acknowledging this in the section titled "Living as Disciples Today: From the Bible to Economic Ethics," the bishops write,

> In addressing policy questions in a pluralistic society, the church does not presume that everyone shares its religious vision or that its theological arguments will be persuasive to all members of the body politic. Therefore Catholic teaching seeks to support its perspectives on policy with arguments based on philosophical reasoning and empirical analysis.[20]

Catholics enjoy the "conviction that human understanding and religious belief are complementary, not contradictory."[21] Faith and reason are "interdependent."

This seems clear enough on first reading, but it conceals several difficulties. It is not, for example, clear whether the bishops wish to say that the undergirding vision and commitments could have been developed without reference to scriptural revelation and theological reflection or, alternatively, that the policy recommendations they make, though grounded in exclusive insights, can be *supported* (though not fully justified) by appeal to general human understanding. When they turn in Section II to the specification of moral imperatives, they make their case so exclusively in the language of rights that a question might be raised as to whether there was any real need for Section I at all. Human dignity is, after all, a conception employed by atheists and agnostics as well as Christians to anchor their moral and political theory. The advantage of such an approach is that it does indeed make possible a broad dialogue in a pluralistic culture; the disadvantage is that if there is something truly distinctive about the

Christian understanding of the world or of human motivation, this approach will not disclose it.

This is, of course, the bargain that Roman Catholic thought historically has struck by virtue of its reliance on natural law, and it is the basis, as Troeltsch acknowledges, of the hierarchical "solution" to the "social problem" achieved by St. Thomas Aquinas in the high Middle Ages. To be sure, the letter on the economy does not explicitly rely on the old natural law arguments, but in its analysis of the structure of the problem and in its employment of the construct of rights, it remains a thoroughly traditional expression of Roman Catholic social teaching, despite its innovative elements and reformist policy recommendations. This has been an exceedingly useful and flexible tradition, not to be lightly abandoned. However, for all its utility, it suffers several widely recognized liabilities. First, as Troeltsch insists, it is the relative and not the absolute natural law that is accessible to right reason operating in a fallen world; natural knowledge of the relative natural law merely prepares the way for the revelation of the absolute natural law. The prevalent habit of thinking that the moral law discoverable by right reason is identical with the divine law revealed in Scripture overlooks

> the fundamental fact that the real Christian moral law does assume a moral aim, which is quite different from the aim of Natural Law, that, in reality, it is not merged with the Decalogue at all, but that, regarding the Decalogue merely as "germ and seed", it can only be called Christian in a very mystical and spiritualized sense, by reference to the real moral law of the New Testament.[22]

We might summarize the first liability by saying that in entering into conversation with "the world" on the world's own terms, this tradition is in danger of losing the truths of revelation. A second liability is the heavily theoretical character of this tradition. It works well for moral philosophers, jurists, and legislators, but it cannot easily move the hearts of common people to the creation of an alternate future. A third liability resides in the fact that despite its rootage in medieval times, this style of thinking is perilously congenial to the rationalistic and individualistic habits of Enlightenment reflection. The bishops thus undertake to ratchet the American public out of its customary habits of interpretation by relying on arguments hardly to be distinguished from the arguments which have produced those habits. It is easier to move a world when you have a fulcrum outside that world to supply leverage.

A pastoral letter composed in a conservative and hierarchical ecclesiological institution might not be the place to expect new theological methods and paradigms first to show themselves. Likewise, this particular letter may constitute an uneasy and unsatisfying alliance of new approaches and old forms of presentation. Yet is has to be said that by refusing to rely too heavily on scriptural revelation and by casting their primary appeal in the conventional language of rights, the bishops have ironically weakened the case they might have made for Christian solidarity with the poor and marginated. One does not necessarily expect the United States bishops to run through the streets in sackcloth crying, "Repent!" Short of that, however, would be recognition of the difficulty of couching prophetic judgments in the language of right reason and of finding in the relative natural law the resources for its own critique.

IV.

I HAVE ALREADY SKETCHED the alternative presented by kingdom theology, but discussion of a specific text representing that approach may serve to clarify the ways in which it differs from the approach of the pastoral letter. *A Theology for the Social Gospel* (1917) by Walter Rauschenbusch provides an excellent contrast because the actual policy directives put forward by Rauschenbusch are remarkably similar to those articulated by the bishops. Both texts focus upon the dignity of work and the necessity for society to provide gainful employment for its citizens; both emphasize just wages and support cooperative movements on the part of workers to obtain a just hearing for and right response to their rightful claims; both support a greater degree of socialization than presently characterizes the economy of the United States; and both strongly support cooperative ownership of the means of production by the workers employed in the production process. Both documents also make much of covenant, community, and solidarity, but beneath the apparent similarity of language, there is a difference of meaning which reflects a significant difference in the theological foundations of the two documents.

In *A Theology for the Social Gospel*, Rauschenbusch pursues the task of defining the Christian's responsibility to seek the common good and to work for social justice by giving central place to an analysis of the doctrine of sin. Traditional Christian treatments of sin have, he argues, been excessively influenced by Greek dualism, with the result that sin has been identified primarily with "sensuousness and materiality." Moreover, "the theological definitions of sin have too much the flavour of the monarchical institutions under the spiritual influence of which they were first formed."[23] The result is a picture of an isolated individual locked in a lonely struggle with a sovereign authority:

> Theology pictures the self-affirmation of the sinner as a sort of solitary duel of the will between him and God. We get a mental image of God sitting on his throne in glory, holy and benevolent, and the sinner down below, sullenly shaking his fist at God while he repudiates the divine will and chooses his own. Now in actual life such titanic rebellion against the Almighty is rare. . . . We rarely sin against God alone.[24]

This heavily individualized and "vertical" conception of sin must be exchanged for the more reliable conception of sin grounded in "the vision of the Kingdom of God."

> The sinful mind, then, is the unsocial and anti-social mind. To find the climax of sin we must not linger over a man who swears, or sneers at religion, or denies the mystery of the trinity, but put our hands on social groups who have turned the patrimony of a nation into the private property of a small class, or have left the peasant labourers cowed, degraded, demoralized, and without rights in the land. When we find such in history, or in present-day life, we shall know we have struck real rebellion against God on the higher levels of sins.[25]

In Chapter 9, Rauschenbusch advances "a social conception of the Kingdom of Evil" which reworks the doctrine of original sin in terms of sinful social structures by means of which the "social tradition" becomes the channel for "the transmission and perpetuation of specific evils." He points to "social idealizations of evil, which falsify the ethical standards for the individual by the authority of his group or community" and to "super-personal forces, or composite personalities, in society . . . [which] add enormously to the power of sin."[26] In light of this massive social solidarity in sin, individual preoccupation with individualized personal failings seems of little consequence—until we realize that it is the aggregate effect of all those individualized personal failings which perpetuates and advances the Kingdom of Evil.

> The life of humanity is infinitely interwoven, always renewing itself, yet always perpetuating what has been. The evils of one

generation are caused by the wrongs of the generations that preceded, and will in turn condition the sufferings and temptations of those who come after. Our Italian immigrants are what they are because the Church and the land system of Italy have made them so. The Mexican peon is ridden by the Spanish past. Capitalistic Europe has fastened its yoke on the neck of Africa. When Negroes are hunted from a Northern city like beasts, or when a Southern city degrades a whole nation by turning the savage inhumanity of a mob into a public festivity, we are continuing to sin because our fathers created the conditions of sin by the African slave trade and by the unearned wealth they gathered from slave labour for generations.[27]

This is what it means to be "in some sense partakers in Adam's guilt."[28] We are all bound under and we all contribute to the burden of "common sins."

In Christian theology, sin and salvation are correlatives, neither complete in itself. If we experience solidarity in sin, then our conception of salvation must have a similarly social dimension. "If our exposition of the super-personal agents of sin and of the Kingdom of Evil is true, then evidently a salvation confined to the soul and its personal interests is an imperfect and only partly effective salvation."[29] The redemption of "the historical life of humanity" is a significant feature of the Christian doctrine of salvation: "When we submit to God, we submit to the supremacy of the common good. Salvation is the voluntary socializing of the soul."[30] Later, he phrases this claim more orthodoxly: "The establishment of a community of righteousness in mankind is just as much a saving act of God as the salvation of an individual from his natural selfishness and moral inability."[31]

This argument, representative of kingdom theology at its most serious, represents a formidable contribution to the problem of specifying the relationship of the authentic Christian community to the temporal and fallen world of which it is a part. It takes history with absolute seriousness as the realm shaped by the human exercise of freedom rather than representing history as belonging to alien principalities and powers beyond the domain of Christ. Moreover, in wrenching the doctrines of sin and salvation out of their privatistic context into the public realm, this theology gives Christianity a central, genuine, and absolutely necessary interest in the unfolding events of the world and time. In stressing the structural and organizational dimension of sin, Rauschenbusch centralizes the duty to serve God through the struggle for social reform. In emphasizing the solidarity of the entire human race in sin through our universal inheritance of the world shaped by the sins of our forebears, he destroys the convenient fantasy that purity can be achieved and maintained by the strategies of detachment. Detachment is at best a delusion; to refuse to work to diminish the sin of the world is to contribute to it and to be all the more enwebbed in it.

This entire argument rests, of course, upon the recovery of the conception of the primordiality of the community. The individual emerges within it, dependent upon it—caught in its meshes like a hawk in a net. Unlike the hawk, however, the responsible self possesses the power (not always perfected) to act as an agent of the eventual transformation of that community which is the condition of the agent's emerging at all. The individual is a function of the community and the other way around, but the relationship of the individuals to their community is a dialectical one, if for no other reason than that the community has no reality apart from the accumulated past acts of its members and the interpretive story of those acts that is told by those who participate in it.

This understanding of the communal dimension of dignity represents a foundation upon which we might begin to construct a "public philosophy" proper to Christians which goes beyond the effort to impose certain moral norms, more or less unique to Christians, upon the public life of a pluralistic nation. The principal contribution is this notion of a "web of relationship" in which we are so tightly knitted together that every gesture of our lives, however gratuitous or trivial, is felt in the lives of others and will make some mark on the framework of human possibility. Thus we come to understand that in everything we do we shape the conditions of possibility within which contemporary and future agents exercise their freedom, even as we understand that our own responsible acts represent free responses to contexts shaped by our forebears and contemporaries.

Such an understanding weights our acts with a terrible seriousness. We are charged not simply with the work of our own salvation but with the work of the salvation of all those with whom we are related—and the edges of our relatedness are not discernible. Through our failures others may be lost—this is the deep and nearly unbearable meaning concealed by the platitude concerning our responsibility for the keeping of our brothers. In creating us in freedom, God has given us the absolute freedom to make the world according to our choices, and the world we make is not some private preserve for the mind in its own solipsistic play; the world we make is the world that others must inhabit. It is our common world that is constricted by our inappropriate choosings. Hannah Arendt, who

understands the weight of action in just this way, but who must contemplate it as one who confesses no faith in God, writes that such
an understanding of action ought to serve the godless twentieth-
century individual as a demythologized version of personal immor-
tality. That it does not function in this way is a result of the inability
of the individual to sustain such a weight of absolute responsibility:

> That deeds possess such an enormous capacity for endurance,
> superior to every other man-made product, could be a matter
> of pride if men were able to bear its burden, the burden of irre-
> versibility and unpredictability, from which the action process
> draws its very strength. That this is impossible, men have al-
> ways known. They have known that he who acts never quite
> knows what he is doing, that he always becomes 'guilty' of con-
> sequences he never intended or even foresaw, that no matter
> how disastrous and unexpected the consequences of his deed
> he can never undo it, that the process he starts is never con-
> summated unequivocally in one single deed or event, and that
> its very meaning never discloses itself to the actor but only to
> the backward glance of the historian who himself does not act.[32]

The Christian understanding of the weight of action is not similarly hobbled by despair. Christians confess the hope, founded on
God's promise, that freedom is self-transcending and that the work of
God is the redemption of history, not the destruction of it. If we are
fallen in the sense that we come to be and live our lives in a context
flawed by the sins of our ancestors, through the grace of God it
remains open to us to begin to reverse this incremental accumulation
of objectified sin. Just as it is open to us to shape a world in which
it is increasingly difficult for others to act in ways that realize the
good, so it is open to us, in faith and hope, to shape a world in
which other agents are increasingly supported rather than seduced,
a world in which the evils among which people must choose are less
destructive and less humanly diminishing. Understanding solidarity
in sin in the way that we do, Christians have a special understanding
of the importance of social structures in the moral lives of individuals.
With this understanding of the way in which individual life is woven
into its context comes a special understanding of our responsibility
actively to seek to shape those structures toward the enhancement
of human dignity and the support of decisions maximizing the good.

While others might not share similar beliefs with respect to our
solidarity in sin and salvation, and thus might fault the Christian

public philosophy that thus emerges, the Christian—with this appreciation of the web of relationship, the tragic waste that transcends fault, and the human responsibility which transcends justice—rightly holds a view of common life which embraces a public which does not share its suppositions. And the foundation of this Christian public philosophy is this conception of human dignity as realizable only in a supportive and embracing community which nurtures, corrects, cultivates, and is transformed by the individuals who come to understand their identities within its structures.

V.

DESPITE THE EMPHASIS given to the notion of community and despite the similarity of actual policy recommendations, the bishops' pastoral letter seems conceptually far removed from the project, strategy, and anthropology advanced by Rauschenbusch. The concept of solidarity provides an index to the degree of difference. Though they speak of interdependence and cooperation, the bishops do not present solidarity as defining the human condition; it is not our common situation but our voluntary achievement. Thus, the removal of most references to solidarity from the second draft made little difference to the argument.

In the letter, solidarity is advanced both as a strategy in the achievement of larger moral objectives, most especially that of social justice, and as a moral objective in itself.

In its treatment of solidarity as a strategy, the pastoral letter reflects the argument of the 1981 papal encyclical *Laborem Exercens*. There Pope John Paul II speaks of solidarity as a movement of response on the part of the oppressed to the injustice of their condition. "Every new movements of solidarity of the workers and with the workers" are essential "in order to achieve social justice."[33] While the specific injustices that gave rise to the movements of worker solidarity in the last century have been remedied, at least in some of the more developed nations, the present global community suffers "other forms of injustice much more extensive than those which in the last century stimulated unity between workers."[34] The picture that emerges is of "solidarity and common action" as a reaction provoked by the violation of workers' dignity and endorsed by the church as an appropriate reaction to social injustice. The Pope declares, "The Church is firmly committed to this cause and considers it its mission, its service, a proof of its fidelity to Christ, so that it can truly be the 'church of the poor'."[35] This deliberate unity is a technique or strategy in the pursuit of justice; we must join our cause with the cause of those who suffer, opposing oppression in a body in order that it may be overcome.

The letter also presents solidarity as itself a positive moral goal which it is our moral and/or religious obligation to bring about. The absence of this desired condition is a situation characterized by strife, indifference, self-enclosure, and the exploitative and manipulative exercise of self-aggrandizing power (injustice). This use of the term has strong affinities with the notion of corporatism advanced by Pius XI as the preferred alternative to the deficiencies of both capitalism and socialism, and it is worth noting that Pius XI was himself reverting to the image of social organization provided by the medieval guild. When Troeltsch describes the architecture of the medieval unity of civilization, he attributes its emergence to the unique cultural situation of the period, the dominant feature of which was the medieval town, a collection of interdependent corporations or guilds constituting "a firmly established fellowship of labour and of peace."[36] The guilds were the paradigmatic achievement of a social organization in which the greatest importance "attached to personal relationships" and in which there developed "a sense of solidarity in the ordering of life, and a widespread community feeling, expressed in mutual help and interdependence, in which all the people living in one place became a kind of united body, based on a spirit of mutual protection and mutual service."[37]

Unlike the notion of solidarity in sin that characterizes kingdom theology, the conception of solidarity as a strategy or as a moral goal preserves the belief that the individual in his self-disposition is primordial and controlling: "Should you *choose* to commit yourself to this moral project, these actions will be incumbent upon you." Thus, it is possible to argue that while the bishops' pastoral letter does move us in the direction of communitarian thought, it does so in a way that can be assimilated to Enlightment individualism as a refinement of that style of thinking rather than as a challenge to it. It belongs to the tradition of reflection on moral obligation arising from the social character of the self rather than from that more radical understanding of solidarity that takes the motif of relationality as the point of departure and thus asserts that we are lost in sin *together* and can move toward salvation only as a people of God.

The bishops' position reflects a coherent theology of the church in the world, but their project is one of revitalizing an endeavor which appears to many (particularly to those theologians at work in the Third World) to be fitted to a sociological situation that differs substantially from our contemporary context. Dignity is presented as an attribute of the valued individual, discrete in the eyes of God. When the bishops describe what they take to be appropriate behavior and attitudes, their fundamental appeal is to the personal virtue of individual agents. This appeal rests on right thinking about the requirements entailed by the self-evident fact of human dignity, buttressed in this case by a direct reliance on Scripture both to ground the assertion of human dignity and to provide normative force for unpopular imperatives rationally derived from the foundational assumptions. For all the emphasis placed upon it, the preferential option for the poor, which supplies leverage for the push for a recognition of the "economic rights" of individuals, has more affinities with the church's traditional social ministry than it does with the radical rethinking of human communities that characterizes kingdom theology. The social ministry of the church, charity, has been and continues to be immensely important in alleviating human misery, but it has been no more successful in directing social policy than the care of casualties has been successful in altering battle plans. Likewise, the hope that virtuous lay people will be able through their individual virtuous acts to bring about the improvement of the world has not been much supported by historical experience.

Insofar as the bishops may indeed be motivated by the desire to advance a "consistent moral philosophy" with relevance to the general culture, the appeal to right reason, human dignity, and human rights seems a well-chosen strategy. One of the strengths of Roman Catholic moral theology has always been its capacity to open conversation with the nonreligious about rectitude in worldly affairs; the difficulty with the conversation that unfolds is that it belongs to the sphere of the relative natural law and is in no wise specifically religious, let alone specifically Christian. Thus this rational discussion, though understood differently by a Christian (who believes it to operate reliably through the creative power of God, who ordained the world to his will even in its fallenness) and by a non-Christian, will nonetheless contain no elements over and above those recognized by the non-Christian. Insofar as the bishops have constructed an appeal that rests upon right reason, human dignity, and human rights, they have not done anything that could not have been done by rational moral philosophy. The appeal to Scripture is puzzling in this regard.

Kingdom theology, in contrast, is unabashedly scriptural and does not pretend to be able to make an appeal to those who do not stand already within the Christian community. However, with its understanding of the importance of history in the economy of salvation, it provides grounds upon which Christians can work side by side with their ideological opponents (Marxist and otherwise) for specifiable historical goals, including the goal of social justice. The advantages gained by kingdom theology fall into two broad groups. First, kingdom theology presents the work of the church in the world as intrinsic to the religious vision rather than derivative from it. Second, by stressing solidarity in sin and solidarity in salvation, kingdom theology offers an alternative to all those divisive representations of the human condition which pit group against group. By this strange alchemy, genuine kingdom theology presents concern for the poor as a feature of our concern for our common life, and the notion of meritorious but fundamentally unattractive self-sacrifice is submerged in an activity of transformation by means of which the flourishing of the entire community is ensured. Kingdom theology thus presents us with a compelling reason for altering our habits by binding our lives inextricably into the web of the lives of the marginalized and disadvantaged.

It is for this reason that I think the letter would have been more successful in altering the lot of the poor if it had been conceptually more radical. The first draft of the letter leaves the readers' individualistic understanding of their own lives unchallenged while exhorting them to deprive themselves for the sake of other persons who, again, are understood individualistically as victims of a collection of oppressors who are also individualistically understood as particular agents of evil. The effectiveness of this moral call rests, then, on the willingness of the readers to identify themselves with the oppressors, a moral judgment that most of us can be expected to reject as implausible if not downright offensive. Before the moral exhortation can be expected to have much impact on the population to which it is addressed, it must first of all break down the atomized individualism and complacent conviction of moral merit which militate against any genuine identification with the poor of the world. A right understanding of "the sin of the world" is the beginning of compassion.

NOTES

1. Ernst Troeltsch, *The Social Teaching of the Christian Churches*, trans. Olive Wyon, 2 vols. (Chicago: University of Chicago Press, 1931 [German edition, 1911]), 2:987, n. 510.
2. Ibid., 2:1012.
3. Ibid., 1:83.
4. Ibid., 52.
5. Ibid.

6. Ibid., 59.

7. Ibid., 100.

8. Ibid.

9. Ibid., 82.

10. Ibid., 85–86.

11. Cardinal Joseph Bernardin, "Religion and Politics: The Future Agenda" [delivered 25 October 1984], *Origins* 14 (8 November 1984): 324.

12. Ibid., 325.

13. Ibid., 326.

14. Cardinal Joseph Bernardin, "The Fact of Poverty: A Challenge to the Church" [delivered 17 January 1985], *Origins* 14 (31 January 1985): 543–48.

15. National Conference of Catholic Bishops, *Catholic Social Teaching and the U.S. Economy*, first draft (Washington, D.C.: United States Catholic Conference, 1984), 337.

16. Joseph Cardinal Bernardin, Martin E. Marty, and Arlin M. Adams, "Symposium: The Religious Leader and Public Policy," *The Journal of Law and Religion* 2 (1984): 369–70.

17. *Catholic Social Teaching and the U.S. Economy*, 316.

18. Ibid., 27.

19. Ibid., Outline, Part One, I; paras. 23, 25, and 330.

20. Ibid., 67.

21. Ibid.

22. Troeltsch, *Social Teaching*, 1:262.

23. Walter Rauschenbusch, *A Theology for the Social Gospel* (New York: Macmillan, 1917; reprint ed., Nashville, Tenn.: Abingdon Press, n.d.), 48.

24. Ibid., 47–48.

25. Ibid., 50.

26. Ibid., 78.

27. Ibid., 79.

28. Ibid., 91.

29. Ibid., 95.

30. Ibid., 99.

31. Ibid., 139–40.

32. Hannah Arendt, *The Human Condition* (Chicago: The University of Chicago Press, 1958), 233.

33. *The Pope Speaks: The Church Documents Quarterly* 26 (no. 4, 1981): 302.

34. Ibid., 301.

35. Ibid., 302.

36. Troeltsch, *Social Teaching*, 1:255.

37. Ibid., 249.

WILFRIED VER EECKE

Justice, Freedom and the Bishops' Pastoral on the American Economy

WILFRIED VER EECKE is a Professor in the
Department of Philosophy at Georgetown
University. He received his Ph.D.
in philosophy from the University of
Louvain.

I. Introduction

THE BISHOPS' PASTORAL LETTER on the U.S. economy is a reformist document. The letter praises the U.S. economy for certain of its achievements, but also criticizes it for its shortcomings. Clearly, such an evaluation rests upon the choice of a model. The one chosen by the bishops is not an existing alternative model, but a vision of a society incorporating morally desirable characteristics such as care for the poor and the possibility for all to participate in creative economic activity.

A reformist document takes a middle position between two extremes, in this case, between the argument that all is well in our society because we have embraced the principle of a constitutional free market[1] and the argument that the source of evil in the twentieth century (just as it was in the nineteenth century) is the technical organization of the economic order, that is, the free market mechanism. Such a position would imply that in order to achieve a good society, the United States would have to give up its free market economy in favor of an alternative economic structure.[2]

The purpose of this paper is to support and defend the bishops' reformist position by giving reasons for rejecting the two extremist positions. For this purpose I will rely on three authors with wide interdisciplinary knowledge: T. Lowi, a political scientist; G. Briefs, an economist; and G. F. W. Hegel, a philosopher.

I begin by rejecting the position that all is well in our society because we have embraced the principle of a constitutional free market, borrowing ideas from Lowi and Briefs who argue that a constitutional free market society and American capitalism in particular have become, in the latter half of the twentieth century, unjust, or are unable to guarantee the common good due to the deeply rooted influence of interest groups. The first part of my paper will be devoted to this topic and will, I hope, establish the validity of what may look to some to be a gratuitous assumption of the bishops' letter, i.e., that certain outcomes of the U.S. economy are a moral scandal.

I also reject the position that the source of all social evil in this country results from accepting the free market mechanism. On the contrary, I will argue that competitive free markets are an unavoidable, if not a necessary, mechanism for maintaining a good society in an industrial or postindustrial world. For this argument, I rely on Hegel who, following the British economists, interpreted the free market mechanism as one of the great institutional innovations of modern times. From the classical British economists we can all learn the technical reasons favoring a competitive free market. From Hegel we can learn cultural and anthropological reasons for defense of the free market. Hegel's arguments thus form a bridge between the technical arguments found in economic literature in favor or the free market and the religious-ethical discourse of the bishops' letter about the free market. The reliance on Hegel's arguments becomes even more rewarding for the turn that Hegel's argument takes. Indeed, notwithstanding his sympathy for the free market and his many profound arguments in favor of it, Hegel ends up discovering some structural problems in the functioning of a market economy. These structural problems are of such significance that morally sensitive people must be responsive to them.

After having considered arguments against the two extremist positions, we are left, then, with the conclusion that there are longstanding problems with the free market, which the current revival of enthusiasm for it tends to eclipse. These are problems, moreover, to which not only socialists or other systematic opponents of the market are responsive. In fact, the three authors under discussion are all sympathetic to what the free market has achieved. This conclusion of critical praise is precisely the point of view taken by the bishops' letter.

In the third part of this study, finally, I analyze the novel contributions made by the letter with respect to both analytic arguments and proposed solutions.

II. Justice: Concern for the Common Good

THE U.S. SYSTEM AND "INTEREST GROUP LIBERALISM" OR "LAISSEZ-FAIRE PLURALISM"

THE U.S. ECONOMIC SYSTEM began to dominate the world scene in the second phase of capitalism, which has aptly been described by Theodore Lowi as "interest group liberalism" and by Goetz Briefs as "laissez-faire-pluralism."[3]

In his book, *The End of Liberalism*, Theodore Lowi analyzes the American scene from 1930 on. He argues that a new kind of relationship has developed between the free market and the state, with interest groups as the moving forces. He does not focus upon the history of ethics and ethos patterns, as we will see Briefs does. He concentrates instead upon the formal changes that have occurred in the political practice of the United States.

According to Lowi, the changes that have occurred in the relationship between the state and the economic order are of such magnitude that he calls the new state of affairs "the second republic." The first republic (which lasted, depending upon the criteria used, until about either 1930 or 1960)[4] was a federation in which most of the governing was done by the states. The scant governing by the federal government was done by congressional legislation. The second republic is characterized by a dramatic increase in the functions of the government and the size of its bureaucracies. In particular, the federal government has taken on the roles of regulation and distribution. The first function leads to a kind of national police power in economic affairs, the second to a fiscal and monetary policy. This extension of governmental tasks means a government centered around the executive and the delegation by Congress of its legislative powers to an agency which is supposed to fill out the details of Congress's intent. There is, in effect, a shift in legislative power away from Congress and toward administrative agencies.

Three presidents contributed in important ways to building this new republic. The first was Franklin D. Roosevelt, with his New Deal. The second was John F. Kennedy, who defined the problems of the United States as nonideological but complex. These problems could be addressed, Kennedy claimed, by the president and a professional bureaucracy. He therefore requested (in his 1962 Economic Report, for instance) vast discretionary powers. The third president was Richard M. Nixon. He requested from Congress and got authority for revenue sharing, which gave the president even more discretionary power.

But clearly, if governmental decisions are not made by the Congress, they do not undergo the mediating process of public debate and modification. In order to have some mediation, the executive substituted for the public debate in Congress a bargaining process with the affected interest groups, giving such organized groups a privileged position.[5] Indeed, the government has been asked, if not forced, to protect industries, corporations, or economic activities that cannot stand on their own, provided that they are organized and can bring political pressure to bear. Technically, the government is able to enter such a bargaining process by using discretionary regulatory or fiscal policies, made available to it by Congress: for example, the discretionary power of the Emergency Loan Board to guarantee loans. Such discretionary power invites bargaining.

Bargaining, which involves the use of power, produces results that have desirable qualities: it creates peace between power groups. However, the use of power in the bargaining process also puts limits on the ability to guarantee justice. Justice has a better chance if decisions are made by using rules which must be publicly defended.

Lowi believes that this can be achieved by what he calls juridical democracy. Such a democracy would return the legislative duty to Congress, that is, it would demand specific legislation from Congress and from federal agencies administering by rule, not a case by case approach. Lowi's hope is that Congress would thereby be forced to debate the legitimacy of governmental actions, thus giving a place to moral concerns.

Briefs presents a similar critique of contemporary democratic capitalism. His specific contribution, though, is an analysis that allows us to locate the U.S. economic order within the context of the whole capitalist system. Indeed, Briefs's writings include reflections on rise and development of capitalism since its beginnings; these writings also cover more than the economic, political, and juridicial aspects of capitalism; indeed, Briefs also analyzes the cultural

components of the capitalist system, such as its philosophical traditions, its religious movements and its ethical convictions and practices. Briefs's work can therefore usefully broaden the razor-sharp
critical analysis of the U.S. economic order made by Lowi.

One of Briefs's main theses is that Adam Smith's or anybody
else's belief that commercial society combined with a constitutional
state embodies the good society has proven to be naive because
commercial society itself was made possible by forces which have
given rise to a new and questionable social order.

Some of the circumstances that made the commercial society
(capitalism) possible also undermined the existing ethics and ethos
pattern. Instead of a communal, religiously bound ethic, a new ethic
has emerged in modern times that defines human relations according
to the model of relations existing among alien classes (for instance,
among traders, merchants, and colonized people). This new ethic
defends the right of individuals to act according to their own personal
interest.

The excitement about the commercial society, however, was
tied to the belief that individuals would act according to enlightened
self-interest, not short-sighted or purely egoistic self-interest; to the
belief that the possibility of self-interest leading to harmful actions
would be checked by economic competition; and finally, to the belief
that individuals would adhere to traditional standards of human behavior.[6]

The rising middle class made the commercial society a reality.
It resulted in major "social disruption and swift decline of marginal
standards" of ethics. These social disruptions are well documented
in the social and economic literature of the nineteenth century, in
the committee reports of the British Houses of Parliament and the
reports of the factory inspectors.[7]

One of the reactions to these social disruptions which had long-
term consequences was the organization of individual economic play-
ers in order to make concerted action possible. The first to organize
themselves successfully were the Amalgamated Society of Engineers
in 1851. This self-organization of workers was followed in Europe
by the organization of peasants. In the depression of 1873 to 1898,
businesses, in turn, organized themselves into cartels. The last to
be organized were the professions and government employees.[8] The
transformation of the free market economy from a competitive relationship among individuals to a competitive relationship among
groups became generally accepted. It made its way into public policy
after World War I in Europe and after the Great Depression in the
United States.[9] The war, particularly in Europe, had led to the belief
that the economy could be directed. It was thought, furthermore,

that the task of directing the economy would be easier if the economic subjects themselves were organized. Finally, social Darwinism was replaced by a "desire for security, for stability, for the good things in life, for the rights of the common (person), and a sense of belonging to a sheltering collectivity."[10] Thus was created a favorable environment for the maturation of interest-groups.

Briefs's thesis is that the emergence of interest groups is but a second phase of liberalism. In the first phase of capitalism there were, or were supposed to be, only individuals and small firms engaged in atomistic competition. In the second phase, group formation is tolerated, even encouraged and legitimated. We can call this second phase of capitalism a second phase of liberalism because it adopts the same ethics of behavior between alienated groups as in the first phase. Indeed, interest groups replace individual interests, defending the proposition that their interests can be maximized without too much concern for the consequences of their actions upon other groups or upon the society as a whole. Furthermore, just as in the first phase of capitalism, competition (now between groups) is hailed as the regulating mechanism. And just as in the first phase, the new economic agents (the interest groups) strongly oppose state interference even though they may welcome the help of the state to pursue their interests.

Thus the erosion of ethical standards and ethos patterns will unavoidably continue. This submarginal ethical behavior will create new burdens. Organized groups will be able to carry their burdens by shifting them upon the anonymous unorganized masses, in large part through inflation. Since the distributive effects of inflation hit different groups in different ways, most drastically the poor, inflation is basically unjust, as Keynes has already argued.[11]

Democracy also underwent change. The first transformation occurred when, during the Enlightenment, rationalism undermined the need for a metaphysical foundation for the state through its contractarian, utilitarian or popular sovereignty arguments. The second transformation occurred when rationalism was unable to define the common good. Democracy then became expediency in the form of a bargaining model of governance. In such a democracy, the state bargains with the interest groups involved. Neither the bargaining interest groups nor the government are willing or able to guide their decisions in light of a common good. What we now experience is "the meeting of the secondary phase of liberalism with the tertiary phase of democracy."[12]

Still, this pessimistic analysis is not Briefs's last word. He does not present a detailed plan of action, though, as Lowi has done.

Instead, he points to the limits and the possibilities which the new situation has created. It is Briefs's conviction that the emerging awareness of these limits and possibilities creates the opportunity to seek and affirm explicitly ethical principles. But let me quote the eloquent words by which Briefs introduces that conclusion:

> A degree of freedom exists, and there are functions of the state that are vital. But we realize now as never before the existence both of a realm of necessity ruled by economic laws and of a variable zone of freedom. Because of this freedom, ethics again has a place in economic life and hence, going even further than Max Weber's admission of "value relations," a place in economics proper. The era of determinism accommodated by silent and implicit ethical assumptions is over.[13]

From the studies of both Lowi and Briefs, it is clear that the combination of democracy and the interest-group phase of capitalism has seriously negative consequences. These consequences are of such proportions that Lowi argues that this type of society is not just and Briefs maintains that the common good cannot be guaranteed.

It is curious that democratic capitalism ends up in this situation because it had been conceived of as a new societal organization to replace the one dominated by the ideals of chivalry. This chivalric ideal had been discredited in the sixteenth and seventeenth centuries by such authors as Hobbes, La Rochefoucauld, Pascal, Racine and Cervantes.[14] In its place, the image of a commercial society emerged as an attractive alternative to the chivalric society with its passionate and savage exploits of the aristocracy combined with the depredations of looting armies and murderous pirates.[15] Hirschman summarizes the situation in concluding his survey of the history of the arguments for capitalism:

> Capitalism is ... hailed ... because it would activate some benign human proclivities at the expense of some malignant ones—because of the expectation that, in this way, it would repress and perhaps atrophy the more destructive and disastrous components of human nature.[16]

If we want to understand the transformation from the optimistic hopes projected into democratic capitalism in the eighteenth century to the critical disappointment noted by twentieth century authors such as Lowi and Briefs, we need to analyze the basic structures of democratic capitalism. In turning to this task, let us look to Hegel's illuminating analysis for assistance.

III. Freedom, Free Market and the Good Society

IN HEGEL'S GOOD SOCIETY, as outlined in his *Philosophy of Right*, there is no need, as there was in Plato's *Republic*, to force individuals to take jobs that they are best qualified to perform.[17] It is also not necessary to share wives and children in common so as to assure a feeling of unity, nor is it necessary to prohibit private property in order to make adherence to the common good possible.[18]

Based upon a reading of the British economists Adam Smith and Sir James Steuart, Hegel was able to invest the emerging free market with the hope of enabling the good society to develop without an appeal to some of the authoritarian or paternalistic methods thought necessary in Plato's *Republic*.[19]

Hegel expects that the free market will be able to achieve three desirable goals. First, providing, in a guaranteed way, the goods and services needed for the members of society. Second, integrating the individual in a preliminary way into his or her community. Third, allowing people to reconcile themselves with nature and at the same time to develop self-esteem.

Hegel has a typical philosophical way of assigning these different functions to the free market.[20] Indeed, he calls the free market one of the three "ethical" institutions. The other two are the family and the state. These three institutions are ethical because they embody and give institutional form to the moral principle. It is typical of the moral principle that the individual has the right and duty to do what is good as he or she sees it. Morality is thus, first, the free choice or free commitment to something; and second, it is the choice of and commitment to a good.

These two aspects of morality are more easily perceived in the family and in the state than in the economic order. Hegel describes the moral aspect of the family as follows: "Hence in a family, one's frame of mind is to have self-consciousness of one's individuality within this unity as the absolute essence of oneself, with the result that one is in it not as an independent person but as a member."[21] He summarizes the two elements of the family as follows: the essence of marriage consists "in the free consent of the persons, especially in their consent to make themselves one person, to renounce their natural and individual personality to this unity of one with the other."[22] The moral aspect in the family thus requires a free consent and commitment to a goal, a common good: the unity of two wills.

Similarly, Hegel sees a moral dimension in the state: the free consent to a common good, which in this case is the discussion, selection, and enforcement of the rules by which the life of the community is going to be governed.

As far as the economic order is concerned, there is a problem. It is clear that one of the two moral components is present, that is, free choice. Adam Smith said it well when he wrote: "Every man, as long as he does not violate the laws of justice, is left perfectly free to pursue his own interest his own way, and to bring both his industry and capital into competition with those of any other man, or order of men."[23] It is not surprising, therefore, that Hegel characterizes the free market as "the system of *atoms* by which the substance is reduced to a general system of adjustments to connect self-subsisting existences and their particular interests."[24]

It is difficult to see how the other component, commitment to a good, is realized in the economic order. Again, Adam Smith is worth quoting. Every individual "generally, indeed, neither intends to promote the public interest, nor knows how much he [or she] is promoting it . . . [they] intend only [their] own aim . . ."[25] Hegel, too, understood this aspect of the free market; he even saw its politically disastrous consequences. He wrote: "particularity by itself, given free rein in every direction to satisfy its needs, accidental caprices, and subjective desires, destroys itself and its substantive concept in this process of gratification."[26] Hegel therefore confirms that one can look upon the free market as the "disappearance of ethical life."[27] In less philosophical terms, he wrote: "Civil society (the economic order) affords a spectacle of extravagance and want as well as of the physical and ethical degeneration common to them both."[28]

However, these negative remarks are not Hegel's final judgment about the ethical relevance of the free market. Hegel, informed by the British economists, accepts the proposition that there is an invisible hand at work which in a quasi deterministic way guarantees a common good. That good is the fact that the free market provides more and better products and services (as they are desired by the consumers) than any other system. The argument advanced is that individuals need products and services in order to satisfy their needs. The free market system does not give anybody a right to a share in the social product unless one has contributed to that product. More technically, the free market guarantees that one gets a claim to a share of the social product of goods and services in direct proportion to the marginal value of one's own product.

This means that if one does not or cannot produce something or if one produces something that nobody is asking for, then one does not have a claim to the goods and services available in society. The free market thus becomes a system that automatically rewards or punishes individuals according to whether they contribute to the useful products of society. No one can be indifferent to a domain in which the free market can reward or punish. Indeed, inasmuch as we are bodily subjects, we cannot afford to be insensitive to the free market system's rewards and punishments; if we are, we will suffer bankruptcy or starvation. Individuals, inasmuch as they are bound to the requirements of their own existence, are forced to accept the laws of the free market. It is in this specific sense that we can say that the free market employs a threat or uses compulsion, and thus that determinism is at work. There are important consequences to this mechanism. It guarantees that even self-interest and selfishness can be mobilized for productive purposes. It also guarantees that individuals will pay attention to each other.

Let us elaborate upon these two points. The fact that the free market is based upon self-interest has long been acclaimed. It is supposed to guarantee a more productive society, and a more reliable supply of goods as well.

The fact that it forces individuals to pay attention to others is an important anthropological feature of the free market. Indeed, a long tradition of philosophy and of Christian thought has affirmed that man is a social being. This social dimension has frustrating aspects,[29] and it is therefore not surprising that individuals prefer their independence rather than their social dependence. The free market thus helps individuals to accept what they might not be willing or able to accept freely: that is, the fact that they have a social destiny.

This brings us naturally to the second goal assigned by Hegel to the free market. The free market is supposed to provide a preliminary integration of the individual into society. This integration is then completed in the state. Hegel strongly emphasizes, however, the idea that the integration of the individual into the state need not "start from scratch." The good citizen is not a magical transformation of the self-interested *homo economicus*. Even though Hegel points out that the free market educates the *homo economicus* toward becoming a social being or an individual integrated into social groups, and even though he notes that the state must promote the legitimate self-interests of the citizen, he nevertheless maintains that there is a radical difference between the *homo economicus* and the citizen. Indeed, the emotional attachment of the citizen to the state (patriotism) means that the individual is willing and able to recognize that the value of his or her life lies in something beyond the self. As citizens, people are therefore in principle willing to accept freely the subordination of self-interest to the interest of the community as it is organized in the state. Willingness to pay one's fair share of taxes and to serve in just wars are the two primary ways in which the citizen transcends the logic of *homo economicus*. But the free market prepares the *homo economicus* to become a citizen.

We have already seen that the free market entices and forces the individual to pay attention to the needs of others. The free market thus automatically makes the *homo economicus* a socially oriented individual. But the *homo economicus* still remains self-interested, even in the attention paid to the neighbor's needs. Through the market, *homo economicus* does not become altruistic, transcending the self. One remains selfish, but not solipsistic. Hegel sees, however, a further integration at work: integration in a class or association[30] or a corporation in the process of integrating oneself into the economic order. In order to become a participant in the free market, one must develop a skill, and choose, therefore, one of the many professions available. One thereby automatically becomes a member of a class (or a professional association). In becoming a member of a professional class, one also acquires an identity in the economic order and is thus recognized by others (and in one's own eyes) as being somebody worthwhile.[31] Furthermore, the rewards of that profession specify the kinds of wishes that are realistically realizable. While in principle desires are infinite, one's acceptance of a specific profession provides the individual with a bundle of attainable goods that others accept as satisfactory for a decent human existence. Inserting oneself into a particular economic class thus provides help in accepting one's finitude.

Insertion into a corporation has the further advantage that we are partially liberated from the threat which forced us into the economic order in the first place. Indeed, the corporation provides a stable basis for the livelihood of the family. It furthermore allows for sublimation of the self-interest motive, that is, the minimally required motive for setting the free market in motion. Membership in a corporation allows the individual to be assured of his or her self-interest while at the same time being free to work for the interests of the corporation. One is thus led—and enabled—to transcend individual self-interest and become concerned about a common good: the good of the corporation.[32]

The third goal assigned by Hegel to the free market is that it can allow for the person's reconciliation with nature and with his or her own bodily nature. Indeed, Hegel saw labor as the solution for the problem of self-consciousness, which entails coming to terms with the challenge of being a self; this requires affirming objectivity even though the self is obviously more than mere objectivity. Hegel provided his solution in his famous analysis of the master-slave dialectic. He also argues, however, that labor does not happen automatically. Because labor requires restraint of desire, it comes about only under a double threat: the fear of death, which teaches consciousness the value of life, and the threat of the master, which imposes on the subordinate (the slave) the burden of service and labor. We are ultimately called upon to discover that work is our essence.[33] Thus we reconcile ourselves with a situation in life that has its negative aspects. The free market economy sanctions this insight by giving a moral significance to the ability to earn a living and by interpreting the failure to do so in a moral sense as well, usually as the result of laziness.

Hegel nevertheless went beyond this optimistic view of the free market. He noted that there were a number of problems in the free market system for which he hoped the state would provide adequate help, for example, the administration of justice and the provision of what are today called public goods, or externalities.

(a) The administration of justice is connected with the idea of the protection of property. It not only requires a legal system but also a police force to protect against thieves and an army to protect against foreign occupation. Hegel, however, does not reduce the problem of property to a utilitarian argument or to a formal entitlement theory. For him, "property is the first embodiment of freedom and so is in itself a substantive end."[34]

As property has this intrinsic connection with freedom, Hegel sees correctly that the state's task cannot be restricted to the protection of existing property rights. The administration of justice needs to be combined with an attempt to remedy the problem of excessive poverty, that is, the lack of property by some.[35]

(b) The problem of public goods means providing things which might benefit a large number of people without the producer being able to receive payment for his or her services. One special form of public good is that of government regulation of goods offered to the public.[36]

There are as well two main problems for which Hegel did not see a solution. They are: (1) the fact that the division of labor leads to meaningless jobs, or more generally, that work is not work for oneself, but for the anonymous market; and (2) the fact that poverty is widespread and derives from accidental phenomena outside the control of individuals (Hegel suggests that it might even be system generated).

A first permanent deficiency of the free market is that the division of labor does not allow the free market to perform its educative function. Work not only keeps a person busy; ideally, it teaches one to master the material with which one works and invites one to cooperate with others. It also helps one to acquire a habitually executed skill recognized by others as worthwhile. The division of labor, though "makes work more and more mechanical."[37] This in turn results in the "distress of the class tied to work of that sort," so much so that they will be unable "to feel and enjoy the broader freedoms and especially the intellectual benefits of civil society."[38]

A second problem of the free market is the creation of poverty. Success or failure in the free market depends not only upon skill and hard labor, but also upon luck. Thus all kinds of contingencies play a role in the creation of poverty. But Hegel points to the fact that the existence of a rabble of paupers "greatly facilitate the concentration of disproportionate wealth in a few hands." Furthermore, Hegel thought that unemployment was the result of overproduction and he therefore believed that the free market was inherently unable to eliminate poverty.[39]

Indeed, the poor can either be supported without being required to work or the state can give them work and pay them accordingly. Hegel would exclude the latter method. Giving work to the unemployed would add to the productive activities of society, but the unemployment problem was created by overproduction. Therefore it is not rational to try to solve the problem by producing even more. However, the first method, supporting the unemployed or the poor without their having to work, also creates impossible problems, according to Hegel. First, it deprives the unemployed or the poor of the means for acquiring the self-esteem and social respect which result from successfully earning a living. Second, if support of the poor is based on private charitable donations, then the poor and unemployed are never certain of what to expect. This uncertainty can be removed if the state uses its power of taxation to guarantee a steady stream of income to the poor and the unemployed. This method, however, violates a basic principle of the free market whereby one establishes a claim to the social product *only* if one contributes one's self to that product. Hegel thought that such a violation of the free market principle would lead to resentment. The state might still attempt some form of welfare program, but Hegel foresaw that resentment would put a limit to its scope.

Hegel is the first great philosopher to have understood well the contribution of the free market to the good society. His appreciation, however, was not uncritical—and neither should ours be. He argued that the centrifugal forces of a free market and the inability of the free market to solve the problem of poverty required the presence of a properly ordered political system in order for the free market to make the proper contribution to the good society. The United States, at least, does not have the required political order for guaranteeing the proper contribution of the free market. Both Lowi and Briefs have taught us how the free market has in fact transformed

American capitalist society into an unjust society (Lowi) or a society without proper concern for the common good (Briefs). This is exactly the point of departure for the bishops' discourse on the U.S. economy.

IV. The Bishops' Pastoral: A Religiously Based Economic Ethic

EARLY IN THE LETTER, the bishops have praise for the American system. This praise is so formulated that it seems to reflect approval of the democratic capitalist arrangement of American society. The document can therefore be seen as being in basic agreement with Hegel's view of the good society in the modern world. Consider the following:

> When we consider the performance of the American economy and its success in reflecting these basic economic rights, we see an encouraging record. In its comparatively short history the United States has made impressive strides in the effort to provide material necessities, employment, health care, education and social securities for its people. It has done this within a political system based on the precious value of freedom.[40]

Still, the pastoral letter points to some very serious failures of the American economic system. In the same paragraph we read:

> While the United States can be rightfully proud of its achievements as a society, we know full well that there have been failures, some of them massive and ugly. Hunger persists in our country, as our Church-sponsored soup kitchens testify. Far too many people are homeless and must seek refuge from the cold in our church basements. As pastors we know the despair that can devastate individual families and whole communities when the plague of unemployment strikes. Inadequate funding for education puts a high mortgage on our economic future. Racial discrimination has devastating effects on the economic well-being of minorities. Inequality in employment opportunity, low wages for women and lack of sufficient childcare services can undermine family life. The blighted and decaying environment of some disadvantaged communities stands in stark contrast with the natural and architectural beauty of

others. Real space for leisure, comtemplation and prayer seem increasingly scarce in our driven society.[41]

The letter also makes a moral judgment about the economy's failures. Indeed, in section 100 it states: "We believe that the level of inequality in income and wealth in our society and even more the inequality on the world scale today must be judged morally unacceptable...." Or, "the fact that so many people are poor in a nation as wealthy as ours is a social and moral scandal that must not be ignored."[42] Or finally: "In our judgment, the distribution of income and wealth in the United States is so inequitable that it violates this minimum standard of distributive justice."[43]

Lowi, Briefs, and Hegel all saw the problem of injustice (poverty in the midst of plenty) as arising from a society built upon a one-sided concept of freedom. Lowi proposed juridical democracy as a remedy. Hegel hoped for other institutional arrangements. Briefs indicated a moral task. What does the pastoral letter offer as its answer?

The letter uses the institutional authority of a major religious organization to introduce a religiously based ethic into the debate about the outcomes of a democratically organized free market. That ethic draws on two themes of the biblical vision of man. First, a human being created in the image and likeness of God has transcendent worth: there is something sacred about every person.[44] Second, the dignity of the human person is realized in community with others.[45] Based on that union, the letter demands from the economy more than productive efficiency; it also demands that the economy "permit all persons that measure of active social and economic participation which befits their common membership in the human community."[46]

The letter does not consider this second goal as secondary in the sense that it is justifiable or desirable only if it helps to attain the first goal of economic efficiency. The letter does not even consider the economic cost or economic benefit of imposing a participatory character on the economy. Instead, it systematically spells out the implications of the communitarian demand. Thus, when describing the threefold moral significance of the economy, the letter mentions explicitly that "work should enable everyone to make a contribution to the human community to the extent each is able,"[47] or as reformulated subsequently: "it (the economy) should make possible the enhancement of unity and solidarity within the family, the nation and the world community."[48]

This religiously based economic ethic is then reformulated in terms of rights and in terms of a theory of justice. Three groups of rights are enumerated. First are the rights to "food, clothing, shelter, rest, medical care." Second, the rights "to free initiative in the economic field and the right to work." Third are broader "rights which set moral constraints on the institutional ordering of the economy, such as the rights of labor unions and the rights of ownership." The language of rights allows the letter to stress in a language that is culturally understood the demand that the economy must in its outcomes provide for the needs of all. The letter emphasizes this rhetorically when it states in italics some ten paragraphs later: *"all persons really do have rights in the economic sphere."*[49]

The language of justice is used to focus more specifically upon the community-building requirement that flows from a religiously based economic ethic. The letter presents several formulations: "justice demands the establishment of minimum levels of participation by all persons in the life of the human community"[50] "Justice demands that social institutions be ordered in a way that guarantees all persons the ability to participate actively in the economic, political and cultural life of the community"[51] "justice is not simply a matter of seeing to it that people's private needs are fulfilled. It is also a matter of enabling them to be active and productive."[52]

The bishops are fully aware of the difficulties in implementing the two major goals of fulfilling the basic needs of all (including the poor) and of increasing the participation of all in the economic process. Thus the letter acknowledges that the American ethos does not give the same privileged position to economic rights as it gives to civil and political rights. In an eloquent paragraph we find the following statement:

> First, the philosophical tradition which helped form our national ethos gives pride of place to the protection of civil and political rights such as freedom of religion, speech, and assembly. Economic rights (for example, adequate nutrition, housing and work), however, do not hold this privileged position in the cultural and legal tradition of our nation.[53]

Furthermore, the letter acknowledges that to this date this country has not demonstrated that it knows how to implement economic rights. Again, this is in sharp contrast with our institutional expertise in ensuring civil rights.[54]

Finally, the letter clearly recognizes difficulties at the level of motivation for the implementation of its goals. Thus it states: "There are forms of individual and group selfishness present in the nation that undermine social solidarity and efforts to protect the economic rights of all." Or, ". . . the sins of indifference and greed continue to block efforts to secure the minimum economic rights of all persons. This selfishness not only distorts the hearts of individuals, it has also become embedded in certain of the economic institutions, and cultural presuppositions of our society."[55] The letter therefore almost naturally asks for "the formation of a new cultural consensus that all persons really do have rights in the economic sphere."[56] What this new cultural consensus entails is spelled out in applying the principles of economic justice to the working of the American economy. It entails seeing that the "fulfillment of the basic needs of the poor is of the highest priority,"[57] that the "increased economic participation for the marginalized takes priority over the preservation of privileged concentrations of power, wealth and income,"[58] and that "meeting human needs and increasing participation should be priority targets in the investment of wealth, talent and human energy."[59]

In discussing "The Responsibilities and Rights of Diverse Economic Agents and Institutions," the letter introduces anthropological and politico-philosophical concepts to give increased weight to the demand it makes on the economy. Thus it introduces a religious interpretation for the three anthropological concepts of work, consumption, and private property.

Starting with the concept of work, the pastoral stresses the fact that work is not just a burden but also an opportunity for self-realization for the individual, as a member of the human community and as a religious person. In paragraph 109, we read:

The obligation to work derives not only from God's command but from a duty to one's own humanity and to the common good. The virtue of industriousness is an important expression of a person's dignity and solidarity with others.[60]

The pastoral relies heavily upon Pope Paul VI's encyclical *Populorum Progressio* for moral directions about consumption. Paul VI argued that in order to alleviate poverty, the wealthy must learn to relinquish goods and services in favor of the poor.[61] Applying this to the American scene, the pastoral observes:

All U.S. citizens, especially parents, must nurture the inner freedom to resist these pressures constantly to seek more.[62]

Finally, concerning private property, the pastoral goes back to the patristic and venerable Christian idea of stewardship, which advocates that

> ... the right to own must bow to the higher principles of stewardship and the common use of the goods of creation.[63]

The letter also introduces two principles of political philosophy. The first is that of subsidiarity. "This principle states that government should undertake only those initiatives necessary for protecting basic justice which exceed the capacity of individuals or private groups acting independently."[64] The second principle is that of the supranational duty to the whole of the human family, even in the absence of international political authority.[65]

But clearly, several of these demands and principles are contrary to the principles operative in democratic capitalism. Indeed, at the anthropological level, capitalism has been heralded as the social arrangement that would tolerate or even legitimize "interests" in order to obviate some unacceptable vices.[66] Arguing that one must restrain the desire to consume, or that one must acknowledge higher principles than private ownership, is to situate oneself outside capitalism as it was originally imagined and as it still is popularly understood.

The challenge at the politico-philosophical level may be even more severe. Democratic capitalism clearly has international dimensions. But its democratic aspect is tied to the nation state. As Lowi and Briefs have shown, the functioning of the democratic political order in the late capitalist phase is not independent of the interest groups that have emerged in the nation state. Interest groups actively interfere with systematic implementation of the two political principles to which the bishops' letter appeals. Indeed, by their very nature interest groups try to use the state to further their goals, and might therefore oppose international humanitarian objectives if these were perceived to conflict with the perceived interests of the group. Even worse, in domestic policy, the refusal of interest groups to accept responsibility can and does easily undermine application of the subsidiarity principle, as Briefs has argued, because that principle can only work if lower forms of organization are able and willing to taking responsibility.

The bishops' letter can thus be seen as an attempt to criticize certain outcomes of American democratic capitalism on the basis of a religiously grounded economic ethics. That ethics goes against the implicit and explicit legitimation of self-interest in democratic capitalism. But it is a powerful challenge.

V. Conclusion

THE BISHOPS' LETTER is concerned with the outcomes of the American economy. Like the three authors I have relied on for my analysis, the pastoral letter maintains that there are such serious deficiencies with those outcomes that one can call them unjust. The authors I have examined present other conclusions, or make different suggestions for improving the capitalist system than those found in the bishops' letter. Lowi puts all his hope in a change in *one* political institution: the Congress. It would be required to write specific laws instead of laws expressing only general intentions whose implementation is left to bureaucracies. It is his contention that this current practice invites group bargaining, at the expense of justice, between interest groups and the bureaucratic agency charged with applying the law.

Briefs's assumption is that the domain of action of the interest groups is far broader than skillful negotiation with bureaucratic agencies. Interest groups can also establish quasi monopolies and use all the techniques available to monopolies in order to increase their share of the national income. They can also go directly to the legislature in order to get specific legislation that benefits their interest. Briefs argued that even though the results of such actions hit people and groups in anonymous and not clearly visible ways, there is a definite moral aspect to the problem. But calling it a moral problem hardly provides a solution.

Hegel's philosophy invites the following conclusion: there are so many benefits to the free market that such an economic arrangement is ethically desirable. Unfortunately, there is a price to be paid: poverty, menial and mechanical work, and cyclical unemployment. The bishops' pastoral differs from Hegel's analysis in that it does not share his defeatist characterization of the free market. This is the case because the pastoral does not accept Hegel's basic assumption that the modern drift toward subjectivism and individualism is irreversible. Instead, the pastoral puts forward a conception of man in which the communitarian spirit is an essential element. It is not seen merely as a dialectical outcome of something that is guaranteed mechanistically, as it were, by an invisible hand.

In the spirit of Briefs's essay, the pastoral addresses its appeal to "human beings" behind the institution, and behind the egoistic model of economic theory. The letter is the heir to a long tradition which holds that man has a task of self-development in and through participation in community. Such a task is claimed, in fact, to be the realization of the true self. The pastoral also holds that individual efforts make a difference. But contrary to Briefs, it is more concrete in that it presents a guide for action. Furthermore, the concrete exhortations are broader than the one recommendation of Lowi. Indeed, the pastoral admonishes people to change their tastes and preferences because of moral concerns so that societies' utility curves, and thus societies' demand curves, will change. The pastoral further urges people to work for a change in the understanding and implementation of rights so that economic rights become as valuable as civil and political rights in our ethos. It also advocates changes at the institutional level so as to create the organizations required to implement economic rights. Finally, the pastoral calls for changes in the political domain such that the solidarity principle, which demands initiatives contrary to self-interest, may become operative in our society.

The pastoral is thus more optimistic than Hegel, and more concrete than Lowi and Briefs. It is a document whose main conclusion is consonant with the research of these important scholars, and the bishops are to be congratulated for bringing this theme of economic life sharply into focus for the public mind. It is no small accomplishment.

NOTES

The author wishes to thank the editor of this volume for the many suggestions he made for improving this paper. It has also profited from the discussions of the monthly faculty colloquim on social and political theory at Georgetown University.

1. Michael Novak, *The Spirit of Democratic Capitalism* (New York: Simon and Schuster, 1982), represents such a position.

2. Richard C. Edwards, Michael Reich and Thomas E. Weisskopf, eds., *The Capitalist System. A Radical Analysis of American Society* (Englewood Cliffs, N.J.: Prentice-Hall, 1972), is an anthropology representing that view.

3. Goetz Briefs, "Staat und Wirtschaft im Zeitalter der Interessenverbande," in Goetz Briefs, ed., *Laissez-faire-Pluralismus* (Berlin: Duncker & Humblot, 1966), 1–317; "Grenzmoral in der pluralistischenGesellschaft, in E. V. Beckerath, F. W. Meyer and A. Muller-Armach, eds., *Wirtschaftsfragen der freien Welt* (in honor or Ludwig Erhard) (Frankfurt A.M.: F. Knapp, 1957). (An English translation of this article is available under the title "Marginal Ethics in the Pluralistic Society," *The Review of Social Economy* XLI (1983): 259–70 (translated by Henry Briefs and Michael Malloy, edited by Elinor C. Briefs); "The Ethos Problem in the Present Pluralistic Society," *Review of Social*

Economy XV (1957): 47–75; and Theodore J. Lowi, *The End of Liberalism. The Second Republic of the United States*, 2nd ed. (New York: W. W. Norton, 1979).

4. It is 1930 if one starts a new period with the emergence of the new republic; it is 1960 if one starts the new period with the maturation of the new state.

5. Lowi, *The End of Liberalism*, 278–79.

6. For a report on the different interpretations of what actually happened, see A. O. Hirschman, "Rival Interpretations of Market Society: Civilising, Destructive, or Feeble?" in *Journal of Economic Literature* XX (December 1982): 1463–84.

7. Briefs, "The Ethos Problem," 53–54.

8. Ibid., 55–56.

9. Cartels, however, remained mostly prohibited in the United States.

10. Briefs, "The Ethos Problem," 56.

11. John Maynard Keynes, *Essays in Persuasion* (New York: W. W. Norton, 1963): 13.

12. Briefs, "The Ethos Problem," 67. See also Briefs, "Staat und Wirtschaft," 48, 77, 264, 281, and 286. Here, Briefs calls it the third phase of liberalism. That third phase he defines as the period in which the interest groups are independent variables, they are a state within the state (48–49).

13. Briefs, "The Ethos Problem," 75.

14. Albert O. Hirschman, *The Passions and the Interests* (Princeton, N.J.: Princeton University Press, 1977), 11.

15. Ibid., 63.

16. Ibid., 66.

17. Plato, *The Republic*, trans F. McDonald Cornford (New York: Oxford University Press, 1979), IV, 423d, 114.

18. Ibid., Ch. XVI, "Abolition of the Family for the Guardians," V, 457b–460d, 155–68.

19. For a book-length treatment of Hegel's dependence upon the British economists in particular from Steuart, see Paul Chamley, *Economie Politique et Philosophie chez Steuart et Hegel* (Paris: Dalloz, 1963).

20. For a systematic exposition of the relation between the free market and Hegel's view of freedom and thus of the moral-ethical aspects of the free market, see W. Ver Eecke, "Hegel on Economics and Freedom," in *Archiv fur Rechts — und Sozialphilosophie* LXIX (1983), especially Parts I and II.

21. G. W. F. Hegel, *Philosophy of Right*, trans T. M. Knox (London: Oxford University Press, 1967), no. 158, p. 110.

22. Ibid., no. 162, p. 111.

23. Adam Smith, *The Wealth of Nations* (New York: Modern Library, 1937), 651.

24. G. W. F. Hegel, *Philosophy of Mind*, Part 3 of Hegel's *Encyclopedia of Philosophical Sciences*, trans. William Wallace (Oxford: Clarendon Press, 1971), no. 523, p. 122.

25. Smith, *Wealth*, 423.

26. Hegel, *Philosophy of Right*, no. 185, p. 123.

27. Ibid., no. 181, p. 122.

28. Ibid., no. 185, p. 123. See also G. Briefs, "Marginal Ethics in the Pluralistic Society." The basic thesis of this article is that there is marginal pressure to undermine legal and moral norms in the capitalist system, because economic doctrine expects too much of competition as a regulator of self-interest.

29. Sartre even said: "Hell is other people."

30. Hegel, *Philosophy of Right*, no. 207, p. 133 and no. 251, p. 152.

31. Ibid., nos. 252–56, pp. 152–55.

32. Ibid., no. 251, p. 152. This aspect is much stressed by Michael Novak, "A Theology of the Corporation," by Michael Novak and John W. Cooper, eds., *The Corporation: A Theological Inquiry* (Washington, D.C.: American Enterprise Institute, 1981), 210–11.

33. G. W. F. Hegel, The *Phenomenology of Spirit*, trans. A. V. Miller (New York: Oxford University Press, 1977), 118–19.

34. Hegel, *Philosophy of Right*, no. 45, p. 42.

35. For a further development of this argument, see W. Ver Eecke, "Ethics in Economics: From Classical Economics to Neo-Liberalism," in *Philosophy and Social Criticism* IX (1983): 145–50.

36. The problem of public goods is discussed in standard economic textbooks on "Public Finance." A survey of considerable depth is John G. Head, "The Theory of Public Goods," in his *Public Goods and Public Welfare* (Durham, N.C.: Duke University Press, 1974), 68–92. Hegel mentions or discusses public goods' problems in his *Philosophy of Right*, nos. 232–36, pp. 146–48.

37. Ibid., nos. 197–98, p. 129.

38. Ibid., no. 243, pp. 149–50.

39. Ibid., nos 244–45, p. 150.

40. National Conference of Catholic Bishops, *Catholic Social Teaching and the U.S. Economy*, first draft (Washington, D.C.: United States Catholic Conference, 1984), no. 81.

41. Ibid., no. 81.

42. Ibid., no. 187.

43. Ibid., no. 202.

44. Ibid., nos. 23, 24.

45. Ibid., nos. 23, 24.

46. Ibid., no. 73.

47. Ibid., no. 76.

48. Ibid., no. 77.

49. Ibid., no. 86.

50. Ibid., no. 92.

51. Ibid., no. 94.

52. Ibid., no. 95.

53. Ibid., no. 83.

54. Ibid., no. 84.

55. Ibid., no. 85.

56. Ibid., no. 86.

57. Ibid., no. 103.

58. Ibid., no. 104.
59. Ibid., no. 105.
60. Ibid., no. 109.
61. Ibid., no. 139.
62. Ibid., no. 141.
63. Ibid., no. 141.
64. Ibid., no. 127.
65. Ibid., no. 137.
66. Cf. Hirschman, *The Passions and the Interests*, in particular Part One, "How the Interests were called upon to counteract the Passions."